Full
Support

Full Support

LESSONS LEARNED IN THE DRESSING ROOM

Natalee Woods

AMBERJACK
PUBLISHING

CHICAGO

AMBERJACK
PUBLISHING

Amberjack Publishing
An imprint of Chicago Review Press Incorporated
814 North Franklin Street
Chicago, Illinois 60610

10 9 8 7 6 5 4 3 2 1

Publisher's Cataloging-in-Publication data available upon request

ISBN 978-1-944995-80-5
ebook ISBN 978-1-944995-81-2

For my parents,
who always lifted me up.

INTRODUCTION

Staring at her breasts, I backed away to examine the fit of her bra. Glaring lights and long, three-section mirrors crowded our space, giving the dressing room an uncomfortable, mystifying feeling as we moved in silence.

"You're in," I smiled, adjusting the straps before running my hand along the bra's underwire. I waited while she analyzed her body in the mirror, moving from her midsection to her new, G-sized cups. "The power these things can hold," she said before she lifted her boobs to kiss them. "Amen."

My customer's memorable sentiment echoed throughout my unexpected trajectory in the lingerie department. For more than a decade, from the time I was nineteen, I fitted women for bras and other pieces of lingerie in a high-end department store. I never imagined just how much the experience would change me—and my relationship with my body. The narratives from inside the dressing room, poignant and raw, have been an integral part of my life for years, guiding me through a long stretch of confusing purgatory and a lot of self-reflection. I'm honored to share them in their truest, most vulnerable form as a listener and a learner. I'm humbled to share what can happen when we let another human being in far enough to teach us something about ourselves, most significantly our worth, as well as the dangers that exist within a culture that continues to cast shadows over our humanity, disparaging those who do not measure up to predetermined standards.

I'd be remiss to not address my total lack of interest in working retail, fitting strangers for bras. The intimacy was downright startling, and the discourse unpredictable yet unflinchingly honest. For years, I struggled to understand the changing nuances and messy complexities of working in a lingerie department amid a cold and critical world. Each day, I'd experience a surge of emotions ranging from utter heartbreak to euphoria, bouncing my own thick flesh off demi push ups and binding string. And though I had many aha moments throughout the years, pushing me to question a multitude of socially conditioned ideals in the context of women and women's bodies, it still took a long time to fully grasp the significance and lasting impact of my role as a bra fitter. The impression that working retail is easy and stress-free was constantly challenged and far removed from the truth. Women shared so much more than their bodies, commanding time and space without even realizing it, which was precisely what made my interactions in the dressing room so powerful.

One of my most memorable customers, eighty-six-year-old Gladys Brown (names have been changed to protect privacy), taught me on multiple occasions about the power of ageism to make people invisible, and the influence of time. She reminded me that the passage of time, daunting and deliberate, carries us to the places we're supposed to be while introducing us to the people we're destined to meet.

Claire Whittler, a transgender woman whose father disowned her for being Claire, defined the true meaning of empathy and what it means to love unconditionally . . . and with gratitude. Nicole, a single mother and bad-to-the-motherfucking-bone stripper, propelled me to dig deep and examine the intricacies of my own sexuality and self-confidence, igniting one hell of a fire. She was fierce and forthright, and it was while listening to her talk about her work with a private will to persist that I realized I had real, authentic stories to tell.

So I began documenting my days by jotting down notes, observations, and words exchanged on receipt paper from the registers. I would come home from a long, exhausting shift, rip off my bra, and all of these beautifully bold narratives would fall from my cups, reminding me about the power of humanity . . . and that I had stuffed my already-packed double-D bra with wads of white paper.

The presence of these valued lessons also got me thinking about the reality of the dressing room and the act of moving alongside a half-dressed or, often, fully naked woman. It's hard to articulate the actualities of the job. Specifically, my place, coupled with my gaze, inside an already vulnerable space as women self-consciously—and assertively—bared their breasts.

I can't tell you how many times I stood silent, having no idea where to stand or what to say as customers removed their clothing. It was awkward at first. But over time, if I'm completely honest, my gaze became a natural part of the process. I was there to examine one's breasts in order to fit them into a bra, which required eyeballs and a lot of trial and error. Throw in a woman's extraordinary capacity to share her fears and insecurities and deeply compelling perspective on loss and love, and I was left scrambling for words with a pair of boobs in my face. It was part of the job, and my focus on each customer's body remained a constant.

When I look back at how *Full Support* transpired and where we are now as a society—most profoundly our unstoppable and steadfast women's liberation movement—I can't help thinking about the timing of this project, especially as we continue to resist, rage on, and redefine a culture by being our true selves. My experience working in a lingerie department was humbling, and I hung up my measuring tape eager and excited to write this book, knowing that most women can relate, or, perhaps, gain new perspective.

Please understand that I'm not here to bullshit anyone. But out of respect for all involved, I've taken the liberty to make some modifications. As you read, please note that the names and other identifying characteristics of the persons included in this book have been changed. The timeline has also been slightly altered in order to preserve people's anonymity.

I'm so grateful for your time. Thank you for reading. Let's continue to share our stories. Let's continue to transform, galvanize, and amplify our inner workings in an effort to lift others. Let's leave our marks behind . . . without apology.

Sincerely,
Natalee

Full Support

CERTIFIED TIT SLINGER

My heart wouldn't stop pounding. I could feel my hands warm up as sweat settled into the creases. Women were running in every direction as the pianist's hospitable tune echoed throughout the store. Coffee and water bottles and colorful balloons strategically placed in every department gave the first day of the annual sale a little bit of friendly oomph—and customers the stamina to keep their plastic out. Seasoned sales associates gathered around the escalator and clapped, welcoming more women as they rushed to collect their sale items before they were gone. I could hear children crying across the way in the kids' department as their balloons found their way to the ceiling, floating beyond reach.

"You can do this," I repeated over and over in my head, looking like a mortician had worked on my smile. I stood beside a panty table and gazed out at the marble walkway at the number of women filling the third floor. I wondered how far I'd get if I hightailed it to the women's lounge to hide. It was absolute mayhem, the height of retail mania, and a shopaholic's dream come true. It was also seven o'clock in the morning—and my second day on the job.

When I had arrived the previous day at the human resource office less than twenty-four hours after receiving a call from the HR manager, Cindy, it was clear the store was still in the process of last-minute recruiting. Shimmying through the office door, I passed a group of Greek Row's finest sporting Ralph Lauren button-ups, fancy neckties, and Bartell's entire stock of cheap hair gel.

"Hi." I smiled awkwardly, moving in closer to the woman passing out paperwork. Staring at her pink, deep-set blush, I worked hard to find words as I stood fighting a whirlwind of nerves. "I received a call back from Cindy in regard to sale help." I anxiously approached the desk, eyeing a small jar of assorted mints and a glass plaque that read "Seattle's Customer Service Excellence."

"Yes, that was me." She smiled quickly while pulling out a legal pad listing the store's departments. "Let's see." She paused, skimming through a list of scribbled words after spelling my name out loud. "I've got a spot left in lingerie."

"Lingerie," I repeated, lowering my chin in confusion, wondering what happened to the process of asking about work ethic, or what makes a team player, or if I've ever killed anyone.

"We really need floor coverage. Are you comfortable working intimately with women?" she asked, moving her eyes along my protruding bustline and then down to the massive wrinkle in the knee-length satin skirt that I had pulled from the back of my closet. I nodded slowly, feeling horribly out of place.

"I, uh, sure," I stuttered, watching her pull a paper clip from a cluster of formalities.

"Great," she replied, guiding me to the chair beside her desk, next to a young man wearing an emerald-green bow tie who was ready to pass over his crinkled-up Social Security card.

Feeling doubtfully well-suited for the lingerie department, I sat motionless as the office continued to buzz with last-minute hires. After a moment, I started in on the paperwork, wondering what the hell had just happened, and how, in a matter of five minutes, I was somehow gainfully employed.

My parents would be thrilled—their welcome-home question when I returned from my freshman year of college had been if I'd found work yet. That was my first clue I wasn't going to spend my summer watching *Days of Our Lives* and MTV. My father had pulled at his finely trimmed moustache, then raised his hand and rubbed the tips of his fingers together in an effort to *show me the money*. He did this often and continued to think it was amusing. My mother, on the other hand, as forgiving as she was, kept up with a steady *don't ask me for a dime*.

I faced the music and went straight for a high-end department store upon my mom's recommendation—and her desire for a discount—hoping to set up women with a new handbag or a nice pastel scarf. And now here I was in lingerie. I felt I was falling into a rabbit hole for which I was unprepared. But it was a job, and I didn't have time to be picky, considering the three dollars and sixty-seven cents in my bank account.

"Our annual sale lasts two weeks, but I know lingerie is looking to fill more hours," Cindy explained, turning to hand me a sheet of paper stating the store's dress code policy, followed by a thick packet on sexual harassment.

"Oh, okay," I replied, moving in closer to the desk, thinking about Cindy's question regarding my comfort level in the lingerie department. I had no idea what she meant. And as she watched me write down the numbers "1" and "9" on the application next to the word "age," silence quickly cut between us. I looked up to find her cheeks raised in a paralyzed smile.

"KEEP MOVING," I HEARD MY NEW BOSS SAY AS SHE PASSED BY WITH a stack of thong underwear and a twenty-ounce latte. I didn't know where I was moving to except under the green neon sign that said EXIT. These women were like vultures that had just been released from captivity, frantically pulling sale items off the racks while attempting to balance a jelly-stuffed pastry and a long stretch of careless indulgence.

"There's a customer who's been waiting in four," one of the sales associates snapped while holding a pile of bras. "Can you take her? Everyone already has more than one customer, and the other new girl never showed up."

"Oh, I'm only supposed to—" barely came out of my mouth before she interrupted me.

"At least see what she wants. We need you on the sales floor."

Wiping my palms down the front of my pants, I turned to look at the lines quickly forming at the registers. I could see my manager, her latte sitting on the counter as she manically waved a bright orange flag, guiding the next woman to step forward with a pile of sleepwear.

"How about some lingerie wash to go with that?" Her voice echoed, shrill and Valley girl-sounding. Quickly, I scoped the department for black and white clothing, hoping the other girls followed directions about what to wear on the first day of the sale as I had—and, more important, were willing to help me. But they all kept zipping by, balancing bras and panties and phony smiles. I suddenly started to regret my decision, falling victim to Cindy's line about "it's the only position I have left."

"Hi there," I said, standing in front of room four. "Did you need some help?"

"Yes," a stern voice replied from inside as the door creaked open. "I've been waiting for twenty minutes."

The smell in the dressing room was borderline unbearable, reminding me of dirty laundry coupled with the inside of one's belly button. My own contribution of fresh B.O. didn't help.

"I'm so sorry about the wait, ma'am," I said, staring directly into the portable fan she held inches away from her extremely large chest.

"I was hoping to be measured for a bra," she said dryly, suddenly taking off her shirt. "And I don't have much longer to waste."

"Sure, I totally understand," I stuttered. "I, uh, just need to grab someone who's certified."

"That's not necessary," she said, shaking her head while pulling a measuring tape off a hook on the wall. "I just need an idea so that I can grab some sale bras and get out of here. I'll exchange them later if I have to."

"Sure, I totally understand," I said again, giving the classic deer-in-headlights look as I moved my gaze from the baby pink measuring tape down to her boobs pouring out of her bra like hot lava, and then back to the measuring tape. I didn't know what I was supposed to be measuring other than Xanax; the top of her rib cage was nowhere to be found. That's when I realized my new job was a far cry from spreading foam over lattes or shelving children's books at the library.

Dripping sweat from my armpits, I took the tape from her hand and moved in closer, wondering if the Bra 101 tutorial my manager had given me the day before would somehow pay off. She had quickly educated me so that I had some idea of what went down in the department—pun intended. Her obscure lingo was scattered and full of words and phrases like "demi cups" and "elasticity" and "tension in the straps." I couldn't help tuning out, watching all of the department's little elves race around the stockroom in preparation for the shit show I was now a part of.

Once again, I was feeling like I should've revisited Seattle's classifieds after HR Cindy asked me straight-faced, while handing me a W-4, if I was "comfortable working intimately" with women. What Cindy was really asking was if I was comfortable engaging in skin-to-skin contact with a stranger and her breasts.

It was difficult to wrap my head around, as I was still learning about my own body. I wasn't remotely prepared to understand the significance of a woman's breasts—and the relationships women have with their breasts and bodies. I started to feel a strange disconnect from my body just being in the dressing room, thrust under the spotlight and suddenly questioning every pale inch of flesh in front of me. My own set of sizable goods, also in the wrong bra size, had formed a new, lasting narrative I wasn't ready to dissect, let alone embrace in that moment. The intimacy was downright startling, and the exposure nerve-wracking. Some things I thought I sort of knew about my youthful parts were immediately up for negotiation. The abundance of mirrors and measuring tapes and size tags had me drowning in more self-reflection than ever before. I was just as lost as my customer when it came to what I needed for my body—and my mind.

Holding onto the measuring tape, I tried to figure out where to stand.

"Again, I just need an idea on size," she said, pulling down the straps of her bra before unhooking it and throwing it in the chair next to her purse. "I think I'm somewhere around a 40 or 42 band."

"Oh, okay" were the only words I could conjure up as I stood staring at her nipples.

With my hands trembling, I tried wrapping the measuring tape under her breasts, cocking my head to the side in an attempt to view its position. "I'm sorry," I said, my voice crack-ing. "I'm going to need you to lift up your breasts so I can place the tape around you."

After I thought I had succeeded, I moved in closer to read the measurement, realizing that the dark bolded numbers standing out from their pink backdrop were upside down, and that my impatient customer was watching me in the mirror, her eyes dark brown and tired. Taking a step back, I stood in silence, staring at large crowds of brown moles and stretch marks. All I could do was stand there, flustered and mortified, choking on air.

I needed help.

"I'm sorry," I finally said again, quickly peeling the tape from around her ribcage and out of the deep rolls in her back. "I couldn't read the numbers."

"I saw that," she replied dryly, nodding her head, while her eyebrows, thick with tinting, sprung up as if they alone finally registered that she was in the hands of a novice.

Inhaling slowly, I wrapped the measuring tape deep under her flesh for a second time. Her boobs warmed the backs of my hands as I continued to stretch my arms as far as they could go without me eating her hair. I held my breath while screaming at myself inside that I should have told her to leave her bra on. I just stood there, cemented in the middle of the dressing room like the Tin Man. The vulnerability we shared was difficult to navigate. I needed out of the dressing room fast.

Something started to happen to my body temperature, as it went from hot to cold in the snap of a finger. The three-way mirror started caving in, and everything around me went fuzzy, except for the two extremely large boobs resting on the skin of my forearms.

What's happening?

"I believe you're closer to a 42 band like you said." I hesitated to reveal my findings, looking down at the wet fiberglass, attempting to identify the numbers above the black lines.

"I'd like to try, what's it called, the Feather Light?" she asked, reaching for the doorknob.

"I have no idea," I responded, hoping I looked like I was smiling. "I need to have someone come back to help me with the cups."

I closed the dressing room door and headed for the sales floor, pushing through a long line of women waiting to try on their sale items. The department smelled like a mix of coffee and perfume, clogging my airway even more, though I would've inhaled anything outside of the dressing room at that point. I looked all around for my manager, but she was nowhere to be found.

"Would you mind helping me with my customer?" I asked one of the salesgirls at the register, looking over her shoulder to find Cindy from HR waving her thumb in the air at me while passing by the department with a plate full of pastries.

"I can't, I'm with two customers," the girl replied in a slow, steady tone, pretending to regret that she was abandoning me and my obvious desperation.

"Great," I muttered under my breath, walking away to find another bra fitter, realizing that I was probably wasting my time, considering their commission was at stake. I started to panic even more when I thought about my customer waiting in the dressing room, again, sitting in the chair with her boobs in her hands, wondering where I had gone. It made me feel awful and anxious, knowing that the only thing my irritated customer wanted was to cut a deal and exit from the chaos. How could I blame her? We shared the same uneasiness, wondering what the hell we had gotten ourselves into, yet my customer had a well-founded sureness about her that I definitely didn't have. She was down to business, and I was downright scared.

I picked up my pace as I moved through the crowd, now looking around each shoulder in search of the largest bra I could find, though it felt like a hopeless search. I realized that the only things I had as a new employee in the lingerie department were overshadowing angst, disorderly heart palpitations, and a seven-digit employee number I knew would take me seven days to memorize.

"Are you with a customer?" I spotted another salesgirl dressed in a knee-length black skirt and a white button-up. But she looked as lost as I was, following her customer who had at least ten bathrobes draped over her arm. I quickly knelt down in front of a display, madly flipping over bra tag after bra tag, hoping to find something that would answer the large question mark I had waiting in the fitting room. Luckily, the same girl who directed me into my nightmare finally came to my rescue.

"I stopped by the dressing room," she said, holding up what looked like two adjoined nets. "Start with this and let her know the Feather Light only goes to a triple."

"Oh, okay, thank you," I said, looking down at the letter G darkly printed into the tag.

When I returned to the dressing room, I noticed that my customer had emerged from her room, holding her portable fan to her face.

"I have a G," I said with caution.

"A G!" she exclaimed loudly, quickly closing the door. "There's no way that I'm fitting into a G!"

"Well, I talked to the fitter who stopped by, and she recommended that I bring this back to you."

"I'll try it," she sighed, throwing her fan into her purse, which sat wide open on the chair. I quickly looked down as it clinked against a bottle of blue nail polish and a round plastic container labeled with the days of the week.

I held the bra out in front of her while she slowly eased her arms through the straps. Accidentally stepping on the heel of her foot with my boot, I worked hard to connect the band.

"That's good," she said, moving closer to the mirror.

I had no idea what I was looking for in terms of a "correct" bra fit, but my suspicions led me to something much larger than what the bra fitter had suggested.

"Let me just get them in." The customer hesitated, bending over while she shook her boobs into the cups.

I quickly found refuge in the corner, watching her boobs jiggle up and down and up and down and up and down.

"Would you mind tightening the straps?" she asked, moving in my direction. "I want to make sure I can exercise in this before I buy a handful."

With my fingertips changing into a light shade of pink, I tugged on the straps. She pulled her shoulders back and tried moving her boobs to the center of her chest, bringing them in from the sides. And then suddenly, without hesitation, while I was still struggling to form words, she began jumping in place. I watched her arms go up, and then her legs, and then her knees, and then her boobs. Everything was everywhere, flailing around. And then she stopped. *This is what you do to test your bra fit*, I thought, storing it for future use as a long, awkward pause crept in. This is what the inside of a dressing room can look like, every bare-boned inch of fear, anxiety, and truth shining under the toughest of glares. Whether I accepted it or not, I was on my way to becoming a legit, bona fide bra fitter.

"I think it works. What do you think?" my tired customer asked after a careful examination, pulling the bra band out from under the flesh on her back.

My heart began to race again as my eyes widened from the sight of a red line nearly carved into her skin as she started to take off the bra. I watched more sweat travel down her face and breasts, shining brightly under the dressing room lights.

"Uh . . ." While watching her hit the power button on her portable fan, I realized my opportunity had finally arrived, knowing she'd be better off without me.

"I think it looks great."

LOOSE-FITTING

Two years later, I thought my bra-fitting days were safely behind me in Seattle. Yet somehow, even in LA, here I was again, despite having promised myself never to return to retail for as long as I walked this earth. I was what Sally—the new HR lady—called a "lucky rehire," because I'd come from flagship territory. I didn't know what even constituted luck, but I was back, burning in the heels, trying to keep up with an ever-changing industry that had slowly become my escape—and my safety net.

On the morning of day six, I buried my face deep into my bed pillow, feeling comatose and achy. My body was toast. I pondered calling in sick with some bogus excuse, but I was already riding the bottom of the schedule as the last of the summer hires, and I had zero luck to push, and zero cash. As my feet slowly hit the cold hardwood floor, I opened my window to hear the rain. The loud drops hitting the pavement, cleaning out the sky, reminded me of my parents' home in Seattle.

I sat on the edge of my bed in a daze, staring at an old picture of my mother and me laughing in our Halloween costumes. Where had the time gone? How had so many months escaped me? It had been a year since she'd passed, and I still couldn't get myself together. Blouses and dress pants and dirty jeans covered my bedroom chair, almost disguising the stack of laundry mounting in the corner. I needed some serious energy to conquer my self-imposed disarray as grief manifested itself in strange ways.

I'd been more optimistic at first. My desperation to break free from Seattle had brought me to the most popular outdoor shopping and entertainment resort in all of Los Angeles, leaving me speechless after the human resource office handed me a brochure of my new home. Was I really going to be fitting women for bras here? I was almost excited at the possibility of having fun working retail. I never anticipated an elevator with gold doors delivering me to my car after a day's work.

The glamor wore off quickly, though. Maybe management would accept a shortened shift. My brain couldn't take another round of trifling discourse about whether or not a string thong rides all the way up one's ass or just halfway. I knew my idea was careless and unaffordable and, unfortunately, not going to happen, despite my strong desire to lie around and watch the Food Network all day. So I did my best to pull myself together, working hard to find my retail smile while wondering what simple and happy looked like.

A little while later, I walked into the department to find my coworker Farah holding up a floral tin and a note from my new eighty-six-year-old customer Gladys Brown that read, "I love my new boulder holders! Happy Sling-her Day!"

"More?" I asked, staring at a pile of chocolate chip cookies.

"You just missed her. She was on her way to get her hair done and claimed she didn't need them because she had bourbon. She also said she'll be back for more bras after her appointment."

I laughed, looking at Farah's expression as she stood with her hands on her hips. We had become fast work friends, sharing the same anxiety for serving the public and, more specifically, certain women from the zip code 90210.

"I got caught in traffic," I said, smiling. And it wasn't entirely a lie. My timing, yes, but sitting at various stoplights on Hollywood Boulevard so tourists could snap their cameras was not. Farah really didn't care if I showed up for work at all. She was about as interested in selling bras and panties as some of the other bra fitters in LA who also worked retail to pay the rent.

Farah was Lebanese-American, an aspiring fashion designer, well groomed, and dating a real Italian stallion fourteen years her senior. She was a toss-up between Carmen Electra and one of Hugh Hefner's blue-eyed bunnies, but with a little less silicone. Her hair was long and shiny and orange along her hairline from the two-inch-thick makeup she maintained on the hour. I'd see her in the bathroom from time to time, digging her fingertips into her compact and smearing her face with a smooth, spongy glow.

She was witty and really good at pushing customers into buying more than one bra. "Are you really going to wear this when you go out?" she'd ask the customer standing at the register holding two "boring, everyday kind of bras." Less than twenty minutes later, she'd have them back at the register adding a hundred-dollar bra and its matching forty-dollar panty to the bill. She was sexually empowering through it all, though, smoldering with suggestive undertones, and her customers felt it. Everyone loved to hear Farah's breakout theme song, "Power Your Flower," which translated into women dressing from the inside out in an effort to feel alive and sexy. It worked almost every time.

Luckily, work was bearably slow, out of the ordinary for a Saturday in the bra-and-panty department. As I started to familiarize myself with the new merchandise the managers had pulled from the back to crowd the floor with, I realized I should've followed my desires and learned how to make the divine brownies I'd seen on the Food Network. I was having a hard time staying focused on anything, especially after talking on the phone to my dad about his box dinner that morning. The image of him navigating the frozen aisles of the grocery store wearing high ankle socks and boat shoes made the twinge in my chest reemerge. It was my choice to move to Los Angeles to attend some radically progressive institute in an attempt to master the art of putting words together, but I'd burned through my student loans like I had Ed McMahon knocking on my door weekly, holding a bouquet of flowers and a long string of zeros on an oversized cardboard check. It didn't help that I'd left my father to find his way through loneliness—and a house styled with vintage doilies—while sending me money to cover the bills.

I made it my mission to study the new patterns of the almighty Hanky Panky thongs the early morning fitters hung on displays. I took the liberty of restocking the shopping bags and dusting the outdated and unrealistic buck-ten negligee-wearing mannequins while listening to Farah articulate her undying faith in the Plan B birth control pill she'd had for breakfast.

"My parents would kill me," she said with conviction, leaning into my ear as I dusted around the mannequins' milky feet.

With the shoe department, the coffee bar, and MAC makeup all on the same floor, I reacted to the inescapable boredom without a second thought and grabbed my wallet for a fifteen-minute break, hoping the coffee line was short.

I decided to sit outside in our coffee bar's nauseatingly crowded seating area, though it was quickly turning into one of my favorite things to do because there was so much to see. All the pandemonium made it easy to sit back and watch the people, especially cast members from *The Young and the Restless* as they passed through on their lunch breaks from the CBS studios next door. And Paris Hilton, of course, who never failed to stop shoppers in their tracks, turning them into gawking fools like myself as she moved through the scene wearing short summer attire and sunglasses the size of ski goggles.

Sipping on my coffee, I listened to a timed recording of Frank Sinatra fill the air as the shopping center's thirty-foot fountain began its notorious "water dance," shooting out a plethora of H_2O from a variety of pulsing jets. Its hourly entertainment added to the ambiance nicely, making you believe you were standing in Vegas's Bellagio Hotel.

I continued to watch with interest as tourists emerged from posh boutiques, tightly holding their cameras while trying to maneuver around small, fluffy dogs suffocated by Louis Vuitton sweaters and rhinestone-clad collars. The jazz band playing on the grass was a nice touch, too. The energy was high as people enjoyed their Saturday outdoors after an unforeseen stretch of rain. I felt stuck and bummed that the department was windowless, especially after noticing a couple of our neighbors working door duty outside of Abercrombie. It took me a minute to comprehend what was happening as I watched the enthusiastic meatheads welcome their customers, wearing nothing but trendy jeans and the layered afterglow of a spray tan. And though I've never been drawn to protein-sniffing Terminator types, they were still easy on the eyes.

Back inside the store, the shoe department and cosmetics counters were booming with eager-eyed women trying on the new summer collections. Salesmen dressed in suits and fancy ties emerged from the stockroom, attempting to balance a stack of shoeboxes in one hand and rolled-up nylon footies in the other. Across the way, alongside Steven Tyler's raspy inflection of "Dude (Looks Like a Lady)," were the makeup artists, patting their brushes into the limp faces of their customers while moving to the music. It was a drastic change from the lingerie department—and easy to get roped into. But before I could even set down my coffee to dip my finger into a display of colorful eye shadows, I heard my name roll smoothly off the tongue of a woman working in the operator's room. "Natalee Woods, please return to the lingerie department. Natalee Woods, lingerie."

Arriving upon command, I spotted Gladys standing by the register.

"Sorry for the wait, Gladys. Your hair looks nice," I said, placing my hand on her back while running my gaze along her stiffly sprayed curls.

"Thank you, honey. Richie always does a good job," she replied, softly patting the sides of her hair.

"And thank you for the chocolate chip cookies. They will go into my belly and settle on the backside as usual."

"You said they were your favorite, so I whipped up a batch. And speaking of favorites, that Feather Lift you sold me a few days ago changed my life. I mean, the girls were really letting me down, honey."

I laughed loudly, placing my hand on her shoulder.

"It's called the 'Feather Light,' but I like the *lift* part better." I smiled.

"Well, whatever the hell it's called, it certainly does the job. We'll call it the Champion of Slingers!"

"I like it." I laughed, thinking about its embroidered feathers floating down the cups of the bra, attempting to give what was deemed by younger women the "Grandma Bra" a little bit of womanly pizzazz. It was generous in the cups, covering every last bit of breast tissue while hindering any desire for cleavage. But in terms of a good "pickup," it quite possibly was the Champion of Slingers for the geriatric society. "I'm proud of you, Gladys. You're taking my bra-fitting spiel about the importance of rotating your bras to a whole new level."

"Well, honey, I hate how a good bra stretches out so quickly, sending the cha-chas everywhere but up! I mean, thank Mary they're not down to my damn ankles yet!"

"I don't see that happening, Gladys."

"I might have a little more time," she declared, shaking one of her breasts. "But they're certainly loose fitting, honey."

"How many bras would you like?" I asked, listening to Farah's laugh grow louder.

"I need to try on some underpants, too, so maybe grab two more nude-colored ones and a few pairs of those full brief lace-trim jobs, and I'll meet you in the dressing rooms. And, honey," she continued as she started toward the back of the department, "let's put the bras on just to make sure the fit is still good."

Nodding my head, I walked toward the stockroom as her voice echoed throughout the department one last time, alarming a man standing by the bathrobes.

"A 36 long, honey."

GLADYS STOOD QUIETLY IN FRONT OF THE MIRROR WHILE I PLACED her breasts into the cups of the bra. They moved like Jell-O between my fingers as I tried to bring them up and above the underwire, pushing them in from the sides before they flopped back down. I shifted away from the mirror so she could see, hovering over her from the side, softly tightening each one of the straps before moving my finger along the bra's wire to make sure it wasn't rubbing against her rib cage.

I could smell the sweat on her skin from the hot summer day as it rolled down the corner of her forehead, smearing her makeup. She tapped on her right shoulder, so I went back in and loosened the strap, giving it one last pull backward to bring her breast up without creating an indentation on her shoulder. She was a difficult fit, as her breasts morphed into mushed softness once I squeezed them into the cups. After pulling her breasts in from the sides again, I backed away to examine the work.

"Go ahead and sit down, Gladys," I said, pulling the dressing room chair out of the corner. "I think the bra fits you just like the other ones. Let's try your underwear on now."

"Oh, honey," she sighed, gazing into the full-length mirror, her fuchsia lipstick bleeding into the cracks of her wrinkled mouth. "It's hell getting old."

I waited for Gladys's cue before unhooking the underwear. She sat staring at me, carefully moving her eyes along the edges of my hairline, making me self-conscious about my extra-wide forehead while reminding me that, though there's ample room for bangs, they do nothing but collect grease.

"You certainly don't look like her, honey," she said, massaging her kneecaps with the palms of her hands. "You know, the actress, Natalie Wood."

"I'm Natalee with two Es." I smiled, moving her stained leather purse away from her feet. "And I have an *s* on the end of Wood."

She continued to stare at me, softly patting her chest with a Kleenex she pulled from her pocket.

"Well, can you at least swim, honey?"

A widow, Gladys was erratic, lonely, and, in the most self-preserving way, disturbed. I saw a glimpse of my future self in her, buying vintage jewelry and mixing cocktails in a floral muumuu before the sun went down. She lived in Beverly Hills in the same house she and her late husband, Archie, bought back in the sixties. "It's my asylum," she told me just days before. "And with too many memories to sell."

Her skin had aged and thinned out, making the dark purple veins in her hands look like implanted IV lines. I could see the sticky aftermath of high-end hair spray sparkle atop her silver-blonde curls under the dressing room lights, making the contrast with my cherry-red hair look like a blazing fire in the mirror.

"Are you doing okay, Gladys?" I asked.

"It's damn hot, and I'm tired today," she replied, pulling on the elastic waistband of her linen capris. Her mouth shifted out of nothingness into a wide, timid smile. "But I've got bourbon and the *Wheel of Fortune* at home. That Vanna keeps me going! Though I wish she'd get some meat on her bones like you, honey."

I laughed, suddenly thinking about Vanna White's well-preserved breasts compared to my nylon tits filled with sand. Glancing at myself in the mirror, I held up a pair of ivory-colored underwear while Gladys started to take her bra off.

"Oh, Jesus." She snickered, looking at her underpants. "Why haven't you told me that these damn things look like a pair of swim trunks?"

I chuckled again, bending down in front of her to help unhook her bra, seeing her nipples, framed with dark curly hairs, disappear into her tummy's small rolls.

"Actually, Gladys, do you want to leave your bra on since I've adjusted the straps for you?"

"No, honey," she replied, standing up from the dressing room chair. "The one I wore in is fine."

We stood in silence in the middle of the dressing room as Gladys kicked off her slip-ons and dropped her linen capris to the floor. I stared at her skinny legs and small waist in the mirror, slowly moving my gaze down to the bunions lining the base of her big toes, and then up to the disarrayed gathering of pubic hair making its way out of her underwear's leg holes.

"It's quite a sight, I know," Gladys joked, following my stare. "Richie can only do so much."

"You're perfect." I smiled, feeling slightly awkward about being caught eyeing her genital area. But it happened sometimes, considering our close proximity with everyone, making me think about how personal our bodies are, and how quickly they become a topic of discussion in the fitting room—and our culture, from the pedicures to the Brazilian waxes.

"It's funny how things change as you get older." Gladys turned toward the mirror. "It's both liberating and sad."

Liberating and sad? I wondered if my own neglected arrangement was happily liberated or sad.

"It all leaves you so fast, honey." Her tone changed. "One day, you're perky and alive, and then the next day you're stopping for air with aching knees and tender hip bones. And I'll tell you something. Our world doesn't let you forget the clock is ticking, yet we still find ways to escape it."

I nodded as she grabbed onto her stomach's flesh, long-faced and dismayed.

"You start out desirable and end overlooked," she added with a sigh.

I stared at her long breasts in the mirror again, quietly noting a gathering of swarthy age spots.

"I thought age was just a number," I said, smiling.

"Oh, honey." She exhaled again. "I think that's just what we like to tell ourselves to soften the blow."

Her words penetrated right through what I thought was sustainable in terms of dealing with aging's unavoidable tricks. Thanks to all the widespread Band-Aids—better known as lifts and tucks and sharp smoothers used to soothe the sting of feeling invisible—women had opportunities to preserve the fallen. Perhaps there was truth in her reasoning, making me question what really feeds our fears as the birthday candles pile up: what we look like, or how we feel?

"Why don't you sit back down, Gladys?" I offered, guiding her into the chair. "I'll help you with the underpants."

"Are these size small, honey?" she asked loudly, plopping down on the edge of the chair.

"Yes," I replied, taking a second glance at the tag.

She sat with her hands on my shoulders as I stretched the lace-trimmed holes of the underpants around each foot and then up and over her thighs. Pulling on the price tag with her finger, she softly placed the thick elastic band on top of her sunken belly button, covering up the frayed edges of her own underpants with the new pair I had picked out for her.

"How are you doing, honey?" she asked, throwing me off guard with the softness of her voice. She was sincere and ready for anything, looking at me with her glossy bug eyes.

"I'm a little tired myself, Gladys." I sighed, carefully running my fingers around the lace stitching of her underpants to make sure it wasn't digging in anywhere. "And this is one hot summer day."

"I know," she replied, standing up again to look at herself in the mirror. I watched as excess skin rippled through the frailty of her short legs. "It's a goddamn inferno out there."

She stood for a second, quiet and consumed, looking into the mirror at her wilted breasts again. "Yours will get here," she said as she smiled coyly and reached for her old Feather Light.

"Especially those," she added, her smile widening as she pointed to my boobs, perched in their nest, ready to take their descending flight with one quick unhooking of the band.

"Do you have a boyfriend who gets to enjoy those?" she asked, moving back over to the chair.

Continuing to laugh at her unwavering candor, I rested my body against the wall. "Nope, I sure don't."

"We need to change that," she quickly replied, casting her finger into the air as I stood staring at the ground. "What about your family, honey? Are they close by?"

Fidgeting awkwardly, I moved closer to the bar, feeling unprepared for a conversation about my dead mother. Visions of hospital beds and morphine drips and heart monitors swarmed my brain, offering nothing but unforgiving panic and heavy heartbeats. I was inconsolable and messy, constantly regressing into a complicated torment I couldn't understand.

"I moved here from Seattle." I looked up to find Gladys staring directly at me. "My father and older brothers live there. My mother unfortunately passed away not too long ago."

Sensing my fear and reserve, Gladys moved her gaze to the floor.

I stared at her breasts.

"Oh, honey." She began rubbing her kneecap. "This is fresh."

My head started to feel lighter as the beating of my heart grew louder. Sweat pooled in my palms, making me feel slippery and exposed.

"It's a beast, isn't it?" she said softly, looking back up at me after her sharp words cut through the dressing room.

Beast. It was a fair description, I thought as I reflected on the sequence of events. My mom had broken the news a few weeks before my college graduation as I sat in front of my bedroom computer typing my last English paper. Listening to her, I felt the burn of my insides coming together in the pit of my stomach, nearly cutting off my airway. She'd spoken tenderly as I saw waves and stars and fuzzy dots. And then everything went dim. Recalling my mother's words, I sat blinking to black: *stage four colon cancer . . . metastasized to the liver and lungs . . . going to need a blood transfusion . . . and a whole lot of hope.*

"You know what, honey?" Gladys stood up from the chair, staring at my fingers tucked into the palms of my hands. "I think I'm set. I'll let you know what I think of these big ole britches. In the meantime, I want you to enjoy a few chocolate chip cookies and remember to be good to yourself."

I stopped short from her comment before smiling, relieved that the beating in my chest had suddenly stopped scattering its sound up my neck and into my eardrums. I watched as Gladys unfolded her short summer pants and smoothed out the creases.

"Thank you, Gladys," I said as I lowered my chin, wondering when I'd see her next. She had such a peaceful strength about her that made me wonder if she was the key holder to all the wisdom one needed to embrace what is—and what will be. Again and again, I felt the weight of the word *dead* and Gladys's comment that everything "leaves you so fast," from the dependence we can have with our ever-changing bodies to the people in our lives. Everything seemed to have an expiration date. Here today, gone tomorrow. And Gladys certainly didn't hide her fear or frustration because of it, which made me appreciate the realist that she was.

I was convinced she had life figured out, yet I couldn't help wondering if her profound takeaways and revelatory aha moments about her aging body, or her deep inner peace, had happened far later than she'd expected, when life gave her no other choice. I wondered what became more clear as she got older. Perhaps that was the point, an ironic certainty paired with wisdom's cheated timeline. But if I had anything to hold onto in that moment, it was an image of Gladys waving a pom-pom and a celebratory bourbon, chanting, "You can do this, you can do this . . . YOU CAN DO THIS!"

LIKE A VIRGIN

"Does he always have to call when I'm the one clos-est to the phone?" Yvonne snapped, slamming the receiver down in disgust. "He's such a per-vert!" There was truth to Yvonne's statement, no doubt about it. The same guy called frequently with inquiries on such minutia as how long the strip of cotton was in our thong underwear. "Would you say it's precisely three inches?" he'd ask, his words quietly coming through the holes against my ear. They were slow and careful and moderately creepy.

He seemed like a man with exquisite taste, or at least that was the conclusion that Farah and I came to after he asked if some of our delicately sewn French-style bras, priced like a pair of jeans, had "authentic silk" along the edges of the straps or if they substituted their intentions with polyester. And he would always ask if they came in red and black, with his first choice being the latter.

Farah was convinced he had naturally curly hair, small square teeth, and mimicked the characteristics of a serial killer. He said his name was Harry, and though he never gave me his last name, Farah took the liberty of giving him a last name for all of us, because she was also convinced that there was another part of him that was curled, like his fingers around Mr. You Know What, standing stiffly below his waistline when he felt the urge to call the lingerie department. So we called him Harry Curly.

Yvonne always tried to handle Harry with as much patience as she could possibly conjure when he called, smiling an uncomfortable smile as she looked around the department for someone to pawn him off to. Yvonne was down to business 99 percent of the time, with the remaining 1 percent dedicated to her husband, whom she called when the department was slow.

"I got some new ones in four," Farah said, sighing as she exited the dressing rooms. "She refuses to let me put her in a double-D—keeps rambling on about not being fat and that her doctor swore on the bible that she was getting 'full Cs.'"

"Shocker," our assistant manager, Rachel, mumbled under her breath before going into managerial mode. "Sell her what she wants, and bring her more than what she needs."

Farah flashed a fake smile. I knew that Rachel had called her out about flaking on fits and not bringing in enough bras to sell the customer so that the department numbers would continue to increase.

"I saw you bring a woman back into the dressing rooms holding only two bras, Farah." Rachel walked off, smiling smugly with an armful of thongs.

"You think I'll go to jail?" Farah asked with a straight face, and I knew Rachel's comment went in one ear and out the other. Farah's boyfriend, Lorenzo, was picking her up after work for some quality time on Rodeo Drive, and her objectives were clear.

"Grab the new Wacoal push up." I laughed, glancing at the phone to see one last blinking red light before Harry hung up.

As Yvonne gathered a pile of customer returns on the counter, I watched a young girl make her way around one of the panty tables, meticulously examining their patterns and thin linings. She was conscious of her surroundings, too conscious, like she was prepared to run off at any moment out of embarrassment. Her hair's golden streaks and dark abandoned roots shone brightly under the department's blinding lights.

"Do you need something?" I asked, moving out from behind the counter while staring at the neon bracelets bunched around her wrists.

"Yeah," she muttered, lowering her voice as she held four pairs of thongs and a small pile of push-up bras clenched in her hands. "Can I have a fitting room?"

I smiled, taking her bras and matching thongs. "No problem. I see you've done pretty well."

Leading her into the room, I watched as she hung her gray zip-up sweatshirt and rainbow-colored bag on a hook. She was quiet yet considerably confident in her pursuit. She watched me organize her bras and panties on the bar adjacent to her sweater, sneaking fast glances at my red cowboy boots. Before I closed the door, I gave her another warm, comforting smile.

"Thank you," she said, moving her arms closer to her chest. I spent the next few minutes putting away bras and panties that had accumulated on the counter and in the dressing rooms. It was a monotonous chore that we were all responsible for throughout our shift, but because the lingerie department had a steady flow of shoppers most of the time, the stray pieces of lingerie quickly turned into tall mounds on the counter and on the table in the back room. I was convinced management tallied our zealous exertions, so in an attempt to score quick brownie points with Rachel before checking back with my young customer, I walked to the front of the department to reorganize one of the disheveled panty tables. As I stepped out onto the walkway to study my tedious undertaking, I knocked a pile of thongs off another table.

"I got it," a deep voice said from behind me. I knelt down quickly to pick up the pile of thongs off the cold marble when I met his gaze.

"Thank you," I said sheepishly, stunned by the color of his turquoise eyes framed with long, dark, thick lashes.

We stood up together as he handed me the thongs he had picked up, smiling crookedly from the corner of his mouth. He was tall with broad shoulders and had an inviting jawline that led my awkward stare down his neck, right along the cavernous edging of his Adam's apple, and then right back up to his slightly messy, dark brown hair.

"Oh, thank you," I said again, my face warming up to a comfortable 99 degrees as he nodded, crooked smile still in place, and walked toward the double doors to where the time clocks were. He moved gracefully, loosening his blue checkered tie, leaving me standing in the middle of the walkway with a handful of chonies and warm insides.

"I saw that," Rachel said, slyly circling a mannequin.

"What?" I played stupid, hoping I didn't look as red as I felt, which would've made me Farah's perfect bull's-eye if she was near. Though, at that moment, as my face boiled down to its pasty normalcy, I wasn't too concerned; I wanted to know who it was that had disappeared through the double doors.

"You know what I'm talking about," Rachel teased as she walked off, smiling, picking up on my sudden intrigue.

At twenty-five, Rachel lived with her parents in a small house off of Melrose, hoping to find a good Jewish boy who knew how to play house. And as a frequent user of JDate.com, she seemed to be getting closer to matrimonial bliss, because she was going on dates at least four days a week, which we were all proud of because she was actually doing it.

Dating—the thought alone made my stomach drop. I pictured it being the other way around. I thought my long hours of pretend playtime burping baby while flipping plastic pancakes on my Fisher-Price kitchenette would have elicited a longing to pencil in the other half. But in actuality, I was one of Dr. Phil's episodes on noncommittal basket cases who fear far more than they should, hindering any possible growth whatsoever.

"You should try online dating," Rachel threw out on a daily basis. I'd carefully swallow her words and nod as their repercussions translated into a box of Franzia. I pictured an oversized blimp drifting through the summer sky with the words *complicated and looking for ass* under my name printed boldly across its side.

"HOW ARE YOU DOING IN THERE?" I ASKED, PEEKING THROUGH THE cracks of the door to make sure I had the right customer.

"Uh, I'm okay," the young girl stuttered, throwing on her shirt.

My eyes were still locked on her body, which stood motionless in front of the mirror. "Do you need some help with a bra?"

She took a second to respond, still anchored in the middle of the dressing room.

"Um, yeah, maybe," she stuttered again, slowly opening the door. "I'm not sure if this fits."

"Do you mind if I come in?" I asked, noticing the fresh coat of baby pink lip gloss sparkling on her lips.

"Sure." She hesitated, taking small steps toward the corner of the dressing room.

When I closed the door behind me, I noticed that she had reorganized the bra-and-panty sets on the chair next to the mirror, all of which shared sheerness in the crotch and thin stuffing in the cups of the bras. I stared at the order she had put them in, admiring her lingerie's seductive charm.

"I'm Natalee, by the way," I said, extending my hand. Tentatively, she placed her clammy hand in mine, her long fingers barely holding on.

"Molly," she said timidly.

"You have good taste, Molly."

She smiled halfway, her pale face reddening with embarrassment as she looked down at her black Converse shoes. I looked at her for a moment under the florescent lights, catching a quick glance at the small mounds of flesh packed into the waistband of her low-rise jeans. I turned to face her again, struck by the blueness of her eyes and the tiny pimples crowding the left side of her chin.

"Let me help," I said abruptly, looking over at her pile of bras and thongs.

Shyly taking a step back, she nodded with a faint smile. "Let's check out what you have on now," I said, hoping to elicit a sense of calmness, but I soon abandoned my intentions and asked her to lift up her shirt.

After a few awkward seconds, Molly took off her T-shirt. Her rib cage poked out as the collar moved over her ears and around her head. She threw her shirt on the chair and moved in front of me, quickly covering her stomach with her arms.

"Molly," I said, sliding closer to her presumably untouched breasts that were stuffed into a black lace push-up bra. "Forgive me if I sound intrusive, but may I ask what these are for? I mean, are you looking for everyday wear or bras to go under something specific?"

She moved her arms in closer to her stomach and stood crossing one leg over the other, nervously rolling her shoe to one side in response to my unexpected inquiry.

"I just need new bras," she replied softly, shrugging her shoulders, reluctant to divulge anything that might indicate her motives. I pulled on the band of her bra and lightly turned her to one side so she could see the back of her bra in the mirror. "This is way too big."

"It is?" she asked, confused.

"We'll fix it," I said, reaching for the doorknob. "Give me five."

Looking discreetly around the edges of the department for his dark, messy hair, I realized my mysterious thrill had not returned. Carrying on with my duty, I was curious to know more about Molly. I felt a pang of familiarity with her as she reminded me of my own youth. There was a unique and daring flair about her that I liked; it transported me back to Pink Floyd laser shows, Janis Joplin, and my parents' well-stocked liquor cabinet.

Staring at a baby pink push up with small splashes of pastels, I wondered if Molly's adolescence summoned the same kind of reckless abandon that mine had. Middle school and high school came, and my uncomplicated purity transformed into a burning need to understand the world and everything in it. I was sixteen and probably smoking more Marlboros than most of AA's twelve-steppers. Curiosity had overshadowed everything, pushing me to soak up as much experience as I possibly could. I wanted to be everywhere else but at home with my parents, because they had rules and curfews and sit-down family dinners with meat loaf and green beans. And as I sat between my brothers in an old wooden pew during Sunday school, still high from the magic mushrooms I ate the night before and listening to the same tired spiel about Noah's unfathomable ark, I prayed that my negligence wouldn't permanently fry my brain.

"Molly," I said, knocking lightly. "You doing okay?"

I watched the doorknob turn slowly as Molly welcomed me in. She hid her body behind the door, wearing a coral-colored push-up bra with her arms pulled tight around her small belly.

"I don't think this fits either," she replied bashfully as her cheeks warmed to a dark red.

"Here," I said, hanging her bras on the bar. "I brought you these."

"A C!" she shrieked in disbelief while looking at one of the tags. "Really?"

"I brought you 32 Cs to try; 32 bands, aside from a couple styles of 30s, are the smallest size we carry, which still might be too big."

She stood blushing in front of the mirror with a soft smile of gratitude. I waited outside the dressing room while Molly put on one of the bras I brought her. I wondered if I should've taken the time to measure her. Considering her small build, she'd maybe come in at around 29 inches; I knew it would've been unnecessary. Plus, I didn't want to make her any more uncomfortable as I tried to figure out what she really wanted.

"Wow, Molly, that looks great," I said, walking back into the dressing room. She blushed again and relaxed her arms, gracefully moving her body from side to side so she could view every angle in the mirror. Her breasts fit nicely in the cups, filling the space with ease and unfledged proposition.

"How old are you, Molly?" I asked abruptly.

"I'm fifteen, almost sixteen."

"You're almost legal," I said, my eyes widening.

She looked at me, confused. "I have, like, three years."

"I mean, for your driver's license," I replied, feeling awkward.

The room fell quiet, and I watched as Molly moved her gaze around the dressing room.

"It's for my boyfriend. We're sort of planning a night," she said in a low, indistinct murmur, looking down at the soft gray carpet with her hands shoved into the pockets of her jeans. Knowing what she was alluding to, I was at a complete loss for words, suddenly struggling to decide if I was Natalee, the open-minded bra fitter, or Mother Teresa on a Sunday wearing cowboy boots.

"Oh, I see. Alright, great," I replied idiotically, moving my eyes over to her lingerie. She watched me as I assessed her pile of bras and skimpy thongs on the chair.

"Here," she said, pulling out a crumpled magazine cutout from her bag. I stared quietly at its commanding overture, wondering how I was going to feel once I made it out of the bra fitting.

"So you like the look?" I asked, slowly studying a lingerie model's perky assets served up with bright red lace, shiny lips, and not an ounce of objectionable flesh or unwanted markings. Every inch of her body was a lean, mean, smokin' machine, making me rethink my rapport with cookies and brownies and tacos and maybe alcohol, and consider jumping on whatever plant-based nutrition plan this page-turner had going on.

The exchange made me feel uneasy, though, especially when I looked up to find Molly comparing herself to the long list of standards warming my fingertips right in front of my eyes and being so serious about it. It was easier when it was just Molly and me—without the model.

"I like how her boobs look in the bra," Molly replied, pointing at their tanned roundness as they spilled out from over the bra's silk edges. "She just . . . looks good."

"Alright." I tried speaking with deliberate intent while feeling guilty about my own reflection upon seeing our nipped paradigm spread open on the page. "You want something that you can get a lot of wear out of."

She stared at me without blinking.

"And something that fits you properly." I struggled, opening the door again.

My head buzzing with disjointed memories, I sunk my back into the padded wall next to Molly's dressing room, wondering if I should've left or stayed or called her parents or stopped asking questions. I was afraid to pick up another customer just in case Molly wanted to pay and get out as quickly and discreetly as possible. There was something inside me that still wanted to honor her wishes without feeling hypocritical or contradictory.

"I think I like this one," I heard her mumble from inside.

"Yeah," I replied, shaking my head at Farah as she came out of one of the rooms with her hands swaying below her belly button, kindly demonstrating the position of her customer's breasts. "Which one do you have on?"

Molly opened the door, dressed in one of the pink pushups. The cups covered just the right amount of breast tissue, giving her a "tasteful" amount of cleavage, though that part wasn't for me to measure.

"I like it," I replied, wondering which one she was going to pick for her boyfriend. I watched as she moved her body from side to side again, sucking in her tummy with every turn.

"Which one do you like?" she asked, looking at me with her big blue eyes and flushed cheeks.

I paused as I thought about her question, trying to decide which response would be the wisest and most appropriate.

"I like the one that Molly is comfortable in," I replied, emphasizing her name as I stuck her magazine page back inside of her bag.

I could feel her beginning to tense up as she ran her hand through her hair and then cracked her knuckles in unison, mimicking the sound of Pop-Its noise makers. I couldn't tell if she was negotiating with her body in terms of what it looked like to her, or if she was thinking about her boyfriend and what he desired to see.

"I've never done this before," she said, moving her gaze from her new perky breasts down to the floor. "I mean, I just want it to be, you know . . . I don't know . . ." She paused.

Suddenly speechless, I took a step back and looked at Molly in the mirror. I didn't know what I could or couldn't ask, let alone say, as a "professional" bra fitter whose dressing room discourse undoubtedly filled the hallway. But for some reason, I took the opportunity to meddle in her adolescence as if it was meant for me to understand, or at the very least, feel. Part of me couldn't believe I was having this conversation, but I continued, throwing caution to the wind without a second thought.

"Is this your first time, Molly?" I asked, lowering my voice. Her eyes widened as she stood close to the mirror. She took a second to respond to my question, which, frankly, was none of my business. But in that moment, as I stood with my back to the door, Molly's disposition, masked with fear, transformed into an unexpected calmness, rendering me even more anxious.

"Yeah," she muttered shyly, lifting her face to mine.

"Wow, okay," I stuttered as she stood with her hands shoved into her jeans. The thinness of her collarbones became more prominent as she shrugged her shoulders.

"What's his name?" I asked.

"Jacob," she said, smiling.

"Jacob," I repeated. "I knew a Jacob at your age. He used to pick his nose and wipe his rolled-up boogers under his desk." I thought about his rusty orange-colored hair and the cluster of freckles on his nose. "I'm sorry," I said nervously. "I don't suspect that your Jacob does that, but, wow, I remember it like it was yesterday."

"His boogers?" she asked, lowering her chin with a disgusted look.

"No, no." I laughed. "Feeling totally unprepared but curious and ready all at the same time."

Molly's eyes got bigger. "I really like him," she said, looking down at the carpet.

I could feel her attachment to Jacob as she spoke tenderly, reminding me of how vivid and consuming young love can be. "That's great." I smiled, glancing at the white lace lining half of her breasts. I tried to understand Jacob and what it was like to be fifteen again, wanting to experience what life had to offer on my own terms. "Is he funny?"

"He is," she replied, laughing.

"Good." I laughed with her, allowing her wide grin to quiet my list of pending inquiries. "Sounds like he's the lucky one."

Our laughter died down. I moved in closer to Molly and tightened the straps on her bra. "I'll let you figure out the bottoms." I reached for the doorknob as I glanced over at her pile of thongs.

Feeling like I was sixteen again, I circled the department quietly. It felt like only yesterday that I sat alone in a Planned Parenthood clinic and rifled through a brown paper bag stuffed with STD pamphlets, condoms, penis-burning spermicide, and a lollipop for good measure. I had skipped class to prepare for my virginity-losing triumph with my boyfriend of nine months, six days, and a hundred and twenty minutes. He was everything I never saw coming, and from the opposite side of the tracks. I loved him; I loved everything about him. And as the bell rang for math class, I flew out of the school parking lot, knowing my father was at work and my mother was at home cleaning away her OCD. The roads were clear, as was my conscience, impelling me one step closer to the very brink of womanhood.

Still circling the department in a daze, I could almost feel the burn below my waist as I imagined my backside exposed on the old down comforter I snuck out of my parents' house. It was two o'clock in the morning, and the only thing between me and my better judgment was Michael Morrison and a forty-ouncer of Mickey's Ice. Dirt and duck droppings framed our makeshift bed in the park next to the lake. It was cold, and I felt unskilled and disconnected, especially because Michael was older and more experienced. But I wanted it; I wanted to experience sex and like it. It was a perfectly planned farewell to my safely guarded virtue, and I was ready to cross over to the other side. I was ready to stand tall and hold my rights like a lioness, which is exactly what I did after I split ways with Michael and high-tailed it out of the park, praying to every god above that my father wasn't up drinking his morning coffee on the porch six houses down the block.

When I realized I was almost home free, I lightened my tip-toeing and slid under my white ruffled canopy, feeling exhilarated as my heart pumped a thousand beats. I gave my elaborate scheme a few more moments just in case my mother was to barge in, demanding answers. She rarely slept for long periods of time, waking up to the faintest sounds. But silence continued to prevail. My send-off was a success. And as each day passed, the numbness wore off, slowly overruled by a sharp vividness, leaving me free from any regret, and with a small piece of stolen memorabilia to hold on to, kindly thanking me for visiting Treasure Island Park.

I passed by a table of bras and thought about what Jacob might be like, and how I hoped, really hoped, he knew what he had. I thought about how Molly was feeling in the dressing room at that very moment, looking over her body with careful consideration. I wondered if I had scared her even more or made her feel at ease. I wondered what sex would be like for her—naked and distorted, moving blindly to the rhythms of unfamiliarity.

"Excuse me." I heard a voice from behind. "One of the sales-girls told me you have been helping my daughter Molly." I turned around quickly, stuffing my armpit with bras, startled by how much Molly looked like her mother.

"Yes. Yes, I am," I replied, looking around to see if Molly had come out of the dressing room. "I'll let her know you're here."

Instead of waiting by the counter as I had intended, Molly's mom followed me back to her room, calling out her name loudly.

"Mom?" I heard Molly ask, her voice trembling with panic. Molly opened her door dressed in her T-shirt with the red push up I picked out for her sitting on the chair next to a red thong.

"I'm not buying that!" her mother snapped sharply, bolting into the dressing room, looking down at Molly's bra.

"But, Mom!" Molly snapped back. "You said I could pick out a bra!"

"Yes, Molly," her mother replied bitterly. "Something prac-tical, something that won't make you look like you're asking for it!"

I took a step back.

"And what is this?" she asked, picking up the thong by its thin lining as her voice filled the dressing room. "These look cheap! You were raised better than this!"

"They're underwear!" Molly yelled, her eyes filling with tears.

I stood in the hallway, motionless, watching Molly's face melt into sadness. I was worried her mom was going to strip her of her selfhood, cut through her soft, unassuming dispo-sition without even knowing it. Though I completely under-stood the protectiveness; Molly was her daughter, navigating a big, scary world.

Noise continued to fill the hallway outside the dressing rooms. "I'll meet you out front," I interjected quickly, brushing Molly's arm with my hand. I walked straight for the counter and jumped on a register, signaling for the next woman in line to step forward with her items. Red-faced from shock and frustration, I tried regaining as much composure as possible, knowing my manager was floating around somewhere and customers were depending on me to do my job. I felt stuck and afraid to say anything, more worried about letting Molly down.

"I don't know what's going on in there," I heard one woman mutter as she joined the line. "That woman is still yelling."

A few long moments passed before Molly and her mother approached the register. I stood still.

"We're going to get these," her mother said firmly, setting two nude-colored cotton bras on the counter with her credit card. Staring at the mascara-stained corners of Molly's eyes, I slid the bras across the counter and scanned them into the register. We stood in silence while I ran the credit card and wrapped her bras in tissue paper. Her mother carelessly scribbled her name on the receipt and then left it, mumbling a quiet thank you as she took the bag by its handles and walked ahead, leaving Molly and her desired bras at the counter.

"I can't get any underwear," Molly said calmly as her mother moved out of earshot, wiping her cheek with the side of her thumb. I handed Molly her copy of the receipt, mustering up a friendly wink as I touched her shoulder. "You won't need them anyway."

She looked up and smiled, fidgeting with the strings hanging from her hood. "Thank you," she said, zipping up her sweater. "Sorry about my mom."

Standing against the counter in a quiet daze, I watched as Molly and her mom disappeared behind a tall, bare-cheeked mannequin. I wanted nothing more than the freedom to roam away from the lingerie department so that I could escape to the calm silence of my car. My brain was on overload.

"I'm off to dine." I waved to Farah as she stood examining her collision of cleavage in front of the mirror.

"If you see George Clooney out there, tell him Lorenzo's chopped liver."

"Yes, of course," I replied, picking up my pace as I headed toward the time clocks, still thinking about Molly and the pressure we can put on ourselves to look a certain way. What had I done?

Hurrying to order my salad from the coffee bar, a memorable voice cut in from behind. "Come on, pony up. I saw you staring down those cookies." Stepping to the side, I struggled for words as my face heated up to the color of the Roma tomatoes atop my pile of nothing. Once again, like a twelve-year-old girl, I stood fighting a speech obstruction born from the sight of my unexpected panty-picker-upper smiling his crooked smile.

"Yeah, they're tempting," was all that came to mind other than another imagined banner drifting into my periphery with four conspicuous words encouraging me to *get it the fuck together.*

"Chase." he said, extending his hand.

"Natalee." I smiled before settling on his eyes.

"You on lunch?" he asked, grabbing his cup of coffee from the end of the counter.

After watching him stir in two packets of sugar, I looked down at my five-dollar arrangement. "Something like that."

He laughed, pulling up a chair next to a crinkled-up *Los Angeles Times.* "Are you new?" he continued, slowly steering me into his corner.

"Uh." I paused, looking around the coffee bar. "New to the trade, no. But I am relatively new to this store."

As he ran his hand through his thick hair, I watched each strand relax.

"Are you selling shoes or button-ups?" I asked, balancing my fork, a packet of salad dressing, and the inescapable fact that I am, more often than not, socially inept when exchanging words with a good-looking member of the opposite sex.

"Suits," he replied, taking a sip of coffee. "We measure things a little differently down here." While I laughed out loud, quickly catching on, he continued, "I've recently started a production company in addition to writing screenplays, and this supports the rejection."

I giggled again, loving his honesty.

"You should come check out a small independent play I produced. It's at the theatre in North Hollywood tomorrow night, the one off Lankershim Boulevard," he offered coyly. "I think you will like it. And maybe even the drink afterward."

"Oh, alright, sure," came flying out of my mouth. "I'm actually off tomorrow, so I'll definitely stop by."

Rising from his chair, he smiled before handing over his timely pitch on Women Monologues. All I could see was Producer Chase Maxwell etched in fine red print. The name pairing sounded just right, sending a friendly flutter down my entrails and another round of self-sabotaging. The words *thank you* and *bye* couldn't have left my mouth faster.

Hightailing it to the top floor of the parking structure with thirty-two minutes to spare, I was determined to break away. I could barely hold still in the elevator as I watched the numbers rise, tapping my fingers against the brass railing. And then the mental probing started. *What will I wear? I have nothing to wear. I need new bras. My thighs are large. Does he have a child/children? Has he paid child support? Why did I eat that frickin' cheeseburger?* I suddenly felt like Molly with a checklist, feeling the influence and overwhelming effects social pressures really can have on women and young girls. This was truth, a collective truth . . . Molly's truth, and I found myself right back inside whatever magazine Molly ripped her page from, self-consciously sinking into its thick, shiny gloss. But why? For what?

Staring at the white bolded letters of the Hollywood sign, I sat in my car and quietly recalled Molly's request for sexy lingerie and well-constructed cleavage. I recollected the pieces of her desired image in my head, moving through the long silky hair, tan skin, sheer lingerie, and lavish backdrop. It was Molly's idea of beauty, which was both personal—and questionably skewed. The model represented only one kind of woman, emphasizing our culture's toxic conditioning and outrageously unrealistic inclusivity-lacking promotions. Molly was still trying to figure all this out, as was I. In our own private quests to feel sexy and control sexy—and rationalize sexy—it was easy to get lost within a set of predetermined ideals, a polished magazine page, or bold lace.

It was a complicated balance between wanting to feel empowered, yet somehow realizing it didn't necessarily require sexy satin. There were so many more variables. And as I continued to stare into the whiteness of the Hollywood sign, a different kind of questioning came beckoning. A dangerous, perpetuated belief that reared its ugly head again, ricocheting off dressing room walls and out into the world.

Choose something that won't make you look like you're asking for it.

BITTERSWEET

Pounding on my alarm clock, my nerves struggled to function properly. My morning ahead already had me feeling like I needed to practice breathing techniques as I prepared for a mandatory lingerie rally, also known as summer's "Feel Good Fit Party" for bra fitters. Fifty-plus women, unending bra talk, and a trip outside of my comfort zone at six o'clock in the morning on the 405 definitely had me questioning my work ethic. I was also eager for Chase's show, hoping that the bags under my eyes would fade by the time I tore my closet apart.

Finally pulling up to the department store thanks to Map-Quest and a double shot of espresso, I looked around the parking lot for familiar faces. I was nine minutes and forty-six seconds behind, and I hoped that Farah had saved me a seat in the back, far far away from whoever was running the show. Surprisingly, taking into consideration her often lackadaisical approach to life, Farah was always punctual when it came to work. I never understood it. Nor did I follow in her footsteps, however strong my intentions were.

"Right through those doors." A rehearsed smile guided me toward Cyndi Lauper's sorority theme song, "Girls Just Want to Have Fun."

The dread deepened.

"Holy shit" flew out of my mouth as I stopped dead in my tracks. Women were everywhere, taking up chairs and corners and small doorways. I watched as lines formed in front of a table prepared with fresh fruit, jellied pastries, cookies, juice, and hot coffee. The spread reminded me of something out of Martha Stewart's magazine, rousing my weaknesses as I geared up for the guilt. I spotted a surplus of colorful bras and panties hanging from a set of rolling racks, and then Farah, who was waving her hand like a Girl Scout while singing along to the lyrics, foolishly mocking our chosen industry.

"Nice of you to join us," she said as she moved her handbag from my chair.

"I made a wrong turn into Starbucks," I replied, still looking around the room, shocked at the number of women who were in attendance. Luckily, Rachel and our lead manager, Michelle, who had recently returned from a well-needed vacation, took note of my arrival as I offered a smooth pageant wave. Sometimes I wondered if Michelle struggled to keep herself anchored, placing way too much pressure on herself. And though I hadn't known her for very long, I quickly picked up on her patterns, noting similar neurotic qualities shared by my first manager in Seattle. Everything that came out of her mouth had the word "sell" in it, which made sense considering the operation. But her approach rested on a fine line between championing our efforts and micromanaging them. I felt bad at times, feeling her pressure as she hunkered down in her office to crunch numbers and plan events, hoping to keep her job, while filling the pockets of the big boys.

Conversations quieted as a tall blonde took center stage. Large bouquets of flowers sat on both sides of the long platform, adding a feminine touch to an already packed house full of estrogen and a pungent mix of perfumes. Every style of lingerie was strategically placed along the stage, from grandma's girdle to an influx of small cheeky cutouts.

"Welcome, sales associates, managers, regional managers, and buyers." The woman's peppy greeting filled the room. "We are in for a fun-filled morning! Are you ladies ready to view some great lingerie, or what?"

I took note of the time on the wall as the clapping grew louder.

"As we showcase the upcoming collection, we're going to go over sizes and colors and proper fitting and, most important, what women want to look like in this beautiful lingerie," she continued, bright-eyed. "And then I'd like to briefly talk about our customer service philosophy before you rock stars go make it an awesome day!"

"Oh, Jesus," Farah whispered as she sat clutching her phone.

Eyeing her doughnut and pile of fruit, I knew I needed to get something in my stomach other than shots of caffeine if I wanted to maintain a steady pulse. I was afraid to move, though, and I was happy that Farah found seats in the back so we could linger incognito. The last thing I wanted was to be accessible and called upon to partake in some bra trivia or, for the love of Mary, asked to model my girls in a new fall slinger. I didn't trust the process; therefore, I preferred the sidelines where I could observe thoroughly and plot my progress to the food table.

After ten long minutes of listening to our rally facilitator talk about her role as a veteran buyer, a collection of bras and panties were rolled onto the stage. Their bold colors and finely sewn lace ushered in an arrangement of whistles and cheers, preparing the crowd for a formal unveiling.

"Now, this is going to fly, ladies." She spoke about anticipated sales, holding up our "one-of-a-kind demi sexy bra" in a pale pink. "It will be hitting stores in the usual sizes, starting with a B cup and—drum roll if you will—going up to a G! That's right, we're going to make that G lady pretty in pink! It's about every woman, team!"

"Stack 'em high and watch 'em fly," Farah joked.

"And for a 'tissue tip,' fitters, you're going to want to pull all that in from the sides and then tighten those straps!"

"Tissue tips?" I repeated out loud, somehow lost within the vernacular.

My mind started to drift. I couldn't keep up with the lingo, and I had never seen so many exquisite bras and panties. I wondered if our morning get-together was an LA thing or if lingerie departments around the homeland were also shaking their pom-poms.

"Now for even better news, ladies," she said, holding up our most popular full-figured bra. "Our much-loved Fantasie line will now be hosting our H-sized customers! Can you believe it? Your Fantasie in an H cup!"

I was suddenly intrigued. It felt good to know that bras were changing and that people were making an effort to revolutionize our wares. It felt good to know that women had choices, whether they accommodated mosquito bites or a couple Dolly Partons.

"And how about this cute little bow?" our cheerleader continued. "I know we're getting closer to making the larger cup bras sexier."

I watched as a hand shot up toward the front.

"Are they only available in the Fantasie line?" a woman asked, her voice flat and far from muted. "What about all the other collections?"

The room grew silent as our facilitator nodded without speaking. It was clear that her propensity for words had suddenly slowed, making them even more contrived as she searched for the perfect answer.

"There are a few vendors who will not be selling G or H cups," she responded with a practiced undertone. "Some will continue to only carry cups from a 32A to a 36D, which is why we're really trying to branch out. We want women of all shapes and sizes shopping in our stores and we've set the tone, hoping to get as many sizes in as possible."

Everyone watched closely as she took a few steps back and pulled a new Spanx body shaper off a rolling rack.

"And speaking of all shapes and sizes, these babies are a gift from God! Look at how tight the fabric is!" She pulled on the shapewear's legs, stretching the eighty-dollar phenomenon in every direction before tightly gripping its waist. "I'm not kidding, ladies, these are pure magic, sucking in that unwanted tummy while hiding any and all traces of cellulite! No bumps and no lumps in the rump either! They aren't called body shapers for nothing!"

Her taxing modulation echoed right into my eardrums.

"I wonder if it comes in a full body?" I heard a woman ask from behind.

"And we're already seeing them fly out of stores. It's fantastic! It really does a great job at sucking in tummy rolls. Nobody wants spillage, right?"

Spillage, I repeated in my head as I looked down to find my backside nearly covering all four corners of the chair.

"Makes having sex exciting," Farah chimed in before returning to her phone.

I laughed, thinking about myself locked in a bathroom, fiercely gripping their promise, and sheathed in sweat.

As more lingerie made its way toward the front of the room, I finally made my way toward the snacks. I loaded my plate with an assortment of fruit and the last of the small pastries, eyeing the rationally-sized doughnuts at the end of the table. I figured my timing was perfect as the feel-good party looked focused, freeing me from any sudden obligation as I slowly moved along the table.

Unable to calm my indulgence until I got back to my seat, I planted my teeth into the center of a pastry, filling my mouth with raspberry goo as I held the soft edges with the tips of my fingers. It felt nice to observe from a different part of the room. And then, from out of nowhere, before I could even move my mouth to chew, music blasted from every corner, giving me a mild heart attack and making me spill cold orange juice down the front of my shirt as a line of tall, booby-bearing lingerie models strutted onto the floor.

"Let's hear it for our French collection!" our leader yelled over Mariah Carey's teakettle pipes. I stood frozen, watching their smooth backsides, swallowing up the thin strings, move effortlessly from side to side. Powdered doughnut remains hung from the corners of my mouth as more models emerged onto the scene. "Retailing at one hundred and ten dollars. Make sure to bring your customer the matching panty!" The enthusiasm carried on.

I could feel the sticky pulp settling into my cream button-up as I stared at other notable draws busting out of small fabrics. I turned toward the back to find Farah tearing up from laughter, gesturing for me to bring her a doughnut. I grabbed another glazed and a stack of napkins and bolted for my seat.

"You jumped a mile!" Farah snorted, obviously amused with my discomfort.

Embarrassed and feeling exposed, I shot her a glare.

"You need to lay off that coffee." She cackled even louder. "It's like crack cocaine for you Seattle people."

"Exactly," I retorted, collecting small yellow substances from off my shirt while chewing the rest of my pastry. I had no idea I was going to be attending a lingerie fashion show with models straight from the runway with legs akin to a set of bean-poles. Suddenly dreaming of celery, I watched as packages of panties made their way down the rows.

"Nude?" Farah asked as she pulled out a complimentary thong, her gratitude implied. "Again, makes having sex exciting."

Her comment instantly brought me to reality as I mentally prepared for her dating expertise, a bone I knew she'd bite.

"I'm going to a show tonight. Some guy from suits invited me."

Lowering her voice, Farah moved in closer. "Like a date?"

"No," I shot back quickly, watching a pair of oiled ta-tas smack against a thin layer of lace. "Like two adults meeting in the same place. One potentially inebriated."

"Yeah," she replied, still trying to whisper. "Like a date."

I waited as she sat quietly looking toward the front. "You'll need new lingerie."

Thanking nearby partygoers for more napkins, I continued smearing pulp into my shirt, still confused as to where Victoria's well-kept secrets came from. I was focused, nevertheless, watching models as they worked every last inch of lace. Their cleavage, however, hadn't quite measured up to a "proper" fit. The bands sat well above their shoulder blades, eliminating any possible back fat, and their breasts, perky and sprayed a golden brown, runneth over like hot fudge.

Something didn't seem right. Our pep talk had missing links. And as Mariah continued singing about her sweet, sweet fantasy, I sat feeling wet and in wonder. Where the hell was our G lady? Why did our feel-good party feel a little disproportionate? The reality of the dressing room didn't exactly transfer over, though I did appreciate the discourse around the importance of body positivity, and the power of women dressing themselves in whatever firm contraption or lackluster lingerie they chose. The enthusiasm around garments that could make someone feel confident and secure was essential.

ESCAPING THE ENCORE, FARAH AND I TRAILED FELLOW BRA FITTERS toward the lingerie department. Bright lights and soft music filled the store as sales associates scurried to their floors. Escalators began their trek while the clanking of register drawers echoed throughout.

"We're opening the doors in five, Redondo Beach," a voice declared over the loudspeaker. "Remember to put a smile in the aisle!"

"Sound familiar?" Farah rolled her eyes, guiding me toward the back of the department after borrowing a dressing room key from one of the employees. "This is what you need."

"You're crazy!" I laughed, flicking the cups of a high-ticket push up. "I barely had enough gas to get here this morning."

Without hesitation, Farah began singing our rally welcome tune, "Girls Just Want to Have Fun," while swinging our new tan thong.

"How about 'Girls just need money'?" I asked, comparing merchandise while looking around the department.

"Charge it," Farah replied, holding four specific bras in double-Ds, all of which I had been eyeing on the sales floor for weeks. Like Harry Curly, I, too, loved a nice black or red lace bra.

"Besides, Natalee"—Farah's tone changed—"it'll make you feel good."

Startled by her seriousness, my eyes met her gaze. I had never heard her speak my name so tenderly before, filling the space with subtle endearment. We had always communicated through playful sarcasm, our lack of interest in working retail, and a deep love for French fries and orange Starbursts. Something had suddenly shifted, and it caught me off guard.

"Don't move." Farah smiled, planting me in the middle of a dressing room before running out to return the room key. I turned toward the mirror and stared at myself, quietly welcoming the mellow draw of morning. I took off my new yellow button-up and paused. My reflection looked older and run-down under the beaming lights. The stretch marks lining the tops of my hip bones appeared deeper and more visible, reinforcing a bitter redundancy.

I stepped closer to the three-way mirror, slowly examining the vacancy in my eyes. I felt a sudden rush of deep understanding as I thought about my customers standing in the same position, under the same unflattering brightness, cracked open and bleeding from the inside out.

"Let's try this one first." Farah stepped back into the dressing room holding a smooth laced push-up bra. "Throw on one of your 1964 vintage finds with a good push up underneath, and you're ready to rock 'n' roll."

My boobs jiggled out of my bra as I laughed at Farah's friendly jab. We both stared at the paleness of their complexion.

"I think they've gotten longer." I looked down at my chest, eager to strap them in. After pushing and pulling and lifting and tightening, Farah stepped back to examine her selection.

"And there they sit." She stood behind me, crossing her arms. "Own it!"

I turned to the side, carefully studying the bra's placement as bits of my back's flesh rolled over from the tightness of the band.

"Back fat or saggy tits, take your pick." Farah's charming benevolence put me at ease.

"I don't want the double bubble," I replied, taking off the bra while thinking about some of my customers' requests. Many similarities came to the forefront.

Pleading her case, Farah slid the straps of a French-made demi off a plastic hanger. It was one of my favorite bras to look at. The sex appeal was spot on, with just enough black lace stitched around the cups. It was the kind of bra that made me understand Farah's push for "dressing to feel good." Her position was valid, and I respected the certainty in her voice.

"This is it!" Farah quickly moved to the side, making one last strap adjustment as I settled into the bra. I stared at the fullness of my boobs, noting two Ds on the tag, and once again found myself lost within a complicated balance between desire, need, and what the bra was *supposed* to look like as it held up my meaty assets and blurred perceptions.

"You should be getting cramps in your toes and sweat down your forehead in that thing!" Farah said as she lowered her voice to the sound of a customer and her toddler son.

I laughed out loud, shaking my head to her gracious conduct and all of its truth. *It's just a bra,* I told myself. One big sexy bra.

LATER THAT EVENING, WHEN I ARRIVED AT THE THEATRE, I WAS pleased to find an open spot in the back. All I could think about was blending in as much as possible, giving me more opportunity to sit and people watch. I marveled at how unique the theatre was: a perfect vintage find equipped with old chandeliers, red velvet seating, and bright, ambiguous paintings that could lead one to believe in fairy tales. The intimacy was just right, as was the creaky hardwood stage furnished with a minimalist's touch and, ironically, a glaring spotlight on a women's dressing area. The mood felt comfortably strange, too, leading my pensive stare directly onto Chase's well-fit blue jeans while I watched him take a seat toward the front of the house, his dark hair perfect. My attack of extreme nerves wasn't lost on him; opening night had to have been the biggest hurdle of them all with more demands than I'd know what to do with.

Darkness settled quietly, the spotlight casting a shadow around a tall woman as she walked across the stage alone. She spoke with a stern face, sharing an anecdote about hating her body. Powerfully uncompromising, she cut the dialogue wide open, making room for other castmates to boldly share their own stories of heartbreak, loss, trauma, and the hardships of being a woman in society, especially a woman of color.

Pondering a barrage of inquests, I thought about some of my encounters in the dressing room and all the women I had met in a short time. There were so many parallels between the stage and the fitting room, bringing forth a deep articulation of fear, invisibility, self-loathing, and the shameful fact that our history's principles were built on misogyny, racism, and bigotry. My experience as a bra fitter had suddenly spilled its glaring contents while I sat analyzing its impact. I couldn't get away from it or make sense of it. And as a band of women formed their presence around me, softly and boldly sharing their truths from a backdrop of mirrors to a hardened platform, I had one realization after another, quietly acknowledging a lineup of maddening disparities. Everything about my evening thus far gave me a mixed bag of feels. The world had so much to listen to and learn from. So much to resist and change. The tensions tightly woven around gender—and my own privilege—came into a sharp focus, making me want to rewind some of my time in the dressing room. A startling thought for sure.

"You'll join us for the after-party, right?" Chase asked with a small nudge. Quickly thinking about Farah's parting words, which were along the lines of "saddle up," I accepted without hesitation. Chase had depth far beyond his three-piece suit, and it rattled my brain, causing another round of ceaseless probing: *Maybe it's just sex. There's nothing wrong with just sex, I don't think, though I'm not on birth control and motherhood is really a stretch right now. He's also slightly awkward, and I like it. I wonder what kind of hair products he uses. I need to invest in a better dry shampoo. There's nothing wrong with "just sex." I'm human. Humans have sex. Women have sex. And then we get labeled for "just having sex." Vodka it is.*

Magnetized by the strip's flashing lights and lively confusion, we entered Hollywood's universe and all its dirty corners. I followed Chase and his group of friends into the bar, taking in the scene while trying to remain carefree.

"So why LA?" Chase asked, moving his eyes along my collarbone as soft music played from a variety of turns. Thinking quietly, I had hoped for different circumstances in terms of what brought me to LA. Ones that didn't require uncomfortable explanations, or a complete evaluation of familial constructs. I didn't have it in me to revisit the tennis-ball-sized tumor bulging from my mom's lower back, or the golf ball protruding from her forehead.

"I needed something different," I finally replied, running my eyes around his mouth. "Something that offered sunshine and culture and purpose. I wanted mileage."

"Mileage?" His eyebrows sprung up. "Open window, Tom Petty." He smirked, quietly understanding my search.

"Sometimes it doesn't make sense to stay with what's familiar," he sighed. "Chicago was killing me."

Silence cut between us. I waited. Candles flickered as the ambiance transformed into a boisterous revelry, making the butterflies in my stomach spread across my sides. Tapping my foot against the barstool, I watched as Chase ran his fingers through his hair.

"Just sex" is perfectly okay.

"So what's next?" he asked intently.

I took a deep breath and looked down at the floor. I could feel my limbs loosening as his open-ended query pushed a blast of panic through my upper body. I instantly thought about my dad and his box dinners.

"I have no idea."

Chase remained quiet. It was obvious that he picked up on my troubling uncertainty.

"Tequila toast!" one of his friends yelled over the music, signaling for the bartender to revisit our end. "And then it's bull riding!"

I nearly choked on my straw at the mention of bull riding.

"Bull riding?" I asked, wide-eyed.

"It's a bar a few doors down. Have you not been to the Saddle Ranch?" Chase asked with a grin.

"Uh, no."

"Bulls and rock 'n' roll!" another friend chimed in. I tried gathering as many images as I could, none of which involved me getting on a mechanical bull. There wasn't a dollar amount in the world that would even prompt me to consider gyrating my lower half in a room full of gelled sideburns and infantile hard-ons. Besides, I would've ended up on YouTube faster than the medic could've rolled out the stretcher, my Hanky Pankys on display from my legs wrapped around my neck. The idea was nonsense. But I was slightly intrigued by the opportunity to participate from the sidelines.

"Bottoms up!" Chase slid a shot of tequila into my reach.

I started to feel a little nervous, making sure my taxicab number was still buried deep in my clutch and remembering that Sunset turned into Beachwood Drive after approximately five turns. I needed to keep in mind that I really didn't know Chase. I wasn't sixteen and riding in cars with strange boys. I was in the early stages of adulthood and riding in cars with strange boys. And though my intuition calmed my apprehension, I had to be somewhat responsible while continuing to foster my "in the moment" mantra. I also had a Ford Escort to find in the morning, hopefully still squeezed into a back alley, and then prepare myself for another long day of bra talk and body parts. But as the crashing of glasses resonated alongside the burn rising in my throat, I couldn't resist Chase's declaration as he reiterated our plan with great enthusiasm.

"Bottoms up!"

STRUGGLE OF
THE JUGGLE

"Excuse me, ma'am? Ma'am. Ma'am?" A voice crept into my eardrums, pushing the pain inside my head closer to a full-on explosion. "Do you work here?" the woman asked, moving closer. Sliding my tongue along the fur growing on my two front teeth, I tried pulling myself together, hoping that the smell of tequila wasn't seeping from my pores. I hadn't showered or brushed my teeth or deodorized or found even the slightest bit of hope to get me through my eight-hour shift, which I was praying to cut to five. I was an absolute tragedy, hauled from the rubble, packing a wad of spearmint gum on the roof of my mouth and dirt along the short white edging of my once well-groomed fingernails. Keeping up with my high-end department store's expectations as far as "proper" appearance didn't exactly earn me poster child status. I was one burning Jameson away from losing teeth, and one tequila shot away from seeing dead people. And for the first time in my life, I hoped it wasn't my mother.

"Yes, I do work here," I replied cautiously, my head spinning like a tumbleweed. "What can I help you find?"

"I was actually just hoping you could point me in the direction of your Spanx body slimmers." *Point?* I thought. *Yeah, I can point. I can point all day from my corner of recovery while pretending to resize a fixture of bras if it meant keeping silent with a long phony smile. Time was all I needed.*

"Can I grab a style?" barely left my mouth when the customer nicely shunned me, walking away to fend for herself. I was momentarily saved, feeling less of the panic due to the severe dehydration I suffered. What the hell happened last night? And are my limbs intact despite any rough handling? Determined to work through the fuzz piece by piece, I turned back to the bra wall and started with the Saddle Ranch. I couldn't understand why I felt so uneasy about my evening. I had found my way back to Beachwood Drive via Yellow Cab after a fare negotiation through Taco Bell, and Chase had kindly walked me to my door, and my limbs had indeed been intact. I didn't do anything that would've led to regret, like premature slumber parties, bull riding, or, heaven forbid, a wet T-shirt contest. I was safe, but really anxious and slightly wobbly and so fucking thirsty I began to have a lisp. There wasn't a person in the world other than fellow sales associates who understood the challenge of being on your game with my department store. There was no time for slacking or multiple breaks or poor hygiene. We were right on par with the Ritz-Carlton, and if you weren't ready to serve the customer, so help you, Prada.

"There's a woman in five who needs a fit." Rachel snuck up from behind. "Michelle and I will be in an interview if you need us."

"Oh, okay," I said slowly as I watched both Farah and Yvonne enter the fitting rooms with a handful of bras, Farah stopping abruptly to give me a suspicious smile. I scoped the front of the department, wondering if Chase had made it to work yet. I was eager to see him, yet a little reserved due to the fuzz.

"Hi there." I knocked twice at the door to five, sniffing a pungent scent similar to what I imagined Woodstock would have smelled like trailing the hallway.

"Hi!" a loud voice welcomed me in.

Looking up, I nearly froze at the sight of a six-foot platinum blonde with a parrot adorning her shoulder.

"This is Raul," the woman said, widening her red lips. "He's very friendly."

"Hello, Raul." I lowered my chin in confusion. "What can I help you find?"

"Well." She paused in front of the mirror, slowly moving her shirt over Raul and then above her head. "I need cleavage to go with a specific dress I'm wearing tonight, and this isn't doing it for me."

"Alright." I continued to respond with a steady nod, quickly eyeing the measuring tape hanging on the wall and then the breasts hanging off her chest, trapped underneath her bra's underwire.

"I'm sorry to be so rushed, but I don't have a lot of time, and Raul, though friendly, can grow restless. I just flew over here, realizing I need major help."

"Sure, I understand" came out as one big lie. I'm not only half alive, but I could potentially get mauled by an impatient bird while fitting a half-naked woman for a bra. Like cats, birds come as unpredictable creatures in my eyes. They present themselves as vultures that could wrap their barbwire claws around one's neck at any moment, taking with them a vocal cord or a chunk of soft tissue. My uneasiness about being over-served at the Saddle Ranch had nothing on my uneasiness about Raul.

"Tell me the cut of the dress." I tried concentrating while looking over a blinding crest of florescent green coverings on Raul.

"It's fairly low," she said as she moved her hands along her chest, stopping at her sternum. "And I want my boobs UP." She moved her breast tissue accordingly. I examined the thickness of her breasts, in addition to their length, hoping I could nail her size based on assumption and determine my work was done. However, I knew it wasn't that easy. Her ill-fitting bra threw me off, and because my cognition was substantially impaired, I knew I needed to go in hands first.

"Go ahead and raise your arms," I said, moving strategically behind my customer while yanking the measuring tape from off the bar against the wall. I could smell a mixture of sweetened pines coupled with the hearty musk of the great outdoors. Eyeing Raul, I carefully wrapped the measuring tape around the woman's rib cage. "You mind picking up your . . ." She caught onto my fragmented guidance, lifting her breasts so that I could rewrap my intentions. I quickly settled on a number and discarded the tape, hoping for a little fine-tuning as I struggled to comprehend the simplicity of the same black linear markings from the day before . . . and the day before that.

"Who's your customer talking to in there?" Farah asked, joining me at the counter with a pile of bras ready to be rung up.

"A parrot," I replied flatly, watching Farah's facial expression transform into a cackling roar.

"You mean a bird?"

"No, Farah, a donkey who also goes by the name *Parrot*."

I waited as Farah gathered herself, watching drool hit the sides of her mouth.

"How was last night?" she finally asked, catching on to my lack of interest in everything lingerie. "You look a little haggard."

"You think?" I asked sarcastically, eyeing the sales floor for a handful of 40 triples.

"You're going to have to—"

My name rolled off the tongue of the operator and echoed throughout the store: "Natalee Woods, 64."

"Shit," I said, setting the bras on the counter. "What's this?"

"A phone call." Farah signaled for her customer. "Hit pound first."

I stood by the telephone and went over a few possible scenarios. What if something happened to my dad? Or maybe Chase never made it home after dropping me off, and the cab driver threw him and his Nachos BellGrande off the Santa Monica Pier. Everyone had always called the department directly, so why, of all days, was someone seeking me out via the operator?

"Thanks for holding, this is—"

"Natalee, yes." A direct voice spoke through the holes. "This is Roxanne, the store manager."

My legs nearly buckled as I gripped the phone cord. "Hi."

"Are you with a customer?" she asked, getting to the point.

"Uh, yes," I responded slowly, certain that I was moments away from filing for unemployment.

"No problem. When you're done with our customer, swing by my office for a second."

"Sure, yes, absolutely" flew out of my mouth as I stood staring at Farah wide-eyed. "I'll be there shortly."

Panic-stricken to hear from Roxanne Michaels, aka Big Cheese, Bitch on Spikes, the "I Couldn't Smile If My Life Depended on It Because You're an Insignificant Peon and I'm a Store Manager," made me rethink my mind-set. She ruled the roost with more Gucci pencil skirts than the Kardashians. And her manner was thunderous when any nonsense got in her way. Michelle and Rachel, bless their severed hearts, bolted straight for the front of the department upon catching sight of Roxanne's five-ten frame musing about. She packed her ass and top-of-the-line Bentley into tight spaces in high places. Her role was nothing short of scary, and I was about to experience its wake.

Barely able to control my nerves, I came to a screeching halt as I entered the dressing room and found Raul eating pellets off his owner's shoulder.

"I, uh, brought you a few styles of triple-Ds to try. I think the cup size will fit you nicely."

"Fantastic! Do you mind helping me get into it since I'm crunched for time?" she asked, tearing off her bra. I stared at the placement of Raul's feet, noting his claws nearly carved into her flesh, reminding me of Freddy Krueger in *A Nightmare on Elm Street.*

"They're really a charismatic species," she said, staring at me in the mirror while I unhooked a black plunge bra.

Moving cautiously two steps closer, I examined the purple rims of her glasses as they boxed in the brightness of her blue eyes. "Does he talk?"

"Does he talk?" She exploded with excitement, suddenly speaking Spanish and French and English while holding out her arms. Regretful that I encouraged life out of Raul as we coexisted in proximity, I helped carefully slide the bra straps up and over each shoulder, listening to my customer engage in trilingual banter with a bright plumage of filth. And though I appreciated her devotion and self-confidence, Raul's responses came out in whistles and squawks and indecipherable "hellos," making the black eyes plastered on the sides of his head appear creepier. I fastened the band and moved toward the door. I couldn't bear another moment as time with Roxanne Michaels pended. Maybe she spotted me hiding in the corner, dazed and confused, like I had just been released from the dark, and the bright department lights finally proved to be everything but advantageous.

"And then there were two! This is fantastic, I'll take this one!" she yelled.

Yes, I thought, cracking the door for air as I watched her breasts shake up and down.

"Oh, and here," she continued, handing me a business card. "Come see me."

Staring at the dark bolded words, "Diane Hart: Psychic Medium and Soul Guide," I wasn't quite sure how to respond.

"Oh, okay, thank you." I flipped the card over to find a picture of a smiling child riding a large stallion with the sun in the background. I wondered whether I should view the image as a metaphor for everything I needed to welcome into my life, aside from Pampers.

"It's pretty straightforward." Diane spoke earnestly. "And it might lend new direction."

I paused at her sudden innuendo, wondering what she saw that I needed to see. I stuck the card deep into my pocket. She nodded quietly, unhooking her new purchase. I could feel a shift within our exchange, something indescribable and unexpected and oddly comforting. I worked against time only to want more. And as the tumbleweed slowed its surge, making room for an assembly of what-ifs, all I could do was hold onto the wall.

"New direction?" I pondered its implications, realizing that Diane was no ordinary customer. We didn't cross paths just for the art of placing her bountiful boobs into a few slingers and calling it a day. Our interchange felt much deeper, knocking me right off my escape-fueled clouds and into the light, mounting every cutting fragment of unwanted reality. Fear and self-doubt had their own mileage, as loud and uncompromising as they can be. A "soul guide" sounded promising.

"Sooo, your work." I prompted her to stop for a second. "What exactly do you do?"

Mentally recording my situation with a naked woman and her parrot, I was prepared for anything.

"I'm a psychic medium," she replied, turning her body toward me. "I can connect with loved ones who've passed on and help guide those who might need new direction. Some people think of it as cheap therapy, others think it's a crock of shit."

"Wow, alright." I nodded as my stomach dropped to the floor. *Connect to loved ones*, I repeated in my head ten times, wondering what exactly it entailed. I'd never experienced such direct handling in the dressing room while in the opposite role. Her bold exposition threw me a little. But I was intrigued. My "spiritual path" was radically untraditional and full of suspicion. I sought tangible evidence, and a lot of amens for fried chicken and sweatpants. I was a realist who believed in nothing and the possibility of everything at the same time, hoping I'd get to my place of rest and find Ryan Gosling working door duty while Snoop Dogg passed out party favors. If Diane could give me something legitimately good to hold onto, I was in.

Watching Raul adjust his stance, I surrendered to the novelty of Diane Hart and all the effects that followed.

"How'd you ever—" I paused before she quickly cut in.

"Figure out who I am?"

"Well, yeah." I stared.

"Since childhood, I've always had a pulse on different planes, I guess. And then my sister died unexpectedly and everything changed."

"You mean like . . . change like . . ."

"I started to hear things and feel things, names and sounds. It's hard to explain. But something brought me to a completely different place, yet I wasn't the one driving, you know?"

"Huh." I stood motionless, completely transfixed in the moment.

"Follow your intuition." She smiled, checking the time. "Listen to *who* you are."

Who I am? I questioned, once again struck by the intensity of insight we experience as human beings. It often comes out of nowhere. Lost in an aching mind while leaning into our insecurities. Confused as a motherfucker. And then there was Diane, a kindred spirit (minus Raul) who seemed so . . . together, almost untouched by all of life's weight. Or maybe she wasn't, but knew how to survive the game. Either way, I was convinced Diane came into the lingerie department to shed light on something I needed to understand about myself—and the great big mysterious world around us. It was precisely the transparency one receives upon letting another person in far enough to make an impact that true transformation can happen, even when it shakes us from our comfort zones and comes from unexpected places. In a matter of seconds, Diane showed me how important it is to take cues from other people, however big or small they might be.

"I'll wear this tonight and let you know how they did." Diane laughed, grabbing her new bra.

"Sounds good," I replied, still spellbound as I caught sight of Roxanne Michaels walking toward her office. "Let's stay in touch."

WIPING SWEATY PALMS DOWN MY SLACKS, I STARTED FOR THE DOUBLE doors in customer service. Farah's assistance in lending mints, deodorant, fruit snacks, a nail file, and a mist of perfume made me feel a little more put together. My desperation had no bounds.

"Hi, Roxanne." I knocked softly on the office door, eyeing one of Van Gogh's tiresome nights above her desk.

"Natalee, hi." She smoothed out the wrinkles in her knee-length skirt as she stood up from her leather chair. "Please, have a seat."

Quickly sitting down to the slow motion of her hand, I felt another booming headrush, hoping that at some point my bloodstream would flow its way back to regularity.

"I won't take up too much of your time," she started in, relaxing into her chair. I couldn't help staring like a fool. Roxanne Michaels was breathtakingly beautiful, a real stunner, as Farah would say. Her skin was Lancôme controlled from her forehead down to her chin, making way for a smooth, golden bronze, dark strategic lashes, and wet Chanel lips. Her brown hair, slicked with style in all the right places, reminded me of Twiggy. It was sexy and controlled, like the rest of her. Roxanne Michaels certainly fit the high-end mold, though I was afraid she knew it.

"First up." Roxanne faced her computer, squinting as she moved her eyes down the screen.

My heart slid down my pants, cutting off all air. I hated being put on the spot.

"I have something regarding your department."

I watched as she moved a piece of paper to the side.

"I received a letter from a customer who was in last week. It involved a different sales associate from your department, but I'd like to bring it to your attention, as I will continue to do with the rest of your team."

"Okay," I said, fidgeting awkwardly.

"The customer said in her letter that one of the girls was a little too forceful with her breasts, and she felt rushed out of the department."

"Wow, alright" slowly left my mouth, adding even more bewilderment to our unexpected exchange. If there was a response in the world to Roxanne's disclosure per our violated customer, I certainly didn't have it. Especially after I thought I'd heard it all.

"It's important that we take as much time as needed with our customers and remember that their vulnerability is heightened. As a professional bra fitter, it's your job to make them feel at ease, which I know you do."

"Yes, absolutely," I replied, nodding my head to a fleeting image of Farah snapping her fingers to the time clock in addition to my raging impulse to get Raul through the exit. I shouldn't have thought of him as filth.

"I know lingerie can get overwhelming from time to time, but I just want to reiterate the importance of acting appropriately. You ladies have an important job to do."

An important job? I'm just trying to pay rent, sister. And figure all this shit out.

"Yes, of course." I nodded.

"Second." She moved another letter into view. "I have a customer who's requesting a seasoned bra fitter and structured one-on-one time."

"O . . . kay," I replied, lowering my head in confusion as to how or why I was an option for the task. *Seasoned* seemed like a lot.

"She's specific about not wanting management," Roxanne confirmed. "And you're working when she'd like to come in. I'll be reserving a room for her in women's wear or maybe up in lingerie. She has requested as much privacy as possible."

My hearing started to fade as Roxanne's words became jumbled. I had quickly come to understand how unpredictable the lingerie department, as well as the human race, was, but lacked the tools to deal with the changeability in a successful manner. Staying on your toes was an understatement at best. Each day brought something new, as did every woman, constantly pushing me to make sense of my place in the dressing room—and every subsequent step that followed.

"Thanks, Natalee. I'll follow up with a time frame." Roxanne smiled while reaching across her desk, clutching every one of my fingers with convincing propriety before I bolted for the double doors.

RUMMAGING THROUGH AN OUT-OF-PLACE CLEARANCE ROUNDER IN the teenage-inspired subdivision, I paced myself back to the lingerie department. I felt even more on edge upon leaving Roxanne's office, and I couldn't quite figure out why. Maybe it was the anxiety from just being in her office while looking like death's latest development. All I wanted was anonymity, which wasn't lost on me as I considered Roxanne's request and whoever needed seclusion in order to buy lingerie. Hiding beneath my bedcovers quickly took priority over everything, including the heart-stopping cheeseburger I had been dreaming about since I rolled off my mattress twenty-six minutes before I was due to shine. The abundance of adult beverages I'd consumed, coupled with unwavering heart palpitations, had me on serious tenterhooks.

"There she is!" I heard a familiar voice welcome me back to the department.

"Gladys!" I wrapped my arms around her small frame, trying to sound enthusiastic. "What a treat."

"Oh, honey, those cute boys are washing my car next door, and I thought I'd come in and see if you wouldn't adjust the fit on this bra and send me with a few more swim trunks."

I smiled as her presence suddenly put me at ease. "Remember what I told you about the straps. When the girls are letting you down, tighten them up!"

"Honey, that's going to take a lot of strap!" She laughed out loud, kindly leading the way.

Helping with her purse, I guided her into the dressing room chair.

"It's damn hot again." She patted her forehead with a Kleenex before unbuttoning her shirt.

"Your hair looks nice, Gladys."

"Beverly Hills has some damn good beauty parlors."

I laughed at the sound of "beauty parlor," thinking about my grandmother's visits growing up. She'd stick me in the corner with a lollipop and a book, and I'd watch as the room filled up with hot air and sticky fumes.

Pushing the chair toward the center of the dressing room, I signaled for Gladys to stay seated.

"Is this still comfortable for you?" I pulled on the straps.

"Oh, yeah, honey. It just feels looser."

"Are you wearing this one more than the others?"

"Well, maybe." She stared at me in the mirror. "I can't keep track of what slinger goes to what day."

"Well." I laughed as her voice carried. "As long as you feel snug and supported, then things are looking up. Just remember to rotate your bras."

She snickered softly, continuing to stare at me in the mirror. "You look tired, honey."

"I am, Gladys." I pulled on the second strap, flooded with splashing tequila shots and an image of me struggling to enter my apartment with my car key.

"Long day at the office?" She sensed my hesitation as I fought her eye contact.

"You ever wonder how nice it would be if we had all the answers?"

"Hell no!" she snapped back, looking up at me with her glossy eyes. "We wouldn't get anywhere, honey. And we'd sure as hell never learn anything."

I let her reaction resonate as the silence stretched between us. Carpet stains shined under the lights as I reached into my pocket to feel the corners of Diane's business card, making sure it was still within reach. I could tell Gladys was deep in thought, moving through my question layer by layer.

"It was sudden and quiet." She spoke carefully. "I went into the bedroom to grab our checkbook and came back out to find Archie keeled over in his reading chair. I remember just standing there, frozen in time, knowing that just seconds before, we had shared our last words. It was so strange. And after I called an ambulance and tried CPR, I just sat staring at him alone one last time."

I stood speechless, choking up from Gladys's reverent honesty. Her words came out in punches as I pictured her standing in the middle of her living room, surrounded by death's quiet grip and the looming wail of sirens.

"Oh, honey, I searched for all sorts of answers until I realized they didn't exist. Why didn't I get his heart checked? Did he know something was wrong and not tell me? Was he really a better pinochle player than me? I woke up the morning after I buried him and felt the loneliest sorrow I've ever known. You're stripped of everything. Damn near dead yourself. But—" She paused, looking up at me dotingly. "Sometimes you have to let time do its thing."

Staring at her half-naked body, I felt every blow of her sadness as her words echoed inside my brain.

"I know it's tough without your mom, honey. My trick is to think about the good, if you can."

"Yeah." I breathed in deeply before exhaling, still holding on to every one of her words. "I just wish she could've known me as a woman. A good one, you know?"

Gladys's boobs swayed as she moved in closer to touch my hand.

"She knows more than you think, honey."

Wetness seeped from my nose. Everything felt clammy and bare, yet reassuring in its truest form. And as I looked down at Gladys sitting in the chair with her areolas peering out through the bra's lace, I realized what she meant about the power of timing. We both had something to say, big and small, with infinite parallels widening our onerous terrain. The moment was ours, given to us freely, and it couldn't have been more complete.

"So . . ." I waited, imagining Gladys alone, gazing at her husband's lifeless body, "you just stared at him? I . . . can't imagine what that felt like. I mean, a man you spent so much life with. Whom you loved. Achingly. Every day. And then . . . nothing."

Gladys stared at me quietly, searching for whatever response would set her free. Momentarily free. Breathtakingly free. "I remember thinking, *I was just in our bedroom seconds before*. It's such a hard testament to how fleeting life is. It goes by so damn fast. You just—" She paused, rubbing her kneecaps again. "You just never know, which is why you have to treat every day as it comes. You gotta take the good and the bad."

I hung my head in the silence that followed.

"How about another black Feather Light and some trunks, honey." Gladys winked, softly brushing my arm. "Sounds like we both need to get the hell out of here."

I smiled, quietly embracing an unexpected reverence. "Are you sure you want another one?"

"Why not?" She looked up with a twinkle in her eye as her mouth widened into a denture-shining grin. "Eat your heart out, Madonna!"

Looking sharper than before, I emerged from the dressing room with Maybelline's best smeared along my under-eye bags. I immediately started Gladys's transaction at the register, discreetly throwing handfuls of sample lingerie wash into her shopping bag.

"They're all yours," I said, smiling as I handed Gladys back her credit card and purchases while we walked toward the women's lounge.

"Damn right." She winked again, giving her breasts one last shake as she headed toward the escalator.

Upon entering the lounge, I took quick refuge in the nursing room, welcoming the dim lights and long strains from exhausted breast pumps. I sat with my eyes closed, knowing that if my department manager came in—or heaven forbid, Roxanne Michaels—I'd be pumping the gas right out of The Grove. My mind drifted as my eyelids grew heavier. I could feel my legs sinking into the soft cushions while I listened for small hints of life. Images of an imaginary Archie took the lead as I thought about him sitting in his reading chair, lucky to have had a woman like Gladys. My own heart pumped gently for the first time all day. And then reality came knocking like it always does, shaking me from my slumber.

"Is the lingerie department on this floor?" a woman asked from behind the darkness. My immediate feeling was to keep quiet and continue relishing in my warm sanctuary. I couldn't possibly take on another customer. No way. I needed French fries and water and fresh air and Diane Hart. I knew it was out of the question, though, especially since I was on Roxanne's radar, with a killer work ethic.

"It is." I stood up slowly and guided the woman toward the door. "Is there something I can help with?" She waited, carefully choosing her words while looking over my sullen black eyes.

"I need to get a few things."

"Yes, of course. I can help," I replied. "I actually work in lingerie and was just taking a quick breather."

She stared at me longer.

"I'll walk with you." I smiled, noticing the same soggy darkness under her eyes.

"I'm Natalee, by the way." I extended my hand.

"Julie," she responded with a faint smile.

"So, what are you looking for?" I asked, still staring at her bleeding eye makeup, knowing that my own mess, suffocating my pores from the night before, was CoverGirl's dream come true.

"I'd love to have some new lingerie. Maybe some bra-and-panty sets," she replied, looking around the department before running her finger along the elaborate stitching of one of our lace demi-cuts.

Picking up on her attention to detail, I waited to investigate her purpose. Meanwhile, I introduced as many bras and bra sets and other stray pieces of lingerie as possible from both the practical corner and the not-so-practical corner.

"I want sexy," she interjected firmly, picking up three sheer bras from our French collection. "I want really, really sexy."

"Done and done," I replied, moving my gaze down to her boobs, wondering if she'd even fit in our French collection. I had no idea what size of tissue she was hiding under her oversized top.

"How about I measure you first, Julie?" I tried saving time. "I can bring you sexy."

She quickly followed me back into the dressing room, promptly hanging her purse against the door. I waited as she slid her top over her head, thinking about how quickly my day had changed and praying that a fourth customer hadn't arrived.

"I've been measured before," she said, moving closer to the mirror. "It's been awhile, though, and two kids later."

"Alright." I moved the tape under her bra, keeping track of how many times she looked at herself in the mirror and then down at the ground.

"I'm going to grab you some 34 Ds. And if you don't mind, I'd love to bring you some of my personal favorites, also in the French collection."

Julie nodded quickly and then tapped on her belly a few times.

"You have anything for this?" she asked, pulling on a thick layer of skin.

"Uh." I paused, still trying to understand her motives. "You mean like a Spanx?"

"Yeah, something that will help suck it in when I'm wearing jeans or something."

"Got it."

Within minutes, I had a few styles of black, red, and white lace bras in addition to a couple florals, bralettes, matching thongs, and a pair of tummy-tucking, thigh-sucking Spanx. I tried my best at keeping the bras sexy, noting where the nipples peeked through the lace.

"Alright." I unlocked the door. "Let's put this on." I stopped short, surprised to see Julie sobbing in the chair, her breasts exposed.

"I'm so sorry," she replied. "I thought I could do this. I really thought I could do this."

I quickly hung her pile of bras on the bar and stepped back over to the door.

"Can I get you some water or something?" I asked, trying to understand what had happened. "We don't have to do this, you know. I don't want you to feel uncomfortable."

"No, no, it's not that. I just . . ." She paused, wiping her eyes before letting out a lengthy sigh.

I waited, trying to figure out where to stand.

"I just found out my husband has been having an affair with a young woman in his office."

"Shit" came rolling off my tongue faster than I could try to take it back.

"That's exactly what I said." She shot me a glance.

I stood in silence, wondering if she needed Kleenex or chocolate or whiskey from the bar next door. Maybe an extra fruit snack from Farah.

"Julie, I can go get you some Kleen—"

She cut me off. "Fifteen years of my life." She sat with her head down. "A twelve-year-old son, an eight-year-old daughter, two miscarriages, and a fucking dog."

I listened, watching her leg jerk up and down.

"I drove here thinking it was me. I'm getting older and fatter and grayer. I wear cotton briefs because they're comfortable. My bras are old and tattered because my children's needs come first. I grocery shop, cook dinner, do everyone's laundry, take the dog to the vet or the park, and then do another load of laundry before reading a bedtime story. I'm always home because that's what he wanted."

I could almost hear her heartbeat, moments away from exploding into thin air, bloody and beaten.

"I can—" I began, but she cut me off again.

"And then to stand in this dressing room, alone and naked while you gather my pathetic efforts to prove lord knows what. My god, my god."

Her last string of words made my stomach turn as they faded into whispers. I tried opening my mouth to speak but nothing came out. I felt awful. Her dejection was profound, yet authentic and admirable and really unexpected. I could see the loneliness cast its spell over her sunken brown eyes, understandably making room for a bank of hard questions and sleepless nights.

"I say you try on a bra." I hesitated, hoping Julie didn't interpret my wanting to make her feel good into an untimely sales pitch. She looked up at me and then at the mirror, quietly standing to her feet. Silence pervaded our tiny room as I slipped a red lace bra off its hanger. Julie watched me through the mirror as I carefully moved the straps up and over her shoulders. After fastening the band, I pulled her breast tissue in tight from the sides, hoping to give her a quick pick-me-up.

"That feels nice." She nodded in my direction, wiggling her shoulders and arms.

"Just know it's an option, and the fit looks pretty good. We could try going up a cup size to see if it feels any better."

I watched as she stared at herself in the mirror, examining every last mole, stretch mark, and bright squiggly vein. Her eyes began to well up as she stopped to study her loose curls.

"I thought I was good to him." She spoke softly, running her hand through her hair. "I just don't understand."

I looked down at the ground, searching for every right thing to say, knowing I had never been in her position and was scared shitless of it.

"You're really brave, Julie." My eyes started to water as I thought about the sequence of my day, including Gladys and Archie and Julie's kids and Julie's dog, whom I didn't even know. The heaviness around their truths came with forceful markings, making me slow my responses in an effort to offer some kind of hope, which seemed imbalanced because I was also searching for hope and all life's answers. Julie was completely drained, stone-cold, carved into nothing, and it was hard to watch.

"I'm so embarrassed," she whispered under her breath.

"You found me hiding in the women's restroom," I added quickly.

She turned to look at me, staring at my disheveled mass of hair and thrown-together ensemble with hair color stains on the collar. I could feel a sudden awareness with her, like we had both implicitly communicated our separate crusades and grasped every second of the hard, lingering woes.

"Embarrassing is that wire popping out," I joked, pointing to her raggedy, discolored bra.

She laughed, looking back at the mirror. I could tell she was ready to leave.

"I'll take this one." She double-checked the price on the tag. "I'll see how I like it and then come back for more."

"Are you sure?" I asked, not wanting her to feel pressured. A big part of me just wanted her to walk away and start all over and have what Gladys had. Not the swim trunks or the heart attack or the crippling anguish, but the bourbon and the clarity and whatever absolute kind of love and honor I'd felt just minutes before.

"I came for sexy," she responded decisively, handing me the tag after ripping it from the side of the bra. "And I got sexy!"

"You did." I smiled, feeling her pulse.

"Thank you." She waited, stopping with her shirt in hand. "I'm so sorry."

The sound of her apology hit hard. I'd heard it too many times, immediately making me question why women have somehow been made to feel embarrassed or weak for becoming "emotional."

"Sorry for what?" I shot back, desperately wanting her to leave the store with some kind of ammunition that I had no business trying to give. I wanted Angela Bassett's gas can from the movie *Waiting to Exhale* in Julie's firm grip and a black silk robe on her back. But she had her own path to pave, and setting her husband's belongings on fire may or may not have been the answer.

Julie looked down at the ground. "Thank you," she whispered, choking up again, her tears heavier. "I'll definitely be back for more when I can."

"Looking forward to it," I replied as I casually opened the door, eyeing her rags one more time. "Don't forget to take out the trash."

MONEY MAKERS

Dragging my feet back into the store after Farah begged and pleaded for me to cover her shift, I surrendered to whatever look I could put together in fifteen minutes, once again the epitome of LA's upscale swank.

"Are you serious?" Rachel peered up from her morning paperwork, her tone far from lost.

"She had an emergency and couldn't really talk." I lied as best as I knew how, using the only key word that Rachel couldn't rebut so Farah could continue her impromptu getaway with Lorenzo.

"Go ahead and restock the tissue," Rachel sighed. "I'll get the money bags and open the registers." Within seconds, Roxanne's voice hit the loudspeaker, offering a nice morning greeting before moving straight into business, trapping everyone in time.

"Remember, sales associates, it's always about the customer. Let's make every effort to promptly welcome our shoppers into our departments." Roxanne laid it out, altering her inflection on every third word. It came as no surprise that the phones started ringing right as we opened, too, with an expectation of three rings tops.

"I can't do it today." Rachel quickly handed me the phone as I approached the register.

"Hello," I said cautiously.

"Hi, Natalee? It's Harry."

I shot Rachel a swift glare, mentally adding one more item to Farah's IOU.

"Hey, Harry, what can I do for you?"

"Natalee!" I sensed his excitement. "I'm glad I got you."

"I don't know why you don't come in, Harry." I tried prodding him as usual. "I told you I'd set you up with a room and you could try something on for yourself." He sighed, evading my invitation while quickly getting to his list of inquiries.

"That new satin bustier set, do you have it in red?" he asked.

"I do" slowly left my mouth as Chase snuck up from behind, setting a folded note by the register before leaving with a sly grin.

Trying to focus on Harry's specifics regarding the cut of the piece, I couldn't help reading the note, excited to see: "My place, tomorrow night?" *Tomorrow night*? I repeated in my head, suddenly inundated with way too many questions. I slid the note into my pants pocket and looked around the department, wondering if Chase decided to stick around, but instead found a woman circling our high-end lingerie and Rachel staring at me while frantically nodding her head toward the customer. "I'm going to have to call you back, Harry." I barely waited for his reply, once again taking down his number with a dried-up, inkless-pen, knowing he'd call back later.

I quickly moved out from behind the counter, conscious of Roxanne's spiel about "promptly" welcoming the customer once they'd hit the department.

"Hi there." I patted down a tree of bras, awkwardly fidgeting with their arrangement.

"Hey." A bronzed-over brunette nicely returned my greeting, already holding a few sale items and Harry's desired bustier.

"Can I start you a fitting room?" I asked, ready to grab her merchandise.

"Yes, absolutely." She smiled. "And I'll keep looking."

She moved fast. It was clear she knew what she liked. And judging from her selection of frilly panties and a few bras, her sizes were consistent, leading me to believe this wasn't her first round in the lingerie department. She picked up G-strings, thongs with ties on the side, a couple sheer crotches, and bright lacy bras matching perfectly with the bottom half. She was a good mixer, making me think I needed to clean out my own panty drawer and start all over.

While she continued to look around the floor, still gathering random pieces of lingerie, I tried looking productive by tidying up the counter area but got stuck on the department's daily overview written down in our team booklet, highlighting Yvonne's impending arrival, Michelle's verbose recap about the order in which bras should hang on the wall, alteration pickups, panty table fill-ins, and our new hire, Tabitha, shadowing Rachel for the day. We had a lot to cover. And with a newcomer on board, I suddenly realized I'd be responsible for most of it.

"I think I'm ready to head in," my customer stated softly, concluding my ill-fated analysis.

"Yes, of course, follow me." I smiled, catching a glimpse of her additions, noting push-up bras, string panties, garter belts, and a couple black satin corsets. "Do you need help with any of the bras?" I asked, trying not to stare at her amazingly tight backside crammed into an old pair of Levi's.

"I think I'm good." She smiled, reaching for the doorknob. Back out on the floor, I figured I would get started on filling one of the panty tables until enough time had passed for me to head back into the dressing rooms. It didn't take long, however, for my customer to appear in the walkway, attempting to mask her naked body with her shirt.

"Is there any way you can grab me a 34 triple-D in this and maybe a pair of black stockings I can try with one of the garters?" She stood, pointing to her boobs as they sat atop the bra's ruched lace, mimicking the roundness of two eight-pound bowling balls, covered in a brownish-orange metallic coat and glistening under the entryway lights.

"Yeah, no problem." I nodded her way, knowing exactly what pairs of lace-top thigh-highs she'd be getting.

After a quick jaunt to the hosiery department down the way and a pit stop at our sidewall of sheer lacy bras, I felt good about my recommendations and, to my surprise, Yvonne's arrival. The top floor was filling up quickly and my curiosity had already determined my whereabouts.

"Hi, there." I crept into the hallway outside the dressing rooms.

"It's Nicole." My customer opened the door wearing nothing but a string between her bulletproof buttocks and a v-shaped patch over her lady bits.

"Alright, Nicole." I stood holding onto her lingerie as I fought hard not to stare at the rest of her body, seemingly inscrutable and firmly intact.

"I hope you don't mind, but I brought you a few suggestions," I continued, struggling to comprehend the words inked along her spine as she turned to grab a bra off the bar.

"That's great!" She lit up, putting her arms through the straps. "I'll try anything!"

"Sounds good," I replied, steadily nodding my head, hoping to find the right wording to remind her about dressing room etiquette and placing her potential purchases over her already-owned panty.

"Do you happen to have your own pair of underwear?" I finally asked, spotting another trail of black ink along the inside of her forearm. And if truth be told, I couldn't care less about one's try-on methods, especially if it brought us to the register, but when I'm left to strategically rehang small pieces of fabric on plastic hangers, moments after seeing them placed elsewhere, aversion tends to come on strong.

"Oh, I'm so sorry." She apologized, then paused. "It's just so hard to get the right look. I promise I'm buying most of this. I'll definitely buy the ones I have on. I, uh, actually don't have my own panty," she replied, making me rethink my need to say anything at all, though the number of panties I spotted on the chair was slightly alarming.

"No problem," I replied, hoping to change the topic as I noticed the bra's band riding up her back. "Have you tried going down a band size?"

"You mean a 32?" she asked, turning her body in front of the mirror. "Yeah." She hesitated, examining her backside. I stared at the dry drippings of dark hair dye encrusted around her hairline and then down at a subtle map of stretch marks along her hip bone. "It's the back fat," she continued. "My job won't have it." I paused at her sudden ambiguity, reeled in by the second and wanting every last piece of the particulars.

"What do you do for work?" I asked after a short delay.

"I'm a good old-fashioned stripper." She smiled, unhooking her bra.

"Oh, alright." We both laughed at her unfiltered reveal.

She was forthright and not remotely timid, moving around the dressing room with little regard for wasted time.

"I tend to clean out your sale racks." She shimmied out of her panties. "I bring a bunch to the house for the other girls."

I fought to stay audible as my eyes moved from the small patch of pubic hair immaculately groomed into a shape I couldn't quite make out.

"You guys all live together?" I asked, swiftly moving my gaze.

"No, no." She laughed. "The house is where we dance. Some of the girls are in school or working another job or playing mommy. It's hard to go shopping with the hours."

"Yeah." I nodded like I knew what she was talking about, wondering who had been helping her from my team.

"I've never seen you in here before." I tried not to sound too meddlesome.

"I just moved here from Vegas a few months back. And I really hate shopping to be honest. I try to avoid as many crowds as possible, which is why I do it all in one swoop."

"That makes sense." I stood nodding again, ready to leave her with her merchandise after my awkward and lengthy lingering act.

"Sooo . . ." She struggled to multitask, studying a pair of high-end panties before she unhooked them from the hanger. "You're not the first bra fitter who's told me I should be wearing a 32 band. Why is that?"

"Well . . ." I paused, looking at her rib cage poking out from her skin. "It's so the band won't ride up your back. The higher the band, the lower the breasts."

"Ah, I see." She looked at my boobs and then down at her own. "Even with silicone?"

"Depends on how old the silicone is. Yours look great. And they're certainly perky. I would wear whatever band size you're comfortable in, to be honest."

"Let's try one for the hell of it."

"No problem." I stepped back to open the door. "I'll be back in a few."

The sales floor was still surprisingly quiet. Michelle was in her usual frantic state, doing her best to be seen in case Roxanne walked by, and Rachel, who had the patience of a small child, had started her intensive tutorial with Tabitha. I tried my best not to stare as the two stood massaging bra cups and fiddling with the intricacies of popular panties. I sensed confusion on Tabitha's face, or utter panic, while Rachel talked a mile a minute, spontaneously cupping her own breasts in the middle of the department. Missing Farah was valid. She was my breath of fresh air, my person.

Knocking on Nicole's door, and somewhat prepared for anything, I stood, organizing my delivery.

"Wow, thank you," she said, welcoming me in. I wasn't sure if she wanted me to stay or go, but I liked talking to her. I appreciated her control as she boldly flaunted every last piece of lingerie wedged into her skin. She was quietly forceful, knowing exactly what she wanted.

"I'll let you adjust the bra," she said, running her fingers along the straps. Following the scent of a soft floral, I stood with my hands on her breasts. They were big and round and in my face. I couldn't help staring in amazement at a job well done as I attempted to readjust their placement.

"First hook," I said, moving behind her. "And you're probably more of a 30 band."

"Thirty!" Her eyes widened. "Not a chance!"

I watched as she turned around to examine her back, stopping at a small pinched layer of skin. "The truth is I don't really wear bras all that often," she said, quickly unhooking the bra.

"I would assume so." I smiled, grabbing the bra from off the chair. "Wouldn't that defeat your purpose?"

She laughed, making me feel at ease for potentially crossing customer boundaries.

"You'd be surprised at what people want." She stepped into another pair of panties, still refusing to leave on a panel of protection.

I waited as she retied the sides of a G-string, carefully making loops with her nails.

"Have you been at it for a long time?" I asked, mustering up just enough audacity to ignore the part about professionalism and pry tirelessly. I couldn't help imagining her front and center, especially as she stood before me stark naked and impeccably groomed.

"Too long," she replied, combing her pixie cut with her fingers. "And it hasn't been easy, but it's paid my bills and allowed me to keep my daughter in private school."

"I can only imagine," I replied, still trying to understand the words tattooed along her spine, as well as a world I knew nothing about. The facets of the trade appeared dark and daunting, leading me back to my last memory of a strip club and the repercussions of disbelief due to its wide spread phenomenon. The mass of attendees was startling and I, a little shell-shocked at how progressive the industry had become, wasn't expecting a game of peekaboo at a strikingly slow rate.

"It can knock the wind out of you sometimes," Nicole continued, throwing a pair of panties atop a growing pile of lingerie. "I've learned to separate my true self from the performance though. It sounds crazy, but I do it for my daughter. The money gives her experience."

"Huh." I stood in awe, marveling at her strength. I felt terrible, too, admittedly trying to redeem myself from any and all preconceived notions regarding her industry. She was a woman, a human being, working to live. "How old is your daughter?" I asked, watching her carefully glide a sheer black thigh-high up her leg, her posture robust and unshaken.

"She's six," she said, beaming, before grabbing her phone from her bag.

"Wow, she's beautiful." I leaned in, feeling every ounce of her admiration as she stared at her daughter's toothless smile. "You doing this on your own?"

She paused, slowly studying her body in the mirror. I wondered if I had meddled unwantedly again.

"Since she was three months old," she replied. "Fatherhood became too much for her dad. He struggled with mental illness and bounced from job to job. I woke up one day and said I'm done."

My heart felt like it skipped a hundred beats as I watched her pull the last of her outfit together. "I don't blame him though," she added after a moment of silence. "His episodes even scared him."

"Wow." I once again struggled to find the right words, realizing that I was at risk for overstaying my welcome.

"Life," she responded quietly, eyeing her pile of panties. "We've been on our own ever since. And money talks."

Her comment hit me like a ton of bricks, especially because I felt like I had started to understand. Survival manifested itself the way it needed to, unmistakable and hard-hitting, yet its offerings kept her going. Staring at the G-string sandwiched between her ass cheeks as she worked every last inch of space between us, I thought about my handful of quarters in my wallet and the clothes on my back, and quietly acknowledged the stark difference between our circumstances. "I have to ask," I said, completely invested in her vocation and all its secrets. "What do they want?"

"Hah!" She smirked, picking up on my vagueness while finalizing her pile.

I couldn't help attempting to do the math in my head, wondering if the entirety of her mound would overwhelm the receipt roll.

"To be honest—" She stopped and looked directly at me. "The men are the ones who want the attention."

I nodded slowly, envisioning Nicole spread-eagle and oiled like the well-built machine that she was.

"Not all, but a lot," she continued. "I have a gentleman who brings me flowers every week. He's a businessman, vulnerable, and a great conversationalist, especially when it comes to politics. And then, of course, there are the dirtbags, drunks, and misogynists who think they know you. They think you're just a piece of meat with a sad story looking to be saved." She shook her head and sighed. "And sometimes there are women looking to be saved because they've never known real, unconditional love. I used to dance with a girl in Vegas who grew up in twelve different foster homes, molested in two, starved in one. Her parents were drug addicts and abandoned her when she was four years old. She didn't choose to experience that. But she's a 'lowlife, a whore, a slut.' I've heard it all. And sometimes it comes from the man sitting right in front of you."

"Jesus Christ," I muttered, my pulse high.

"I dance with a girl right now whose boyfriend beats the shit out of her, years after her own father did the same thing, so she's trying to save enough money to leave town and, well, survive. It is what it is, you know. We've all taken to the stage for different reasons. And like I said, it's fast money, it's good money, and money talks, especially when you're out there trying to stay alive with the cards you've been dealt."

Silence crept in again.

"Right." I stood catching flies while circling back to the businessman and the flowers and the great conversation. I was perplexed, yet oddly empowered. Nicole had purpose, fighting round for round, escaping into steadfast resolve, presumably fueled by an exit strategy. I admired her command. I admired her willingness to open up about a trade that society has long deemed dirty, desperate, and demeaning without any real context. It felt so unfair, too, because it all started with people, real-life human beings with brains and beating hearts.

It has been the very people of our society, lost in bigoted doctrines, positions of power, and blinding privilege, who have created such dehumanizing judgment, casting aside those who are "less than." Casting aside people of color. Casting aside women who have been wrongfully trapped inside the binding folds of patriarchy. It is the very essence and vulnerability of humanity that other fucking people have discarded and objectified and pointed fingers at, constructing an even larger system of spiraling ignorance. It's just never made sense. People vs. people. Man vs. woman. Survival vs. advantage. Ignorance vs. everything.

It came as no surprise that my quiet rumblings brought me right back to where it all started—my own sexuality. Boldly accentuated with Victoria's Secret body sprays, Maybelline mascara, a flowing mane, and a winning pair of red velvet G-string thongs I bought for Michael Morrison, my developing mojo felt on point. Hot AF. And as commanding as I wanted it to be, yet still guided by a list of standards I fell prey to as a young, sexually curious teen. My thin velvet strings carried a strange power that made me feel validated, though still controlled by a culture that criticized—and continues to criticize—

women for our chosen attire, our behavior, our desires. Don't speak. Cover up. That makes you look like a hoe. Have some self-respect. Shame on you.

The juxtaposition between my teen customer Molly and me came back tenfold as I stared at Nicole. Though years apart, sadly so, we still followed a similar set of criteria, eager to explore the unknown while searching for an unrepentant tone, because, somewhere deep within sexism's glaring ridicule, we've had to. We have been taught to control our sexuality, our bodies, and our minds, never to experience a gender-equal playing field. Men aren't told "cover your chest, I can see your nipples." "You should really wear a bra because your pecs are saggy, but only the ones with underwire because you'll get a better lift and it will help smooth your gut." "And by the way, your penis is making you really emotional. Is it that time of the month?" "Are you really going to wear that in public? It makes you look fat." "It's okay if your pants are a size 44x30; you have a handsome face." "You should really trim your balls. My god. It's like a plantation down there."

"You look confused." Nicole smiled, bringing me back to the conversation as she zipped up her jeans.

"No, no." I looked down at the carpet. "I just, I don't know." I struggled to articulate my thoughts. I liked her too much, too soon, to have my words misconstrued. Plus I felt uneasy and pissed off. "I'm—"

"Fascinated and bothered all at the same time," she finished for me.

"Yeah," I replied, dumbfounded and still probing. "Do you ever enjoy it? You know, the job?"

Nicole paused and stared at her pile of panties.

"You know . . ." She spoke with careful thought. "I do. Some nights I go out there and feel so sexy and in control of myself that I almost black out. I tell myself every night that I'm in charge; it's my house."

I laughed, loving her attitude. "Damn right," I said with a smirk, trying not to look overly obvious as I snooped inside her bag.

"You should read it." She followed my gaze before pulling out a thick blue book with the title *Cunt* printed across an orange daisy. "It's a good reminder of all things wonderful in the world."

I laughed again, immediately intrigued as she passed over her book. I had seen it at some point in one of my women's studies classes. I also nearly exploded with adoration as I went on to read the subtitle: *A Declaration of Independence*. It was meant to be. The timing, the book, the words . . . Nicole.

"I had a lot of reclaiming to do," she said, scooping up her pile of panties. "So I read it a couple times and wrote myself a love letter, realizing I had to stop hating myself for what I do and don't do. And most important, I had to stop caring about what other people have to say. The world will always judge you."

Her words lingered. *The world will always judge you.*

More silence came rolling in, putting a swift halt to any sensible formation of words on my behalf. Her honesty was, quite possibly, the rawest I'd felt, igniting a long string of penetrating thoughts and the burning need to break away.

I had a book to buy and work to do.

Nicole's bravery and boldness packed a punch, leading me to examine my own ideas about sexuality, identity, intimacy, and survival. I never expected to feel so much empathy as reality came knocking. In a matter of minutes, I began to feel wildly liberated, following my new client to the register like the lost puppy dog that I was.

"Do you have a business card?" she asked, handing over her pile of panties, bras, and a set of thigh-highs.

"I do," I replied, eager to take down her information, quickly making note of her purchases and her telephone number and her words, knowing I'd see her again.

"A declaration of independence." I repeated my new claim, turning the register screen around so that she could see the numbers more clearly and bail if she wanted to.

"Exactly," she said and laughed, handing me five hundred dollars in cash before locking in another smile. "You'll never be spineless."

I quickly looked up, finally comprehending the words boldly inked into the ridges of her backbone. *A declaration of independence*, I repeated internally, smiling at the thought of my own departure as I watched her walk toward the elevators.

WITH RENEWED WIND IN MY SAILS AND A MERITED LUNCH BREAK, I was hot on the heels of a Barnes & Noble associate. "Excuse me, sir," I repeated twice, realizing I was too close for comfort as he turned around. His lips were straight as a ruler, and thick magnifying glasses rode the tip of his nose. "I'm, uh, looking for a book titled *Cunt*."

I quickly checked my surroundings.

"*Cunt*," he restated my request louder than I liked, over-enunciating the "t" before leading me to a wall full of organized promise.

I immediately spotted the bright orange daisy as it adorned an arrangement of book spines. "That's it!" I yelled, grabbing the book and making my way toward the register. I knew I was cutting it close—that is, my budget, or rather, lack of a budget. It was a quandary: Do I neglect my mound of laundry and attempt to live on peanut butter and jelly sandwiches for the next three days? Or buy the book? Eyeing the register one more time, I stood smack dab in the middle of the bookstore, mentally registering other food items I had left in my kitchen, while noting my half tank of gas and a bottle of wine for Chase's house. *I can do it*, I thought, slowly making my way up to the counter, holding tight to the edges of Inga Muscio's *Cunt* and the embarrassment that enveloped me as I quietly dug for quarters, knowing I had just enough to declare a win and total stupidity.

It didn't take long for me to settle into the hospitality of our outdoor seating, far removed from the doorway. My mind raced as my time with Nicole erupted into bits and pieces of ceaseless inquisition. Her fearless declaration and commitment to herself and her body reminded me that I had been failing at so many things, carelessly clipping my own wings. My fear of intimacy and vulnerability was bigger than anything I'd ever known, pecking mercilessly at every organ in my body until the madness came spilling out. She was a game-changer, though, fortuitous and unpredicted, pushing me to create my own unapologetic declaration and actually live it.

Nicole also propelled me to really think about the position of women in our current society. I started to reexamine what I had learned about feminism and power and my own inner roar. The act of "reclaiming" continued to ignite a revolution within myself, yet the very notion of women repeatedly reduced and ranked by society exacerbated an already present rage. Why are we still fighting to claim and reclaim a place in the world?

Just a piece of meat with a sad story. I reworked the words over and over in my head, wondering if my housewife Julie from the day before felt the same way. Did she believe her place in the world only existed within the confines of her male counterpart, the husband she thought she knew? My job as a bra fitter began to worry me. Gladys's struggle with age, Molly's skewed perception of beauty, her mother's perception of other women. I had come to experience too many alarming patterns.

So I sat, staring up at the sky before opening my new book, refusing to feel anything but sexy and grand and full of moxie, like Nicole. I was ready to get turned upside down and inside out on my terms, shamelessly starting with "The Anatomical Jewel."

BEING YOU

I nching my way down the dressing room hallway in women's wear, I called out Nina's name in a small whisper. Considering she had requested her own private space with Roxanne, I wanted to be respectful and not yell her name for all to hear. I had no idea what I was walking into or, more important, how much privacy was needed.

"Back here," I heard Nina reply, causing me to wait until the door cracked open.

"Wow." I stopped, gazing around the room at piles of jeans and dresses and some of fall's early arrivals. "You must be shopping for a whole new wardrobe."

"Sort of." She tried to laugh, pushing aside a tennis shoe with her foot. "Please, come in."

I watched as she inspected the measuring tape dangling from my hand.

"Roxanne mentioned that you need some bras."

"Yes!" she replied without hesitation. "It's been years. And I mean *years*."

My eyes darted down to her breasts bulging out of an undersized button up.

"What do you usually wear for support?" I asked.

Nina exhaled slowly, fidgeting with her hands.

"Honestly . . ." She seemed anxious to share. "Because I'm so big, I wear about three tank tops . . . every day."

"Oh, okay." I paused, hoping I had decent stock upstairs in lingerie. Nina clearly didn't shop much at all and her uneasiness about the process was obvious.

"Are you comfortable taking off your shirt so that I can measure you?" I asked cautiously, bearing in mind that I wasn't in my department and everything about women's clothing felt off. The ambiance had a specific style to it, hipper and cooler and a little more relaxed, yet not relaxed because there were jeans hanging everywhere, and jeans had the power to really change a woman's day, for better or for worse, sort of like lingerie. It was just different, I guess.

"Do you measure around my boobs?" Nina asked, still fidgeting.

"I measure around your ribcage for the band size and then–" I stopped mid-sentence, hoping a string of professional words came out. "And then I'll bring a couple different sizes for the cups, eyeballing it."

"Eyeballing it?" She looked confused.

"Well, them, eyeballing . . . your breasts."

Nina turned to look at herself in the mirror, stopping abruptly at her chest.

"Let's do it." She started to unbutton her shirt, leading me to feel her extreme discomfort, acknowledging that she was on the fence about being fit for a bra at all.

"Do you prefer that I measure you with your tank top on?" I asked.

"I think so," she replied, facing the mirror again, but with her head down.

Trying to move quickly for the sake of Nina's time and nervousness, I noted a 36 on the measuring tape and a possible H for the cups.

"Give me about ten minutes or so to gather a few bras. Once we determine a comfortable cup size, I'll bring down some more to try."

Nina waited as I opened the door, struggling to respond.

"Alright, thank you. Um, uh, what cup size am I?"

The vulnerability in her voice forced me to stop and turn around from the hallway.

"I'm going to grab a couple Hs." I waited. "And a double-H."

"Wow, okay." Nina's eyes grew bigger. "Really?"

Her response, fraught with concern and disappointment, guided me right back up into our stockroom, prompting me to think about Nina's need for privacy. The place was a mess with bras hanging everywhere, some resting on empty rolling racks, others alone atop file cabinets. I went straight in for our Hs and gathered as many styles as I could find, which wasn't my initial response, but I had a feeling Nina was downstairs still thinking about her proposed size, and it suddenly seemed better to try more than enough.

When I returned, she had already changed into a pair of dark denim jeans and a long blazer. Her face was flushed and her skin blotchy, making me wonder how much longer she had in the dressing room. Her other personal shopper, a spunky saleswoman who loved plaid, was on her game, which also made me wonder how close Roxanne was and what I needed to do to make sure our transaction ran smoothly.

"That looks nice," I smiled, organizing her bras on the bar.

"You think?" She asked, hesitant to claim anything.

"I love fall." I kept moving around her, unhooking two Hs from a hanger while contemplating which one she should try on first. "Leather jackets, boots, and blue jeans. Can't beat it."

Stripping back down to her tank top, Nina remained silent. I could almost hear her pulse rise as she became more wary of the process, especially as I moved in closer, holding a bra.

"You mind stepping outside while I put this on?" she asked abruptly.

"Oh, I'm sorry, of course." I hurried to close the door. "I'll be right outside."

Pacing the hallway, I took it upon myself to glance in each one of the open rooms, still caught up with the flashy décor and the amount of clothing brought to some of the rooms. Heaps of late summer trends and fall's upcoming charm sat on floors and hangers and chairs, reminding me that women really do appreciate options.

I didn't want to rush Nina, but my time outside of her room was becoming longer—and quieter. She wasn't moving at all. For a second, I wondered if she was also stuck inside the conversations happening in other fitting rooms, specifically the one directly across from her where a woman felt the urge to release sharp, random profanities and deep grunts. But then I realized, from the sight of her feet planted in the middle of the floor, that she was stuck inside her own room. Motionless.

"Nina?" I called out softly. "You okay?"

I signaled for her other sales associate to stay back as she came whippin' around the corner with another pile of clothes, smile still intact.

"Yeah, I think so, I . . ." The door creaked open.

Nina looked tired and discouraged, saying what I already knew.

"This doesn't fit."

I eased in closer and pulled on the straps of the bra, hoping to rearrange her breast tissue and give the girls a sustainable lift, but it just didn't work. Her breasts were too large for the cups, which made her posture difficult to control.

"I might have a . . . J." I tried stalling.

"What?" Her response plummeted straight into silence.

"We don't really carry J cups in the store, but they exist."

I stopped myself, thinking about our much-needed bra evolution and how far we still had to go.

"Well." I paused. "They're starting to exist."

"This is why I don't shop for bras." Nina's response cut straight through whatever negotiation we might've had coming.

Although I had no idea what it felt like to carry around breasts that could seldom find comfort, I felt Nina's deep need for privacy, along with an overwhelming need to make it right.

"This is why I don't go up to lingerie. This is so frustrating."

I stood listening as her words hit every corner of the room. "Let me see if I have a J upstairs. If not, let's order one."

Nina didn't respond.

I quickly moved toward the door to make room for her personal shopper, who in all fairness didn't quite understand all the layers that go into a woman's wardrobe, or the mounting tension that began to rob Nina of hope.

"I've got more blouses!" Her tune fell flat.

I hurried back up to our stockroom, keeping in mind that we never hung whatever Js we came across on the sales floor. The reality of my travels, aside from briefly working in another department, suddenly hit me: I had to go to the stockroom to find her size, because J cups never made it out onto the sales floor. And Nina knew this; she knew her bras had never been hung alongside double-Ds and triple-Ds and Gs. And though it made sense to separate A cups from Gs for organizational purposes, the seclusion still made me rethink our strategies, along with the shame and self-loathing that often crept its way into a woman's entire being because of it.

Rifling through a section of Hs, I flipped over every tag, carefully noting the band sizes while hoping for at least one J. When I found the size ring with the letter J carved in white, I noticed two customer-returned bras dangling, a 38 J and a 40 J. They were both tan colored and stitched with a "feminine" bow, but if anyone could work their magic, it was our alterations department. Tightening the bra's band wasn't out of the question just yet. Anything was worth a shot at this point. I didn't want Nina to leave the store feeling completely defeated when it came to her lingerie, nor did Roxanne. So I snatched the 38 J and bolted down the escalator.

"Nina?" I knocked twice, trying not to peek through the cracks.

She was quick to welcome me in, wearing one of her three tank tops and another pair of jeans.

"How are you feeling?" I skipped the small talk.

"Well." She stared at the cups of the bra. "Not really sure where to go from here."

"Let's try this," I said firmly. "The band is going to be too big, but I'm thinking we might alter it. I'll step out—"

"It's fine," she said jadedly, moving her tank top up and over her head. Her boobs flopped back down as her arms hit her sides. I held onto the thickness of the straps as she moved in closer and lifted her breasts into the cups. With a small push forward, I resituated myself behind her and held on tight to the band so that she could get a look in the mirror.

"Not bad." I nodded over her shoulder. "The cups are good."

As I continued to pinch the band together with my hands, Nina examined the fit, moving her eyes around every part of the bra, from strap to bow.

"This has been such a nightmare," she said, shaking her head.

"I bet," I replied, hoping I didn't sound insensitive. "What are you shopping for anyway? You've got a lot of clothes in here." I tried moving the attention off of her breasts.

She waited to respond, looking around the room at her piles of jackets, jeans, shoes, and shirts.

"I recently got a new job and, well, need some new clothes."

"Alright, congratulations!" I spoke with excitement. "New beginnings."

Nina's head jolted up at me in the mirror as I continued to stand behind her.

"I don't get out much. It's a new beginning for sure."

I waited, still holding her bra in place.

"I'm sorry I don't have all that you need." I started to talk slowly and deliberately. "I'm happy to order whatever style of J cups you'd like to try. You don't even need to come in. I'll deliver them to your house so you can try them on in the comfort of your home and then mail back what doesn't work. We'll pay for the postage."

Nina thought about my proposition, her arms beginning to relax.

"Yeah, maybe." She continued to acknowledge me through the mirror before breaking her pose, letting her breasts fall back into their freedom place. "I can't keep doing this."

I backed away to give Nina space, eyeing her tank top. "Have you been off work for a while?" I asked, really trying to understand what Nina needed without sounding pushy or insincere.

"Yeah, about a year, maybe more." She spoke softly. "I had surgery and then sort of lost motivation for life. Fell into a dark place for a long time. And now here I am."

"Showing up," I replied, holding onto every one of her cues.

"Barely," she added quietly. "It's easy to escape, you know?"

If I understood anything in that moment, it was the act of escaping. I got the gist of wanting to become numb and invisible, a stranger to the world because people and circumstances and truths were so fucking hard. Life had a way of eating us up whole sometimes, dragging us dirty. And Nina didn't have to say anything for me to comprehend what I presumed to be a year of hell. Vagueness can reveal a lot sometimes.

"Why don't you let me mail a couple bras to you," I said. "Let's try one in your correct band size."

I watched as she began layering each one of her tank tops, overwhelmed with thought.

"A J?" she scoffed.

I stood waiting for more cues, wondering how to respond. There was a coldness to Nina that kept me present. I appreciated it because it wasn't phony or longwinded. She just came in, explaining her needs, while trying her best.

"Let me get dressed," she responded for me. "I might take the 38 and see what I can do."

"No problem." I smiled, slowly backing away. "Take your time."

As I moved out into the hallway, a woman stopped me from inside her dressing room, trying to cover her naked body with the door.

"I'm so sorry to bother you, but I'm desperate," she said. "And I couldn't help eavesdropping." I stood waiting, wondering if I'd ever make it back up to lingerie.

"Is there any way you can measure me, too?" She opened the door wider, her magenta G-string in full view. I stared at her breasts settled into an old bra and then over to the piles of jeans spread out on the floor. Thinking about Nina and her request to engage away from the lingerie department made me feel apprehensive about having any more bra talk with her still nearby. I didn't have it in me to assign C cups while another woman struggled to come to terms with her J cups. It just didn't feel right. Size wasn't supposed to matter, but it mattered in this moment. And I hated that it mattered because its imprint was dark and punishing, moving through hearts with shards and spikes.

"Can you meet me upstairs in the lingerie department?" I asked the woman, mentally noting her cup size again. "I'll grab a couple bras for you to try."

Satisfied and eager for my help, she closed her door and scrambled to put her purchases together. I continued to wait for Nina and thought about knocking on her door again to make sure she was okay, but figured she was also gathering her purchases. She'd been at it for a while, which led me to think about my conversation with Roxanne and her comment about "having an important job to do." I had been too quick to dismiss her point, feeling its verity as Nina's quiet struggles came to light. It was an important job, a hard job, and a lot to make sense of. I'd go from feeling stuck to feeling utterly confused in a matter of seconds, fighting time and running in circles.

"Hey, Nina." I smiled, standing at the counter ready to put in an order. "One 36 J. If you don't like it, send it back." Nina weighed her options quietly, making me wonder if I was too insistent again.

"Do you think this shirt will be okay for the first day?" she asked. "I don't know what to wear. And the bra—" She hesitated, her face long and tired.

"I think you're going to look great in whatever you choose. I say pick something that you will be comfortable in and if it includes a tank top, or three, so be it."

Nina looked up from her pile of loose-fitting shirts and baggy sweaters, her gaze occupied and difficult to follow.

"Here." I helped move things along, sensing Nina's urgent need to remove herself from the store and anything that had to do with bra shopping. "This is my direct line. Call me anytime, and I'll mail you something to try."

Pulling on the corner of my sloppily written note, she refrained from responding. I knew in that moment that one of my biggest cues had arrived. The tension balling in her hands, and the presence of her personal shopper, led me to back away, knowing that Nina wanted to free herself right back into her own quiet makings. Alone. And allowed to do so.

WITHOUT A MOMENT TO BREATHE, I FOUND MY NEW CUSTOMER WAS already waiting for me back at lingerie. Her energy was completely different from Nina's, and it took me a minute to adjust. Everything was moving so fast, a lot of shifting gears and a lot to think about. I rushed to grab a few C cups for the customer to try and then immediately brought her back to a dressing room, trying not to be seen by management—or Roxanne.

"I grabbed a few 38 and 40 Cs," I said, moving them across the bar. "I'll fine-tune as we go."

"Wow, that's it?" she asked, laughing. "That was fast!"

"Well, I figured you've been here for a little bit," I replied with a grin. "I saw all those jeans."

She laughed again, and then shrugged her shoulders, letting out a long, thoughtful exhale.

"Thanks for letting me just jump in. I didn't mean to interrupt."

I sensed her need to keep going.

"I started seeing this guy and we're, I don't know, moving things along. It's making me all weird inside."

"Moving things along," I repeated with another smile, pleased that she picked up on my signal about staying in the room while she tried on a bra.

"It's so hard sometimes!" She tossed aside her shirt before moving her arms through the straps of a black lace push up. "Dating, man. And then all the stuff that comes with it, like feelings and new lingerie and lots of insecurities."

I stopped to think about her situation and all its ambiguities, still trying to absorb the changing of emotions—and cup sizes. But I really valued her honesty. She was candid about just being human, and I liked that it showed up so quickly.

"Insecurities are cruel, aren't they," I said, tightening each one of the straps before pulling some of her breast tissue inward. "Especially when you're dating someone new, or trying to date. I get it."

"Right!" Her eyes widened, reminding me that I had plans with Chase in less than three hours and was in desperate need of tactics to calm anxiety about being intimate and vulnerable.

"So you like this guy?" I asked, watching her study the fit in the mirror.

"I think so." She took a minute to respond, shifting her gaze to her stomach. "We met online not too long ago, and I'm staying at his place tonight."

She moved her eyes back up to her boobs, assessing the fit for a second time.

"I'm so nervous," she said, her voice amplified. "And my boobs are so small!"

I wasn't sure how to answer to the "small boobs" part, but I could certainly relate to her angst. Although she was far more experienced than I was due to the age difference, I still understood how easy it was to fall into self-doubt while moving through all the awkward stages.

I threw out an option. "I can get you some lift enhancers."

"So they can fall out of my bra when I'm lying on his bed?" she joked before changing her tone. "Why does this have to be so hard?"

I waited for a second, considering everything she had disclosed in a matter of minutes, recognizing a familiar fear.

"You look great." I tried calming her inner voice, knowing I needed the same.

"A 38 C ain't great," she replied, pushing her boobs together. "But it's what I got."

"Did you find some jeans?"

"Sort of," she replied, looking down at her shopping bag. "They'll have to do for now."

I grabbed another bra and unhooked it from the hanger, hoping she was okay with less fabric.

"This one is a little thinner." I smiled, holding up iridescent white lace.

"Ohhh, I like it." She moved in closer and then stopped right as I hooked the band from behind.

"You'd think I'd have this all figured out." She turned to study the fit. "I've only been dating for fifteen years now."

"Timing." I looked up to meet her stare, thankful that Gladys's wisdom found its way back into the fitting room just when someone else needed it.

"Yeah, maybe." She thought about my response. "It takes a lot out of you for sure. Just trying to get it right."

"What do you mean?" I asked.

"Well, there's the fear of failure, the fear of being vulnerable, the fear of being hurt. So many fears that come with—" She paused. "Loving."

I swallowed hard and listened as her words rolled effortlessly into recognizable narratives. Fear had too many covers to count, too many codes to crack, for everyone.

"I never wanted any of it to stop me from actually experiencing something though, something good, someone worth investing in, because if I've learned anything, losing is inevitable. It's all part of the game."

My head spun in circles as I swallowed hard again, trying to fight off every one of my shortcomings. Who was this woman and how much did I owe her? The inner concessions molding our private universe made me excited and scared all at the same time.

"I'm so sorry, I didn't even ask your name."

"That's okay," she replied. "I know you have a lot going on. It's Janelle."

"Hi, Janelle."

We laughed, realizing our introduction surpassed the norms and went straight into business, which I liked because small talk was really hard.

"I sure hope it's my time," she said, checking the price on the tag. "Because this is the most I've ever spent on a bra in my life!"

"So you like it?"

"I'd like bigger boobs more." her nagging wish reappeared. "But, yeah, I like it."

I waited as she looked over her body in the mirror, thinking about all the things that push us to escape the world—and everyone in it.

"Thanks for this." She looked right at me.

"Yeah," I replied with a grin, acknowledging our brief time together. "A lot to think about. Sounds like you just gotta be—"

"You." She smiled, snapping her fingers with custom-made flair.

AGAINST A SUCCESSION OF BASS AND THE COOL VIBE OF NIGHTFALL, I burned hard rubber down the 101 to Chase's house. Beyoncé poured out of my lungs and into thin air, heralding my own potent sovereignty and a few trimmings below the belt. I felt like Baby's sister, Lisa, in the movie *Dirty Dancing* when she arrived at the cabin of comforts, unbeknownst to Robbie Gould, raring to free her faithful offerings. And though we had different intentions, and she unfortunately walked into an unforeseen rodeo, I understood her resolution. I, too, was firing on all cylinders, hearty and bold, bouncing snowcapped mountains off lace and a large, pasty backside off binding thread. Thanks to my conversation with Janelle, I held onto a small spark of excitement. She set me up for an experience and didn't even know it, pulling me out of my comfort zone and into the great, scary unknown.

"I hope you brought your appetite." Chase smiled as I stood in the doorway. His voice never failed to pump my vitals, setting flame to my waxy complexion in seconds.

His apartment was what I expected: a bona fide bachelor pad furnished with a minimalist's touch. There was an armchair, an old leather couch, a well-broken-in recliner, and clusters of drunk people robbing every inch of space.

"Good eye," I said, leaning in to examine his photography above the couch, remembering that I heard about his hobby at the Saddle Ranch. He had a way of making people and places look like you could reach out and feel every part of their being, broken and unbroken.

"If I remember correctly, you're a meat-and-potatoes kind of lady." He winked, pulling out a tray of food from the refrigerator.

"Don't say that too loud," I replied, picking up a framed picture of three generations of women smiling against a mountainous backdrop. "I don't want my tires slashed for eating cattle around here."

He laughed, catching on to my subtle overtone in a landscape full of trending health fads.

Stepping closer, Chase watched me analyze the picture. I could feel his eyes resting on my face before slowly traveling down my arms and breasts and then my legs. *Be you*, I thought. *Just fucking be you.*

"My grandmother, mother, and sister," he explained, running his finger along their faces. I stood for a second, quietly remembering what it felt like to have a family of women in my life before they all started dropping like flies. The timing was uncanny as the progression of exits unfolded, presenting too many mysterious circumstances to casually dismiss. As soon as my mother's existence began to crumble, her mother's did, too, and yet I steadfastly refused to make any presumptuous claims about who controlled what from behind the stars.

But I waited. I waited for two days at the foot of my grandmother's bed as she lay comatose and depleted. Part of me was anxious to see what dying was all about, at least what it looked like for her. And just when I thought she was coming back for round two, not yet done with life on earth, I caught her shit-eating grin followed by a final gasp, relieved she had preceded my mother, paving one hell of a path.

Moving poolside, Chase found us a corner spot.

"Thanks for having me," I said, lowering my feet into the water.

"My pleasure," he replied, filling the gap between us. "It's nice to be out of that place."

"Yeah, it is." I automatically checked out. Chase's sentiment about being free had contrasting layers as Nina's isolation bared itself. I hoped, really hoped, that she had found some kind of comfort alongside the wounds. I wanted her job to be exactly what she needed it to be. And I wanted her first-day-back attire to give her ammo to keep going. I hoped Nicole was dancing her ass off right at that very moment, proud and momentarily free from life's restraints. I wanted her to know my working "declaration of independence" was set in motion, already beginning to liberate my good intentions as well as my anatomical jewel. For once, I wanted to keep the incessant analyzing to a minimum and have fun for the sake of living in the moment, letting Janelle's affirmations slowly become my own.

"You good?" Chase asked, his side grin still in place. "No closing down on me." Whistles hit the air as he popped more bubbly.

"I'm wide open" were the only words I got out before someone cannonballed into the pool, delivering perfect form and the sweet spell of emotion.

LIGHTNING BOLT

Still smelling like chlorine and a blend of masculine spices, I was impressed with my ability to get to work on time after another late night. The pep in my step was steady as I exited the elevator and made my way into the pending mayhem, blessed by the greatness of Sunday's hours, which gave unholy employees like myself more time to sleep off any poor decisions from the night before. And luckily I didn't have any, except maybe the bag of Goldfish crackers I ate in front of my kitchen sink after I cabbed it back to my apartment at four o'clock in the morning.

"Welcome," Michelle said, barely smiling as she stood studying sales numbers. "There are a couple women in the fitting room who might need some help. They told me they're okay on their own, but you might check on them just to make sure."

"No problem." I grabbed a measuring tape from off the counter and headed for the dressing rooms, wondering how many piles of bras I would get stuck rehanging while Michelle stood nursing her mania.

"Can I help back here?" I asked, slowly moving my way down the hallway toward an increasingly loud conversation.

"Mom, stop it!" I heard from inside a room. "Look at me!"

The door flew open, and a woman stood with her hands deep into the cups of an elderly woman's bra.

"Hi," she said, doing her best to sound welcoming. "I'm trying to get my mom into a good-fitting bra, and she's not having it. I think today just isn't our day."

"Oh, okay," I replied, waiting as the elderly woman narrowed her gaze in bewilderment. The whites of her eyes looked tangled into jagged lines of red, and her lips, noticeably chapped, bled from the corners of her mouth.

"I don't need a damn bra, Anne! Katherine has plenty!" the woman snapped, pushing away her daughter's hand.

"Katherine is a woman at the nursing home whose clothes she's been stealing."

"I see." I nodded slowly, uncertain how to respond. "I'd love to help you . . ." I stopped, waiting for someone to fill in the blank.

"Mabel," her daughter chimed in, carefully watching her mother's response.

"Hi, Mabel." I smiled, softly touching her forearm. "You don't want your own brassiere?"

She laughed like it was the most comical thing she'd heard in years.

"I'd dump the underwire and try something that will be both comfortable and supportive, which I have."

"Her breasts are so saggy, though. Doesn't she need an underwire for support?"

I looked at Anne and then at her mother's boobs, free as free could get.

"You sit a lot, Mabel?" I asked loudly as I caught her trying to read her daughter's lips.

"Sometimes," she responded, placing her hands on her hips. "I'll go to the bank and maybe the commissary."

"She has Alzheimer's disease and lives in a well-secured wing," Anne added, trying to be discreet with her disclosure. "She spends a lot of time sitting, which is why I'd like to get her something with some lift."

I could sense frustration in Anne's voice. She wanted her mom to have what she needed. But Mabel didn't give a shit if her tits sat under her chin or over her shoulders; she was missing bingo and Katherine's nap time. I wanted Anne to leave feeling reassured, though, and useful, knowing her mom was content. I could see that they had been at it for a while.

"Let me grab something." I opened the door.

"You don't want to measure her?" Anne asked, touching her mother's arm.

"Not yet."

I knew exactly what bra was going to work for Mabel and hoped we had enough in stock for a decent rotation. As usual, the stockroom was a maze—cups spilling over, tightly packed and sorted appropriately onto high and low bars.

"Do we have G cups in this?" Tabitha, the new hire, asked, holding up a sports bra.

"We should," I responded slowly, trying to gather a few different sizes for Mabel to try in our top-selling, non-underwire bra. I could tell Tabitha was beginning to have trouble suppressing her restlessness as her voice shook with unsteady regard.

"Is Michelle or Rachel helping you?" I asked, looking up to see her standing with a variety of bras in her hand, her eyes dark and weary.

"Sort of," she responded, flipping over size tags. "Michelle had to take a phone call in her office, and Rachel is in a prostheses fitting."

"Alright," I said, snagging one more bra for Mabel. "I'll be in shortly."

Upon my return, Mabel had already taken to the chair in the corner, comfortably sitting with her arms crossed as her nipples peeked out from under her forearms.

"Let's give this a try." I slowly slid the straps up her arms, noticing thin layers of bruised skin as I pulled her to her feet. I gently fastened the band before giving her breasts one last tuck, hoping we hit the jackpot with a little lift.

Mabel stared at me, and then at Anne.

"What do you think, Mom?" Anne asked at full volume, running her hands along Mabel's rib cage.

"I think it's nice," she replied, still staring at Anne while lightly rubbing her breasts in a circular motion. I noticed that the whites of her eyes were more glazed over than before.

"I rarely take her out of the nursing home because it's just too hard now," Anne said, looking at her mom. "And I haven't seen her for a little while. I wasn't prepared for this."

I waited for Anne to finish, wondering if I should let them be or attempt to keep helping.

"Here," I said, grabbing her shirt. "Let's put this on for the full look."

Mabel struggled to get her arms through the holes.

"Right here, Mom." Anne quickly expanded the armhole, trying to move the process along.

"Ta-da." I smiled with my hands out. "I'd say they're dining-hall ready."

Anne laughed, slightly putting me at ease. I could hear Tabitha's bra pitch down the way, hanging by a thread.

"Are you comfortable, Mom?" Anne asked loudly.

Mabel just stared at her, unable to utter a sound, her eyes hollow.

"Mom?"

I watched as Mabel looked down at the ground and then at her breasts, not once turning to face the mirror. It was like it didn't even exist, at least for her. I saw the glass as cruelly taking up space, leaving a long reflection of sweeping memories and only transitory rays of guiding light. Trying to understand Mabel sparked a wistful desire to turn back time. I suddenly saw my grandfather sitting, wearing Velcro sneakers on the wrong feet—alone and disoriented and floating into darkness. And maybe nothing felt as varnished or forgotten for them, just for us, the outsiders, whose wanting and needing and bargaining ended up actually shielding the brilliant moments of clarity.

"Mom?" echoed into the space between us again.

Mabel continued to stare at Anne. Waiting. Her lips pinched tight along her teeth. Small traces of blood began to rise, building darker remnants around the edging of her mouth.

"She doesn't know me anymore," Anne whispered, painstakingly. "She doesn't even know my name."

I didn't know what to say. I just stood between them, staring at Anne and then at Mabel and then back at Anne.

"I'm sure she appreciates you taking the time to get her some bras," I finally said, wondering how much Mabel understood, if anything. Her long gazes, however, led me to believe she was full of great secrets and quiet teachings.

Anne remained silent as she moved in closer to adjust Mabel's bra straps. I watched as Mabel's breasts jiggled up before resting in the cups, her shoulders slouched over and frail.

"It's hard to watch them age . . ." Anne's voice trailed off.

I looked over at Mabel, who stood staring at her hands, weathered into a deep blue. I thought of my own mother and how I was granted a moment to see and feel, a different proportion of longing. I still had my mother's youth preserved in tethered pockets, her green eyes infinite. And what I had come to understand was a harsh raid of seemingly reliable time; I never made much room to think about what it would've been like to watch her hair color change from black to silver, or her skin wrinkle into soft layers. I was frozen in time, stopping at her smooth fair skin. It was all I knew. And though slightly grateful and feeling saved, I still wondered what was worse as I stared at Anne, if the difference was even measurable.

"Are you comfortable, Mom?" Anne's voice shook as she tried for a second time.

Mabel looked down at her breasts again and then directly at Anne. I watched as she quietly studied her daughter's graying hair and big brown eyes, rendering us both speechless as her tenderness filled the room.

"I need to double-check a fit down the way," I said, softly touching Anne's hand. "You can try another band size or, if you'd like, go ahead and wear the bra out. It's a start."

Without waiting for a reply, I slid out quickly and knocked on Tabitha's customer's door. I could sense Tabitha's confusion as I caught the last of her words before letting myself in.

"Hi there." I spoke in a low tone, gazing around the room at the enormous piles of discarded bras while trying to focus. I wanted to cry, but then, in the next instant, I wanted to laugh, feeling the swift-moving pendulum from Mabel's sliver of light.

"She's wanting to minimize her breasts," Tabitha quickly stated, looking at me wide-eyed.

"Okay," I replied, turning to examine the young woman's breasts as they sat tightly squeezed into one of our heavy-duty sports bras, pushing her breast tissue in every direction but up.

"Is this for everyday use or . . ." The words barely left my mouth before the customer interjected with demanding urgency, her tone desperate and pleading.

"Yes, and I need to look as small as possible."

"Alright," I replied calmly, picking up on her loss of patience.

My mind was on overdrive, tenderly holding on to Mabel and Anne and their gentle beneficence. I wanted to get back to them, but I knew I was now facing a far-from-easy challenge. And with disappointment spilling into puddles around me, I also knew the customer needed as much time and attention as we could give her so that she could find whatever was going to ease her mind. The significance of feeling comfortable had quickly carried over, propelling me to acknowledge what it looked like on the inside, too, for both Tabitha and her customer.

"Let us grab a few minimizers to try," I said, opening the door while quietly pondering our availability. "We'll get it right."

Tabitha followed me down the hallway, stopping abruptly as I crept closer to Mabel's room. The stillness was startling as I peered through the cracks of the door, seeing only a couple bras dangling on the bar against the wall.

"I'll meet you in the stockroom," I said to Tabitha, moving toward the doorway.

And there I waited, watching Mabel lean into her daughter's arm as they exited the department holding onto a small shopping bag and the transient gift of remembrance.

BUBBLEGUM TUM

With our big annual sale right around the corner, stress levels were on the rise. Incoming merchandise continued to pile up in the stockroom, and Roxanne's stealthy rounds magnified the frazzled levels of Rachel and Michelle. We all worked around the clock in preparation for the sale, packing racks with as many bras and panties as possible. Garment bags, soaps, negligees, and heaps of Hanky Panky thongs lined the walkways, making our stockroom the most organized disaster I'd ever seen.

After an hour of lunching on a gourmet grilled cheese a few doors down while listening to a celebrity chauffeur spill his backseat dirt at the bar, I returned to the madness to find a warm reminder about Jessica Simpson's store visit and how imperative it was for employees to *not* abandon their departments to see how much she weighed in real life.

"Are you available?" A voice crept in from behind as I stood reading over Michelle's frenetic words one last time.

"I am." I smiled, turning around to find a woman and a young girl staring at me. "What can I help you find?"

Within seconds, my new customer set free a series of commands, her tone stern and coldly controlled.

"My daughter will be in a pageant next week, and we'll need a few pieces of shapewear, as well as just a little bit of a padded bra to smooth things over."

"Okay" slowly left my mouth as I stood looking over the young girl. I studied her highlighted blonde hair tightly twisted into a thick bun and then looked down along her false eyelashes, trimmed and positioned immaculately. Her breasts, akin to a couple donut holes, protruded slightly, making me question the need for a bra at all.

"We're also going to need some help from the cosmetics counter. Is someone available to come up?" The woman pushed with unyielding regard as her daughter stood silent.

Nearly tongue-tied by the tone in which she delivered her orders, I inched backward and nodded steadily, knowing the second half of my shift had taken a turn for the worse. I would've welcomed the sweatiest pair of sisters in 96 degree heat over a demanding pageant mom any day. The discomfort intensified as I took one last look at the young girl, visibly uncomfortable and confused; she couldn't have been older than ten.

"Uhhh." I struggled for words. "What sort of shapewear are you looking for? Like a little bicycle short?" I asked, hoping for a quick and easy "yes."

"No," the woman replied flatly. "I'm talking about the kind of shapewear that sucks in the rolls, smooths out the tummy, and shapes the behind."

I couldn't help flinching from the seriousness of her tone again and her long checklist. I stood while she looked me up and down. My body suddenly felt like an extra-large marshmallow thrust under a microscope piece by piece. This woman had expectations, not to mention a clear vision of what her daughter was supposed to look like as she sashayed across a stage. The glare did not go unnoticed.

Leading them over to one of our shapewear displays, I waited while she carefully examined the midsection of a pair of Spanx. Pulling the hard-wearing fabric sideways and then up and down, she grabbed four different styles of tummy tuckers before heading toward the fitting rooms, graciously reminding me that she'd like a small seamless padded bra in a 30 band . . . delivered.

With a lot of deep confusion, I studied a few different options of smaller bras with some kind of removable padding. All of them were way too big for my customer, but I figured time was of the essence, and my patience had already been tested. I couldn't pass her off to a fellow fitter, but I also couldn't find any comfort in my situation. What the hell was I doing bringing back shapewear and padded bras for a little girl to wear and somehow maintain a level of professionalism and tact? I felt stuck and considerably challenged by a swarm of moral dilemmas. *What had happened?* I thought, squeezing the pre-cut foam with the tips of my fingers. My day had started out on a good note.

Knocking lightly on a dressing room door, I hoped I had the right customers after striking out on my first try and accidentally walking in on a woman who sat naked in the chair, talking on her cell phone while rifling through receipts.

"Yes, come in." The girl's mother quickly opened the door and stepped to the side, carelessly exposing a carpet covered with discarded shapewear.

"I'm going to need a smaller size in this one." She held up a light nude body slimmer with extra tummy control.

"This is a small," I said, reading the tag. "We don't carry anything smaller."

"Someone in alterations could take it in from the sides though, right?"

"Umm, I can inquire," I said, looking over at the girl as she stood hovering in the corner with her arms tightly wrapped around her tummy, wearing only her cotton underwear.

"I can also check the girls' department for some kind of undergarment to go under whatever she's wearing."

The mother shot me another glare, reminding me who had the lead.

"That won't be necessary," she replied sharply, unhooking one of the padded bras. "I like the tummy control on these, which she needs."

I glanced over at the young girl again as she promptly looked up for my reaction. Hoping to cut the tension amid a disturbingly awkward exchange, I tried sounding excited about their chosen extracurricular event, about which I knew nothing.

"So, you're going to be in a pageant next week?"

"Yeah, it's the finals," the girl replied cautiously, her short teeth gleaming.

"That's cool," I lied, feeling uneasy and annoyed as I watched the mother lay out her child's wardrobe bit by bit, including previously purchased shapewear, nipple pads, flesh-toned tights, and a pair of sparkling silver shoes with a noticeable heel I'd probably only manage to walk three steps in.

"Did you have an opportunity to contact the makeup counter? We're pressed for time," the mother interjected while unveiling a strapless, hot-pink sequined gown. "And let's also see what a small strapless bra would look like under this. She should be able to wear a 30 band like the others you brought."

She, I repeated in my head, disappointed that I hadn't even taken the time to get the girl's name, because I was so taken aback by how impersonal and detached and presumptuous her mother was. Her child was invisible, as ironic as it might sound, and there I was assisting the behavior, utterly perplexed. A controlling pageant mom with a really shitty perm was new for me, and all I wanted to do was run in the opposite direction, fleeing every penny of commission I never wanted to earn.

Attempting to keep my composure, I quickly noted her requests and set out for a moment of freedom and a makeup artist who was willing to come up to the lingerie department and play Barbie. The department had picked up considerably. Poor Tabitha hadn't even been on the sales floor for more than an hour, and she already looked used and abused.

"Do you think you can come check a fit for me?" she asked, pleading with her eyes as she noted Farah talking to Lorenzo in the corner. Knowing I was mere moments away from tripling up on customers while drowning in the same undercurrent of helplessness, I put in a quick call for a makeup artist, snagged the first "small" strapless I could find, and grudgingly followed Tabitha back to her fitting.

We were welcomed by a middle-aged woman who immediately began pointing to the exceptionally tan, thin roll of skin hanging over her bra band.

"Absolutely no back fat!" she exclaimed loudly. "No back fat!"

Staring at the woman's B-sized breasts and all around her buff, spinach-packed frame, I moved in quickly and double-checked the size on the tag.

"This is disgusting," she continued, grabbing parts of her back's skin before tapping on her boobs. "I can't be seeing this," she repeated in cold whispers.

"I'm . . . sorry," I sputtered, trying to understand what was going on while grabbing the measuring tape from off the hook against the wall. "You mind telling me what you're looking for?"

"She can't have any traces of back fat or flesh pouring out from anywhere," Tabitha tiredly chimed in before staring at me with wide *save-me* eyes.

"Okay." I lowered my chin, feeling a mix of uncomfortable feels as I tried to piece everything together and somehow connect all the protruding veins in her forearms.

Repositioning the tape around her rib cage, I barely read the number 32 before running my hand around the band, attempting to change the placement of her skin and her breasts.

"Way too tight!" she repeated over and over before ripping off the bra and throwing it onto the chair. Tabitha quickly looked in my direction before landing her gaze back on the woman's naked breasts.

"Okay, okay," I replied. It certainly wasn't my first time dealing with a *no-back-fat* request; however, the sense of urgency, paired with a firm plea, left me baffled. There was no budging, and I knew it.

"The 36 band you picked out is just a little big for you, which won't offer any support for your boobs," I continued, staring at her deep-set eyes.

"I still want to try it," the customer insisted, unhooking one of the 36 Bs. Stepping aside, we all waited in silence and watched while she dressed herself in another bra. Before she could even fasten the hook completely, the band had already crept up her back, eliminating even the slightest skin roll as the cups loosely transformed themselves into a couple nipple guards. The bra did nothing but hang on her chest.

"See!" The woman turned to the side. "No rolls. NO rolls!"

"Nope, no rolls," I repeated while cocking my head so that I could side-stare at Tabitha, who also stiffened in utter bewilderment as her customer continued to chant "no rolls" while sternly pointing at herself in the mirror as if she was moments away from charging the center of a WWE wrestling ring wearing Wonder Woman's accessory kit. I had absolutely no sense of direction, or any arrangement of words that would've offered the slightest bit of . . . really, anything. It wasn't my beast. And if Tabitha wanted to survive the complex nuances of a lingerie department and put money in her pocket, she needed to keep moving.

That said, her customer's vision was strangely commendable, masterful in its most vulnerable form. I sensed some serious discipline that, had I understood the term and embraced its principles, would've catapulted right off my hamster wheel and straight into my own self-regulation. She knew exactly what she wanted, as obsessive or unrealistic as it might've appeared. It was hers. All 36 inches of it.

"Looks good," I said, reaching for the doorknob before reminding Tabitha of her role. "It's really important that you rotate your bras. Tabitha will grab you a few more to take home."

After this brief whirlwind of disorder and disillusionment, I took in a deep breath to prepare for what was next and knocked on the dressing room door of my mother/daughter duo. I was somewhat ready for the long tirade that greeted me.

"As I said before, we're on a tight schedule, and I really need to get this done," the mother said, making final adjustments to her daughter's Spanx before taking the strapless bras from my hand. "I also have someone in alterations coming up to alter the shapewear."

I looked over at her daughter, who stood moving from side to side in front of the mirror, thoroughly examining her new tummy tucker before quietly raising her arms to the side. I stood motionless while her mom fastened the strapless and forcefully squeezed her breast tissue into the cups.

I waited, still fighting for skillful phrasing after stuttering on my first three words.

"Are you comfortable?" I asked, eyeing her small, round tummy pinched into thick elastic fabric.

"I'm okay," she responded gently, looking up at her mom.

"Maybe all you need is just a thin hipster short," I suggested, watching her mother pull the pink strapless dress over her bun and strategically place it around her body. "The Spanx seems like a lot."

"She's fine," sharply cut through the room as I turned around to welcome our makeup artist, Benny, to the party. Without a second to lose, I backed away to give them room and watch while our beloved pageant manager assessed her requested help.

The mother looked over his bright blue eye shadow and colored collagen lips. "I'd like to get her makeup done to go with this dress."

"No problem." Benny nodded before turning on his well-rehearsed sales pitch. "But I'll need for you to come downstairs."

"I'm not sure we have time to do that," she replied, running her hand along the sequins. "Are you able to bring some makeup here that we can apply quickly and then buy?"

I could tell Benny was as excited to put makeup on a young girl in a lingerie department as he would have been inside a mortuary. The search for words was almost too much to bear. But it was real life. And we had real customers. All I could think about was moving them out as fast as possible, which made me feel anxious because there was a young girl standing in front of me, unknowingly accepting a set of predetermined rules and standards and wildly unacceptable notions about what she was supposed to look like.

It wasn't reasonable. And for the first time, while feeling angry and overpowered, I saw the bare roots spinning in circles around me. I had failed as a bra fitter—it came rushing in blows as I noticed the young girl tearing up from exhaustion. The confusion on her face, framed by an uncomfortable familiarity as her tears magnified, made my escape route wider and my loathing stronger.

Quietly stepping out so that Benny could plan his makeover after he succumbed to the pressure, I found Farah standing outside, completely immersed in my exchange.

"JonBenét Ramsey?" she asked sarcastically, offering a pageant gesture to a woman from our alterations department as she made her way through the hallway and into my customer's dressing room.

"Funny." I sighed while on the lookout for Michelle, Rachel, and Roxanne. "I'm ready to get out of here."

"Perfect," Farah replied, launching right into her grand plan. "I need you to come on a customer delivery with me."

"No way," I shot back, noticing her boobs sitting in one of our new French numbers. "I need peace and quiet before this shit show of a sale starts."

"Come on," she pleaded, far too close for comfort. "I'll buy you a couple drinks afterward."

"What did you do?" I asked, picking up on her desperation while reminding her about a pending IOU.

"Cece Jones."

"You pissed off Cece Jones?" I asked, following Farah into the stockroom where she had already begun organizing her employee carry.

"I might've forgotten to mail a few bras and panties, and she's heading out of town." Farah clenched her teeth. "And we don't even need to go to her house. She's offered to meet up over this way."

Staring at Farah, I caved out of sheer curiosity and free drinks, knowing I'd roll out her IOU during the sale—right in the nick of time.

"Your customer is asking for you." Michelle charged into the stockroom, her eyes bulging in my direction.

"Yes, of course." I smiled, watching Farah quickly try to hide Cece's large bag of lingerie by pushing it to the side with her foot. "I'm on my way."

Welcomed back by Benny and a couple women from our alterations crew, I paused at the sight of a thick makeup brush moving along my young customer's cheekbones, leaving traces of widespread pinks along the way. Her eyelids had already been marked with hued purples and a few sharp sparkles, and her lips thinly coated in gloss.

She was left standing in nothing but a pair of Spanx so that our seamstresses had room to pick and pull and prod their way around my customer's body at the mother's request. She looked like a different kid, almost disturbingly different, making the air feel toxic and suffocating as I moved closer to the dressing room to clean up a pile of go-backs.

"Can we start ringing these items up?" the mother asked while passing over two strapless underwire bras with alteration tickets attached.

"Sure." I grabbed the bras, noticing her refusal to make eye contact. "I'll meet you out front."

Not remotely interested in her timeline, though eager to get her out of the store, I began prepping the purchases until Tabitha found me. Again.

"You mind checking another fit?" she asked timidly.

Looking around the department, I realized I was the only one somewhat available, so I quickly followed Tabitha back into a dressing room, happily greeted by a woman wearing only her thong and a man sitting in the chair covered in panties.

"How we doin'?" I smiled, trying to keep my gaze near the woman's collarbone.

"Let me throw on this bra so you can tell me if it fits okay." The woman hurried, stuffing her triple-Ds into single-D cups.

Staring at their placement, I was hesitant to go in with my hands due to her not-so-sober counterpart sitting against the wall.

"I'd try going up a cup size or two," I said, looking at Tabitha. "We can grab some for you."

Following her smile, I turned to open the door, knowing it was my job to boot the gentleman, as men weren't allowed in the fitting rooms due to privacy concerns and many other reasons. But before I could turn around to kindly ask my customer to leave, I heard pageant mom's voice grow louder, stopping everyone in their tracks.

"Actually," I said, closing the door. "Let me measure you first."

Time sped up as I slowed the process. I tried everything to not have to go back out onto the sales floor, like repositioning the measuring tape five times while her breasts brushed my forearm and a hard-on prospered in my peripheral. But to no avail. Farah didn't waste any time coming to get me either, and Tabitha had gone full deer-in-headlights.

"You need to learn a thing or two about customer service," my beloved pageant mother said, pointing her finger at me while catching everyone's attention at the register. My heart started to race and I could feel my chest tighten as full-blown hives materialized along my neck.

"I'm not sure I understand," I replied, watching Benny continue to ring up her purchases.

"We've been waiting," she declared, handing over her credit card. "How do you just leave your customer? Don't you have a job to do? How hard can this be?"

All movement stopped.

I turned to look at her daughter, knowing my job was to remain as calm and tactful as possible. It was obvious she was painfully embarrassed, having been no stranger to her mother's uncivilized antics. I knew better than to engage. Plus Michelle was right around the corner listening to every word. The last thing I needed was a lecture. So I took the high road, thanking Benny for his excellent customer service before handing over my business card to the mother with a big ole smile on my face.

HAPPY TO BE OUT OF THE LINGERIE DEPARTMENT, I WELCOMED THE cool night air. I couldn't help finding humor in Farah's debacle as we sat parked in a convenience store parking lot in West Hollywood, ready to pass off a bag of purchased lingerie to one of Farah's personal customers, Cece Jones. It was common practice at the time, and a surefire way to iron out any discrepancies while ensuring good faith with the customer.

As usual, Farah was good at smoothing things over in a pinch. She was also really good at handling Cece Jones, who by all accounts was a force to be reckoned with. How Farah dropped the ball and managed to land us in the parking lot of a convenience store holding more than five hundred dollars' worth of lingerie was beyond me.

Sharing bags of Gummi Peach Rings and Cool Ranch Doritos, we watched cars make their way into the parking lot while we waited for Cece's arrival.

"What's in the bag anyway?" I asked, eyeing a group of guys buying beer at the register.

"A few of her staple bras, a lot of panties, and that new black garter," Farah replied, pulling out the mile-long receipt.

"And an emergency," I added, turning around to the high-pitched release of the song "Stayin' Alive"— and Cece Jones enthusiastically maneuvering a black Cadillac Seville.

"Holy shit" barely left my mouth as she screeched her way into a parking space, full of life . . . and the potent rush of nicotine. It was perfect.

"Hey, girl!" Cece smiled wide while walking over to Farah's car. "Thanks for doing this."

"No problem at all." Farah's retail tone emerged. "I messed up, and I know you need these."

Handing over the receipt, we watched as Cece began rifling through the bag, still smoking her cigarette and full of excitement.

"This is what I'm talking about." She pulled out a black-laced bra and held it up to her full double-Gs, slowly moving her hips from side to side while dressed in an extra short denim skirt. "This is where you spend your money, ladies. You got to make sure your shit is straight, with your girls up, and your panties proud."

Farah and I laughed as people stopped to watch Cece present her new lingerie outside the convenience store. She reminded me how beautifully bodacious one woman can be with her unrivaled spunk and zest for life. Her lead was all I needed in that moment. And before the sunset and cold malt liquor whisked her away, I held on tight to her parting words.

"Keep it real."

Turning to look at Farah, who couldn't stop laughing from the rawness of our moment, made my own stomach hurt from cackling.

"Who does this?" Farah asked, snorting from her nose. "Who delivers lingerie in a 7-Eleven parking lot?"

Laughing uncontrollably at the absurdity of our reality, I knew Farah and I weren't ready to call it a night.

"Where to?" I asked, trying to gain composure.

"The promised land." Farah smiled, pulling out a joint from her console before running her finger along its well-packed leanness. "And then to a jukebox."

Wrapping my lips around Farah's kind offering, my body began to float as we puffed and passed on the depth of our clouded flight.

"Work was crazy today," Farah barely choked out as the inside of her car began to fill up with smoke.

"Crazy," I repeated, sinking into the passenger seat. "I've been thinking about that little girl, too, wondering if she really gives a shit about being in a beauty pageant or if it's just her mom's personal failure."

"I'm sure it's her mom's long-lost dream," Farah said, going ten miles under the speed limit upon pulling out of the parking lot. "I could hear her demands from all the way down the hallway. She sounded desperate."

"Right," I mumbled, taking my last drag while thinking about the long list of ridiculous demands and the poor young girl stuck in the corner of the dressing room, embarrassed and confused. "She was so young. I can't imagine what this is going to do to her."

I sat staring out of the window, high as the night sky, and really hating my job.

"She was just a little girl."

Pointing to an old lit-up tavern on La Brea Avenue, Farah half-assed her one and only attempt at parallel parking and headed straight for the entrance. "No more shop talk except for Chase Maxwell and maybe that new guy down in shoes. The tall one with all the tattoos."

"Deal." I laughed, relieved to see a wide-open jukebox as we turned the corner and walked into a dimmed ambience full of seemingly tempered vibes. "I'll meet you at the bar." Eager to set the mood and forget about tiaras and back fat, I sifted through the jukebox's crowd pleasers, leisurely punching in my long catalog of bad and bluesy ballads.

"Tequila!" I heard Farah yell from afar, already schmoozing the male bartenders with her charming wordplay. The feeling was just right. Cece Jones was just right. And as the shuffling of music seized our moment, landing on Joplin's "Piece of My Heart" before greenlighting my heels across the floor, I took the plunge, grateful to have felt free.

UP FOR GRABS

Staring out my kitchen window, I tried bringing in order with a moment of meditation. The time on my microwave turned in flashes, making me feel rushed as my day ahead had already crystalized into sheer madness inside my head. The first day of our big annual sale had arrived, and I had no choice but to pony up and ride the riptide. Marking my fifth or sixth sale, I expected my nerves to be slightly curbed, but they weren't; the buildup was well fortified and it was up to me to stand and deliver, free from error, as best I could. The expectation on opening day had always carried its own set of demands: You moved, and then you moved faster.

AFTER PARKING IN A MAKESHIFT EMPLOYEE LOT, I HEADED STRAIGHT for the first floor and huddled around Roxanne's circle of love, slowly absorbing my surroundings as she closed her morning pep talk. Colorful balloons hung in clusters around each department, overworked waiters from our café were stationed with small pastry bites, and our pianist, dressed to the nines, had already taken to his bench, playing everyone a friendly jingle as we prepared for the rush of frenzied shoppers.

"Stay hydrated and make it a great day, West Hollywood!" Roxanne cheered us on. "You are here for the customer!"

Hurrying to get up to the lingerie department, Michelle stopped me before I could land both feet on the escalator.

"So, your customer from the other day, the pageant mom."

"Yes," I replied warily.

"She wrote a letter to Roxanne about her experience in the department, and I thought maybe you could give her a call."

"A call?" I stared at Michelle blankly. "To say what?"

"Well." Michelle checked her tone. "She's a high-level customer, and she spends a lot of money with us."

"Ahhh, right," I replied, noticeably agitated. "And you want me to smooth things over?" I asked, walking off the escalator. "I already did that . . . for a ten-year-old girl," I added in jest, though burning with resentment just thinking about it.

Michelle shot me a look and proceeded toward her office. "Let me know when you call her." She left with a smile.

Sinking to a new morning low, I pondered Michelle's suggestion and took it as just that: a mere suggestion. I didn't have time, nor did I have interest in making a phone call to a woman who I'd love to watch eat shit. However, I was interested in reading her complaint letter, hoping to make room for it on my refrigerator . . . after I sought counsel with the Employment Development Department down the way in Van Nuys.

"Five, four, three, two, one," I heard Rachel and Michelle chant from the front of the department while nonstop clapping ensued. And within a matter of moments, just after seven o'clock in the morning, the floor was crawling with shoppers. Women began grabbing items all around them, stocking up on sleepwear, T-shirt bras, push ups, and panties. It took a moment to get going, as I always stood in awe of the people who arrived so early in the morning, wondering how they did it.

"Three customers need help by the sale bras." Michelle pointed to the corner of the department, leading me right to my first customer and officially beginning the longest day in retail history.

"Do you need help with a fitting?" I asked, glancing at the size on one of the tags.

"I'm not sure I'm comfortable being measured," she replied, holding a growing pile of bras along with a stack of shapewear. "I was just hoping I could throw something on and you could double-check the fit."

"Follow me." I smiled, hoping to keep things moving.

As soon as we entered the fitting rooms, constant chatter surrounded us.

"You want to put one of the bras on first and I'll come back to check it out?" I unlocked a door.

She looked around the room and then nodded, noticeably relieved that I was leaving her to change out of her clothes. However, I didn't make it far. Women came rushing; I had no other choice but to stand and wait, knowing that if I tried to make it back out onto the sales floor, I'd get eaten alive by questions, requests, and pestering demands, all of which came with the taxing operation I'd signed up for.

The moment my customer opened the door, I could tell something was wrong. The energy had shifted drastically and her facial expression read emptied and overpowered.

"Alright," I said, glancing at her boobs' tissue that overflowed in great portions from every corner of the bra.

"I know, I know." She cut me off, quickly putting her hands on her hips. "You don't have anything for me."

I paused for a minute, knowing I had to get creative with her bras due to her size. She was a larger woman and not just in the breasts. She was also really uncomfortable, making the room tense and my replies tougher.

"We have options," I said, grabbing the measuring tape from off the hook. "Can I at least get a starting point?"

She looked down at the ground and then toward the mirror.

"I don't want to know my size."

Hoping to create as comfortable a space as possible, I moved in slowly and helped raise her arms to the side. Her skin jiggled with every movement as she tried finding a place to stand.

"I'll be quick," I said, extending my arms as far as they would go in order to get the measuring tape all the way around her. I tried three times until I could read a number.

"It's okay if you don't have anything for me to try." She backed away after I peeled the tape out from under her.

"I have ideas," I replied. "Give me a few."

As soon as I stepped out, I noticed the line to get into a room had moved well beyond the doorway. Empty coffee cups had already been left in random places, and women were flying high. It was a madhouse, making me wonder what the shoe department looked like.

Rifling through a rounder of sale bras, I gathered as many 42 double-Ds and triple-Ds as I could find, and then headed for a box of band extenders from the stockroom, hoping they would offer more comfort as I began the trial-and-error process. When I returned, I found my customer sitting in the chair against the wall, fanning herself with a folded piece of paper.

"How we doin'?" I asked, following her stare over to the package of extenders.

"I've tried those," she replied abruptly. The firmness of her tone reminded me to tread lightly, as I could feel the mood shift again.

"Okay." I searched for all the right words. "I think we should try them again, but with a different cup size."

She waited for a minute before asking me to step outside while she put one of the pink lacy T-shirt bras on.

"It's okay if you don't like the pink." I continued to pull from every angle. "I have it in black, too."

Trapped against the wall, I waited in the hallway as a long stretch of customers crowded the narrow space, modeling their sale items in front of one oversized mirror. I focused my observations up and down the pathway, noting a lot of moving sports bras, push-up bras, butt cheeks, and . . . Raul. "Shit," I whispered, watching Diane turn the corner. I felt scared, and oddly grateful to see her all at the same time. Her presence had a way of making me feel secure, no matter how intense she was. As I did with Gladys, I valued Diane's perspective on life and the deep thought she put into it. Though different from a lot of customers, Diane had a special spunk about her that really made me think outside the box.

"Natalee!" Her smile beamed.

"Hey, Diane." I smiled back, eyeing her stack of bras, underwear, and clothes from downstairs draped over her arm. "You need a room!"

Carefully looking through the cracks of a few doors, I found Diane a spot right as a woman exited.

"I'm with a customer right now, but I'm happy to check back."

"No rush at all." She welcomed herself into the room. "I'm going to be a while."

Moving back down to my customer, I responded to her hand gesture and shimmied back into the room as she held the door only halfway open. I noticed that the cups were still too small and that the band was savagely pinching her back, creating the same amount of overflow as before.

"Let's try another cup size." I didn't bother adjusting the bra.

"You know what," she replied, looking around the room. "I'll come back when it's not so crazy and I have the energy to actually do this."

Staring at the heavy circles under her eyes and along her dark, blotchy skin, I felt a surge of hopelessness, which was nothing compared to what she was feeling.

"Let me grab one more sale bra that I think will work." I kept at it, hoping she'd consider the offer.

Silence crept in while she sat down in the chair.

"I so thought this was going to be easier." She spoke calmly. "I would come in early, grab a couple bras, and bail. I wasn't prepared for the mass of people or . . . this."

I hesitated before I replied, though in full agreement with the overload of people and feeling unprepared.

"Is this your first sale?" I tried not to fixate on her breast tissue pouring out of the bra.

"I came years ago . . . and many pounds ago. I didn't realize it was a morning thing."

"Yeah." I nodded steadily. "We have some real diehards."

She sighed before the uncomfortable silence came back. I wondered what she was thinking about as she assessed her sale items. Turning around to exit seemed unfair, yet I didn't want to pressure her into trying anything else on.

"Can I have a moment?" she asked, looking up from the chair.

Nodding silently, I squeezed my body out the door and back into the pandemonium and immediately grabbed a couple more bras from a sale rounder. Merchandise was already strewn about and I could see that Michelle and Rachel were stuck at the register, leaving Tabitha to drown in a sea of chaos. I thought about knocking on Diane's door, but stopped when I realized I couldn't get stuck in the room with her. I had a woman down the way hating everything about her experience, and I couldn't abandon her.

"How's it going?" I asked, returning to the customer's room. "I snagged one more bra to try."

It took her a minute to let me in, as she was in the middle of trying on one of our slimming body garments.

"I didn't catch your name," I said.

"Christine," she mumbled, quickly closing the door. The air was still tense, and I noticed a pile of body shapers folded in the corner.

"Am I too early?" I asked with hesitation, holding onto a black-laced minimizer.

"It's okay," she replied tiredly. "Nothing seems to be working."

"Well," I said, resting against the wall. "Can we at least try this and an extender?"

Frustrated and run-down, Christine stepped to the middle of the room and quietly raised her arms to the side. I watched as she examined her stretched-out underarm skin.

"I hate being fat," she said, pushing me to quickly fasten the extra piece of fabric onto the band and shove her boobs into the cups. I could feel her discomfort as I rearranged her breast tissue with my hands, carefully pulling it in from the sides and out from the splits of my fingers. "I did this to prove something to myself, not to stand here and look at all this."

Loosening the straps, I backed away confused.

"You're doing good, Christine," I replied, relieved that the bra extender helped. The fit was far from great, but her breast tissue was covered and the ladies had risen to some extent. "Do you want to see how it looks under your shirt?" I asked.

"Sure." She lowered herself into the chair. I waited for a response.

"I feel dizzy," she said, staring at the ground.

"Oh, okay." I quickly moved over to her. "Umm, what do you need?"

"I think I'm having a panic attack," she responded while trying to catch her breath.

"Shit," I said, beginning to feel my own panic. "In through the nose and out through the mouth."

She followed my lead and continued to sit, breathing in heavily as she ran her hands back and forth along her legs.

"Breathe, Christine," I recited like a chorus, hoping the panic would subside.

I didn't know what to do, considering life outside of the dressing room was bound to exacerbate whatever was happening inside of Christine.

"You can stay here for as long as you need," I said, awkwardly rubbing her back while checking out her bra fit. "Are you okay if I grab you some water?"

Responding to her intensified head nod, I bolted straight for the café and fought my way toward the front of the line. Of course, Roxanne was ever so present, making sure things were moving at the speed of light. It was a well-oiled operation with a lot of money at stake and a reputation on the line.

Balancing two large cups of ice water, I headed straight for Christine. The door was a tad cracked when I arrived, and I could see that her blood pressure had found its way back to some kind of order.

"Water on the rocks?" I handed her one of the cups as she continued with her deep breathing.

"I'm sorry," she said, placing her hand on her heart. "This is so stupid."

"It's not stupid, Christine. Whatever it is, it's not stupid."

"I went through your sale catalog for weeks," she went on. "I circled shirts I liked, jeans I wanted, and a few bras I thought were cute and sexy." She paused to take a sip of water. "I knew it was all out of my league, but I wanted to somehow prove to myself that I can leave the house and actually go shopping, like every other woman. I can buy things. I can walk out with shopping bags and feel good about my purchases."

The depth of her agony became clearer by the second. And I felt like I had nothing to offer except water and band extenders and really awkward stances.

"I appreciate your help," she said, reaching for her shirt. "I'll take the bra and extenders, but I've got to get out of here."

I waited while she slowly stood up from the chair. "Remember that you did this, Christine," I said, looking at her straight on. "You might not have purchased what you wanted, but you did this."

She stopped and nodded her head slowly. Tears began to camouflage the rich brownness of her eyes. "'Chub with the rub,' my dad used to say. And, man, I hated him for it."

"Is he still around?" I asked, holding her water while she put on her shirt.

"No." She took in another deep breath. "He died a few years ago, and it was fine by me."

Taken aback by her comment, though appreciative of her honesty, I responded by saying nothing, once again standing in an awkward pose. She reached up into her shirt and ripped the tags from the bra. Silence continued, unkindly marking our space. But before I had a chance to utter anything, Christine left me standing in the middle of the dressing room holding onto a pile of body shapers and a stirring mix of emotions.

I turned to face the mirror, stuck and moving through the relationship we carry with our bodies, which often bears a wearing dialogue—a sharp reckoning that can lead us to dark places in an instant. Christine's dressing room experience, and my own body image, forced me to take note of how complicated these sharp reckonings really can be.

As an "early bloomer" myself, packin' C cups in sixth grade before moving into years of constant vacillating from the idea of loving my "thickness" to sometimes hating its company, I began to truly understand its toll, but not until I arrived at the lingerie department, anchored in solidarity and struck by the harshest of realities that started with one's thinking. So many of us get stuck between a sufferable love and an enduring hate when it comes to our body image. We can lose to the toughest of critics within us, attempting to shrink every facet of our humanity as we try our best to balance the two, landing on a snack pack of broccoli, a promising batch of Botox, a tried-and-true pair of Spanx, or . . . when the light conquers the shade . . . ZERO FUCKS comes reigning, perhaps offering the greatest gift of all.

As I continued to stand alone in the dressing room, inches away from the mirror, I thought about my relationship with my body and how much it had changed since working in lingerie. The complex underpinnings of "self" had turned into a sizable mix. My full double-Ds, thickset thighs, and round planet earth of an ass were exactly what science served up. Throw in an insatiable appetite and bodily inheritances, and my job was to find a way to honor these working parts. Every day. No matter the feat. But there lay the catch, the transformative bit about solidarity and commonality shared within the small confines of a dressing room, that slowly began to teach me how to lean in . . . and love.

ALMOST FORGETTING ABOUT DIANE, I WALKED DOWN TO HER ROOM and let myself in freely, knowing that we had broken all the ice. It was all out moving forward, which is why when I found her standing in her tall-ass birthday suit, conversing with a bird, I wasn't the least bit surprised.

"Natalee!" She flashed me head on. "I've found some really good bras and now I'm trying on a few negligees."

"That's great! I'm so sorry about my delay in getting back to you."

"Oh my goodness, no worries at all! It's busy in here. And I've done well, especially now that I know my size."

"So the bras are good?" I asked, referring to her earlier purchase.

"Yes, I love them! Thank you."

I continued to stand against the door, eyeing her growing pile of bras close to spilling over on the chair.

"You never came to see me." She turned my way again.

"Ah, yeah, I know," I replied, remembering exactly where her business card sat in my apartment. "My time management is compromised on the daily."

She laughed, placing her breasts in the last sale bra.

"I think you'd actually enjoy it," she said, speaking on behalf of her practice. "Needed change and movement for sure," she added, nonchalantly cupping her boobs in front of the mirror.

"Needed change?" I asked, hooked immediately.

"I don't know exactly, but you're certainly in movement. You'll make the right decision."

The right decision?

I guess I was in movement, constantly thinking about new faces and places and whatever else aimless wanderers discovered. But needed change? I thought hard about Diane's proclamation and its relevancy and how "right decisions" had a way of masking themselves in fear before materializing into one big Yellow Brick Road. "I hope so," I finally replied, still startled by her statement.

"Remember to trust the process." She reached for her own bra. "And start paying attention to the feminine spirits around you. You have guides, you know."

What? Guides?

Feminine spirits?

Holy shit.

My mind took off again. I instantly thought about my mother and her mother and my dad's mother. Were they watching me? How exactly did their presence manifest? My libido was finally steel again. *Goddamnit.* What in the hell was going on? My hands started to moisten with sweat as I thought about the prospect of "connecting with loved ones."

"I hope I didn't overstep," Diane said, readjusting the collar on her shirt.

"No, not at all." I struggled to make eye contact. "I, uh, appreciate the—" I stopped in midsentence, unable to articulate anything. Once again Diane had me cornered. I wondered what she knew that I needed to learn.

"Can I at least help you to the register?" I asked.

"Nah." She flapped her hand at me before walking out of the dressing room. "I'll have one of the cashiers ring me up with your employee number. You keep going!"

The door flung shut and I stood motionless in the middle of the dressing room again, wondering if I was really alone. It was hard to comprehend life beyond earth. And then Diane came in, with just a few words, and gave me something to hold onto, even with the skepticism I couldn't push aside. But it really wasn't about what I believed or needed to hear, and everything about the power of people.

TWELVE HOURS AND TWENTY-TWO MINUTES LATER, I WOBBLED TO my car. The bottoms of my feet felt like a burning firepit, and the amount of grease I collected on my forehead was enough to keep a crew of bicyclists on the road.

Reflecting on my time with Diane, I drove home in silence. I envisioned my mother paying visits to the lost and heartbroken, moving my dad along each aisle of the grocery store. It all seemed peculiar, yet worthy of believing. There had to be something. Life, though messy and incomprehensible at times, was far too magical to end in nothing.

"Hey, Dad," I said, detouring down Sunset Boulevard.

"Hey, Nat," he replied, turning down the TV. "How was the big day?"

"It was alright." I sighed, telling myself four times to drive past In-N-Out Burger.

Larry, my dad, hated small talk, as did I, but sometimes it was all that transpired because of work or driving or because it was emotionally easier. The distance between us had a funny way of transferring sentiments, often leaving me in a state of fear. He was all I had—but he was 1,136 miles away.

"You know, Pops," I eased in slowly. "I've started thinking about something." Sirens blared by, stalling my proposition. "How would you feel about me coming back up to stay with you? I'd maybe sublet my apartment for a little while. Plus I can get your expertise with my résumé and figure out what's next."

Silence spread to every corner of the car.

"I'd get a job in the meantime, of course. And it's not like it'd be tomorrow. It was just a thought."

I could almost hear the wheels turning in my father's head. Maybe he wasn't lonely after all and preferred living solo with his newfound freedom.

"I thought you wanted to stay in LA," he said.

"Well, I do," I replied. "But I thought I could, um, spend some time with you until I found a stable job. I'm not really sure I can afford this place. Slingin' bras isn't cutting it. And I just want to make sure you're getting by okay."

Larry laughed softly.

"I'm getting by just fine, Nat. Stop worrying about me. And know that you always have a room here for as long as you need."

My heart gave way.

Why couldn't Christine's dad just say that? Why did he have to call her "chub with the rub"? His own daughter . . . forever up against those words.

"Where is this coming from anyway?" he asked with a concerned tone.

"I don't know. It all just hit me." I tried sounding slightly apathetic so things wouldn't get too mushy. "I just don't want to be in a position where I'm working retail for the next ten years."

"Okay, I get that. Remember you went to college to become a teacher, Natalee." My heart gave way again. Larry rarely addressed me by my full name. Plus I didn't want to tell him that I wasn't mentally ready to embrace the complexities of adulthood due to my lack of fortitude and overpowering need to keep escaping. But I appreciated that he reminded me of my big, burning passion that he had faithfully championed since I was in the first grade—the minute I came home and declared my future profession as a teacher. I'd line up all my stuffed animals and lazy-eyed dolls around the ping-pong table in our playroom and demand that everyone listen as I guided them straight into the Berenstain Bears' concerning family paradox and Charlotte's beautifully entangled web. It felt like magic. My parents would listen from the bottom of the stairs, their movements far from crafty as their giggles overlapped, leading me to kick them out of my classroom for the duration of most days . . . after I retrieved the workbooks, sliced apples, and juice boxes my mom would leave at the top of the stairs.

"Thanks, Dad." I sighed, waiting for his retort after I expressed uncertainty about a specific timeline.

"Whenever you'd like, Nat."

The thought of leaving LA was hard to digest. I loved LA. It had become a significant part of my life, yet there were times when it felt transitive and heavy. And then I met Diane Hart and fucking Raul who really got me thinking: *Stop worrying about the future. Everything will fall into place. Trust your instincts. Larry isn't going to have a heart attack on the golf course; he's going to have a heart attack in his sleep. You should call him back immediately and tell him you love him and appreciate him because you don't always say it and you're going to regret it once he dies of a heart attack.*

Turning onto Beachwood Drive, I got a clear shot of the Hollywood sign, giving me the sharp reminder I had asked for just moments before. I didn't want to leave LA forever, plus people sublet their apartments all the time for various reasons and greener pastures. Something was pulling me back to Seattle, but I didn't know what. I had to trust the process like Diane said, knowing change was a part of it. Time had a way of working things out. I suppose.

MISSION
ACCOMPLISHED

Preparing for another round of the sale, I faced a long Saturday night closing up shop. Luckily Farah shared in the same misery, reminding me that whatever kind of shenanigans unfolded, she was bound to get me through the evening. Being only the second day of the sale and a weekend night in the lingerie department, endurance was key. People came from all over, swiping plastic left and right.

In order to maintain a good dose of staying power, I put myself back together with a handful of anti-inflammatories and Starbucks' panic attack brew. Navigating through a swarm of shoppers, I made my way back to the stockroom where I found a note stuck to my personal box. Carefully unpeeling the tape, I freed a lengthy set of hard penned words starting with the generic salutation: *Dear Ms. Roxanne Michaels.* Anger bristled inside of me as I read pageant mom's note: *It wasn't a good experience for my daughter. Natalee was unprofessional and failed to meet the demands of the job, often leaving us to fend for ourselves.*

"Unprofessional?" I repeated out loud, sharing my new badge of honor with Yvonne and Tabitha as they searched for bras.

"Yep," Rachel said, holding onto a handful of replenishments as she emerged from behind.

"Did Roxanne drop this off?" I asked, preparing for another office visit.

"Yep," Rachel said again.

I did my best to shove the complaints as far back into my brain as they would go. I also ran through the entire transaction from start to finish, noting any discernable time gaps I was willing to own up to, and recalled my strong desire to spend very little time in the dressing room with this woman and her absurd antics. Perhaps I did slow the process, but I wasn't totally convinced my lack of tolerance warranted such an exhaustive complaint. So I went on with my day, semi-prepared to plead my case with Roxanne should it come up.

"A customer needs help with Natori Bras, and I've got a double mastectomy," Rachel approached the counter, still short with me. Walking briskly, I wasted no time in greeting the woman.

"Hey," I said, following Rachel's lead over to a petite blonde with long deliberate curls.

"Hi, thanks for coming over." She offered a warm smile. "I'm desperate for a few basic nude bras."

Perfect, I thought, moving my watchful eyes along the ridges of her collarbone. "I've got you covered."

I soon learned that my use of the word "covered" was an understatement. Emily, who kindly shook my hand upon entering the dressing room, needed all the coverage she could get.

"Go ahead and take off your shirt," I said, anticipating an easy fit.

She stalled shyly, setting her glasses on the chair.

"I wear a garment," she said, sliding her shirt over her head.

I stared at its shiny white fabric and loose-capped sleeves, wondering how a bra was going to fit into the equation once I realized the undershirt stayed on. The stitching designed to sit under the bottom part of her breasts sagged down to her rib cage. I was at a loss.

"Umm, okay." I moved in closer so that I could mentally place her breasts.

"It's my temple garment," she said. "The bra must go over the top. I can't take it off."

"Oh," I replied, admittedly baffled and totally uneducated on the Book of Mormon. All I knew about the community was that they congregated in Utah, rode bikes, and that the male missionaries wore crisp, white-collar button-ups and backpacks strategically filled with scriptures for when they knocked on people's front doors uninvited. Emily was my first garment-wearing Mormon, and I had no idea what I was doing.

"You're pretty tiny." I continued to examine every inch of her polyester undershirt. "I say we find what's going to be most comfortable and stick with that."

"Sounds great." Emily smiled while pulling on her sleeves to ensure that her shoulders were covered. "Aren't you going to measure me?" she asked as I opened the door.

"Nope." I smiled back, hoping she trusted my instincts. "I'm just going to grab a few sizes, and we'll start from there."

The sales floor was slammed. Semi-bored men, women, and loud children packed every corner of the department, making it difficult to pull bras from any of the sale racks. And with my name crossly inked on pageant mom's "we'd love to hear from you" stationery, I needed to remain steady.

"Sorry about the wait." I hung a couple more bras on the hook. "How about we start here?" Carefully sliding a nude, smooth-cup bra off its hanger, I helped Emily get her arms through the straps. She quickly adjusted the placement of her garment while I moved behind her to fasten the band. It took me a couple tries to hook the bra, as the material from her shirt bunched around her back and everywhere along her chest, making it difficult to properly place her breasts into the cups. Once I finally got it on, we both stood in front of the mirror and stared at the shiny white polyester spilling out from underneath the bra.

"Let's try the C cup," I said, still looking at Emily's boobs. I could tell she was uncomfortable, yet determined to make it work.

"I know it's hard with the garment, but I need some kind of coverage," she replied, backing away to take off the bra.

"Are you mostly concerned about your nipples?" I asked, trying not to stare at her arrow-like teats. They were in charge. And I could tell they bothered her.

"Yeah, I am," she replied, embarrassed. "I can't have my nipples showing."

Picking up a 32 C from off the hook, I helped Emily into another bra.

"May I?" I asked, moving in closer with my hands out so that I could place her boobs and the garment fabric into the cups.

"This is a little better," she said, touching the cups before putting on her shirt for a final look. I nodded in agreement, running through a number of questions in my head about her life as a Mormon and when exactly the temple garment came off, if ever. The whole setup created a lot of confusion and fascination on my end, and I was ready for whatever kind of Q&A Emily was willing to participate in as I awkwardly touched her breasts. And my rationale seemed reasonable, given that I've met a few doorbell ringers in my day, also with a lot of loaded questions at inopportune times.

"Does the garment ever come off?" I asked, relieved to see Emily smiling as she kindly accepted a no-holds-barred exchange.

"Like during sex?" She smiled again, giving me a coy look.

"Yes." I didn't hesitate to respond, shamelessly imagining missionary position.

She laughed, reaching for another bra to try. "The garment does come off," she finally replied. "I'm not a robot!"

I liked her response.

"There are a lot of misconceptions about the Mormon Church and our undergarments, trust me!" she resumed with certitude.

Stepping forward, I helped fill the bra cups again, lightly pulling on the garment's bottom edging. I appreciated Emily's willingness to share as I learned about her values and beliefs. We couldn't have been more different, living two drastically different lifestyles, with two radically different mind-sets. Perhaps it was what made our exchange so interesting and worthwhile and unexpected. A devotee to a rigid set of rules, and a roving eccentric without any. The discomfort was inevitable.

"Are you familiar with the Church of Jesus Christ of Latter-day Saints?" she asked, delivering a mouthful.

"Um, no, not really," I replied, mentally trying to organize LSD into LDS as my freshman year of high school came rolling back in waves. "Have you been a part of the church for a while?" I asked, helping create a "yes" pile as Emily handed over bras that she liked.

"Uh, sort of," she replied. "I'm a baptized convert from Seattle."

"Me, too!" I exploded with excitement.

"You are?" she asked, surprised, darting her eyes down to my cleavage-packed double-Ds I strategically placed between a few unfastened buttons.

"No, no, I mean, I'm from Seattle, too."

"We're actually here visiting friends," she said, assessing her nipples in the mirror. "You grew up in Seattle?"

"Yeah, about twenty minutes south of the city. It's a lot different now."

"I started out at Holy Rosary." Her soft nature started to shift.

"No shit," I replied, again doing a fine job of knowing my audience. "How did you ever become—" barely left my mouth before Emily interjected.

"A Mormon wife?" She took a second to gather her thoughts. "I fell deeply in love," she said, laying three flesh-toned bras into a pile on the chair. "This was his life and there was no changing it, so I found a way to make it work for me, to commit wholeheartedly. And I've never been happier."

I appreciated her conviction.

"Wow." I nodded, totally enamored. "That's a pretty big compromise."

"Yeah, it's caused a lot of tension with my family, my mom especially. She thinks I need psychological help."

"That's tough." I followed her gaze to the ground, wondering if she was worn from the permanence of it all. "She doesn't understand that you're happy?" I asked.

"It's not what she wanted for me. It's always been about her."

"And that's why you chose you," I replied.

She took a minute to think about my comment, again staring at the ground.

"Well, you can't choose your family, right?" she said, looking to break her stillness. "But then . . . you can."

I instantly drifted off, thinking about Seattle's boxed suburbia and how much I wanted nothing to do with it. Every inch of its unfurled despondency had run its course, pushing me as far away as I could get. My mom died downtown. Her mom died in a room across from the Narrows Bridge, right off Interstate 5. A duck bit my finger at Treasure Island Park, causing me to bleed into the holes of my Wonder Bread. I didn't want Seattle; I just wanted my dad, and I hated how the two came together.

But there was something about Emily's presence that compelled me to choose, like she did. She chose love, even under its most stringent shadows. She gave its potency and madness the power to guide her, trusting every overlay of its command, as scary and beautiful and life-altering as it was. Emily's good love liberated her, and I could feel the realness and truth surrounding us, which was exactly what I thought about when I thought about love. Deep, authentic love. Intoxicating love. Vulnerable love. And as I continued to acknowledge the sharp contrast between us, quietly pondering her pledge, I suddenly felt as free as a bird, floating into the unknown on a new level of consciousness, wanting everything chosen love had to offer, but without the pamphlets and polyester garment.

Staring at Emily's winning pile, I offered a last call for nipple pads. "I've got gels and petals," I said, gathering her purchases. "They might feel cumbersome at first, but you'll get used to them."

The wheels started to turn while Emily put the pieces together, layer by layer.

"Let me try the bras first and see how they look," she replied with a confused expression after I held up a set of round gel pads designed for extra-large areolas and voluminous nipples.

"I get it." I smiled, guiding her over to the line for the register. "Next time."

MERCHANDISE COVERED EVERY CORNER OF THE DEPARTMENT. I LOST count of how many times our store operator had to get on the loudspeaker to tell our thoughtful sale shoppers that the store was closed. She even gave everyone exit strategies and kindly thanked them for shopping with us. But people continued to wander around as if we were invisible. It was maddening, which is why I was so relieved to see Farah's and Yvonne's names printed along the closing hours on the schedule. Neither of them put up with it, ruthlessly turning customers away so that we could move down the departing checklist and call it a day.

Rachel and Michelle had already left for the evening; therefore, Chase had free rein to sprawl out on our velvet couch next to our half-naked mannequin, Mary Beth, and wait until we had completed our tasks.

"How many times do you think these were tried on today?" I asked, folding the elastic band of a pair of Spanx into the clips of a plastic hanger.

"With panties, ten. Without panties, fifteen." Farah stood counting money from one of the tills.

"Seriously?" Chase perked up from the couch.

Noting the time on the clock, I hustled to put merchandise away.

"Uhhh," Yvonne groaned, approaching the register. "We still have a customer."

"What?" I chucked a pair of panties on the counter, knowing it was me who forgot to double-check all the dressing rooms. "Tabitha?"

"Yep," Yvonne replied with a side snarl. "I'll call the operator and let her know."

Hesitant to walk back into the dressing rooms for fear of losing my cool, I stood by the entrance and waited for Tabitha, but she never came, so I was forced to intervene.

"Hello," I said, softly pushing on the door after I noticed that it was cracked open.

"We just finished," Tabitha said anxiously, moving to the side.

Staring at her customer with one of Yvonne's side snarls, I noticed prickles of dark facial hair and a prominent Adam's apple covered with golden self-tanning streaks.

"Did you find what you needed?" I asked, promptly changing my tone once I realized the customer was really uneasy and half-naked in a pair of small satin shorts.

"I think so," Tabitha replied again. "We weren't totally sure on the size."

"What exactly are you looking for?" I turned toward the customer, hoping to move things along.

"Something smooth that I can wear under dresses and skirts." A deep voice filled the room. "Something with shape."

Studying the customer's slender frame and lopsided wig trimmed into a bob, I quickly assessed the pile of control garments and noticed that our top-selling Spanx body slimmer was not in the pile.

"What about something that goes up to your bra band?" I asked. "It covers all of your stomach."

"I looked for one, but I think we're sold out," Tabitha cut in.

"I've got one," I replied, gathering a handful of hangers. "Hold tight."

Finding Chase still lounging on the couch next to a very white Mary Beth, I interrupted his light snooze and gestured for him to leave.

"You should probably go," I said, tugging on his tie. "I think our customer needs a little privacy."

"Really?" he asked, more curious than anything.

"Does she understand we're CLOSED." Farah interrupted loudly while placing a stack of frayed bras into a plastic bag.

"Yes," I replied, helping Chase up from the couch.

Hurrying to pull the last body shaper from the "customer holds" rack, I noted a size medium on the tag and dropped it off for Tabitha, discreetly motioning for her to move faster.

"Thanks for shopping with us; we are now closed," the operator rambled on from overhead.

We all hovered by the registers, waiting. Farah prepped each one of the money bags, Yvonne delivered alterations and tidied up the department, and I padded down the racks, making sure all the hangers were even so that nothing looked noticeably out of place for when Michelle arrived in the morning.

"What are we doing?" Farah asked, agitated, as she started to pace the department.

Finally, Tabitha and her customer emerged from the dressing rooms, holding the entire store back from going home in addition to a pile of sale bras, ten high-ticketed Hanky Panky thongs, two garters, a flesh-toned body shaper, and a black silk negligee.

"I'm so sorry; thank you for your patience," our late-night shopper pleaded nervously. "I'm trying to figure all of this out and I . . . I . . . I . . . don't know what I'm doing. I'm . . . so sorry."

The sound of the stutter made my stomach sink as panic surrounded the space.

"It's okay," I repeated three times, trying not to stare at the shiny beads of sweat making their way down the customer's multi-shaded forehead. "It's okay."

Flustered from the presence of our store security, Tabitha rushed to complete the transaction.

"Nine hundred and fifty-two dollars," she said, quickly prepping a shopping bag. I moved toward the front of the department, hoping to calm any uneasiness while the others roamed close by, observing the customer's trembling hands.

The intensity of the situation was troublesome and markedly palpable, causing me to feel heavy-hearted for our customer as the struggle became clearer. The words "I don't know what I'm doing" led me to believe there was something going on inside Tabitha's customer that was far bigger than I could grasp in such a short time. My observations, however, brought me to an unexpected rumination on the complexities of gender identity, and what a profoundly internal experience it can be for so many people. My job was to make sure that all the things needed inside of a dressing room, like access to comfort, privacy, and even femininity remained constant, at least for the most part. If I learned anything in the lingerie department, it was how humanly negligent it is to create assumptions about the character of another human being. Our quiet dialogues had undeniable depths. Support was needed. And just when I remembered to have Tabitha pass off a business card, the customer sprinted out of the department like one would during a track-and-field event or an armed robbery. I'd never seen anything like it. The swift flight flashed in my peripheral, leaving me, and the remainder of my restless team, speechless.

LATER THAT EVENING, AT MY APARTMENT, NEVER IN A MILLION years did I think I'd have a Mormon on my mind while pulling myself together with some G-string thongs and shimmery body lotion. Emily's garment came back with a bang, strangely guiding me through every bullet point on my checklist before Chase's house, regrettably earning the sharp rescue of a BIC razor and Skintimate's Raspberry Rain shave gel. My shit was on fire. But my intentions were clear.

Somewhere within the bulk of our exchange, in the private confines of a dressing room, Emily gave me the confidence to choose what felt right for me. Her commitment to love—and her own sexuality—made the pulse beneath my fearful thinking dissipate for the sake of experiencing something, and someone, freely. And the irony was far from lost as I unraveled deeper parts of her promise, which didn't seem free at all, considering her chosen scriptures. But that's what made it infinitely her own. Every word, every line, and every shoulder-capped garment. She chose to own it for herself. Every day.

FREEDOM CALLS

S tanding half dead next to a table of sale panties, I watched as shoppers continued to fill every last section of space. Their movements steady and pulses still flying high, making the store vibrate for another long week of retail paradise. Freedom couldn't have been more on my mind as the light at the end of the tunnel began its slow flicker.

"This is Pamela," Michelle said, irritably grinning as she marked my tired stance. "And she would love a bra fitting."

"Yes, of course." I quickly snapped out of my daze. "Right this way."

Inside the dressing room, and without delay, Pamela began to take off her tank top and bra, exposing what was left of her breasts after advanced breast cancer. "Lots of good cocktails and a double mastectomy," she said with her hands out. I instantly picked up on her definition of a "cocktail," having remembered my mother's oncologist calling chemotherapy the same thing. Maybe it was an easier way to swallow the blow before sinking into a lonely imprisonment.

I stared at the remains of her chest with its deep, dark, pink scars.

"I've got my prostheses," Pamela said, proceeding to take out two large silicone breast forms from the cups of her bra. I examined the floppiness of their existence, as well as the light brown color of their flesh-like layers. Everything about the prostheses looked "normal" with a fairly realistic representation of the nipples. And though an abundance of breast forms lined the corners of our stockroom, it was the first time I actually saw their functionality move alongside a woman, a young woman, who'd been prey to some of the cruel and barbarous certainties of illness. I was at a loss for direction, even though Pamela's presence made me feel otherwise.

"I don't usually assist with prostheses fits," I replied, still staring.

"I'm not filing anything with insurance," she replied. "It's been a nightmare, and I'd rather just buy new bras and have the alterations department take care of the cups."

I stood staring at a prosthesis as she held one in the palm of her hand.

"Will that be okay?" she asked, suddenly worried.

"Oh, yes, absolutely," I replied quickly. "Let's get your bras done first and then I'll grab the alteration tickets."

Somewhat apprehensive, I continued to follow Pamela's lead, quietly admiring her control. The last thing I wanted to do was mess up a prostheses fit.

"These are double-Ds," she said. "I'd like to try a couple of your pocketed bras first to see if I like them."

"36, 38?" I guessed correctly on the band.

"38," she replied. "To go with my new double-Ds."

Repeating her size out loud to myself, I immediately started to assemble an array of styles that would be easy to sew pockets into. I grabbed non-underwire smooth cups, T-shirt bras clos-

est to her skin tone, half lacy numbers, and then precut prostheses bras from our stockroom per her request. Studying the
first batch of bras, I envisioned where the pockets would go,
hoping Pamela had enough to work with as we found ways to
place her adhesive.

On my way back to the dressing rooms, I noticed a woman
modeling lingerie for a man pacing the entrance. She spoke in a
high pitch that became increasingly louder the more string-sized
merchandise Yvonne brought back for her to try on.

"What do you think, baby?" she asked the man, flaunting a
white lace bodysuit.

"I like it," he replied, resting his arm against the wall as he
slowly moved his eyes along her well-toned body. "I like it a
lot, baby."

Quickly moving my stare away from the customer's well-
groomed sites, I noticed Pamela waiting for me outside the
door.

"I've got some choices," I said, lining the bras along the bar
from pre-pocketed options to the collection of strays I picked out.

I paused while she looked over each one of the bras, cup by
cup.

"It used to be so easy," she muttered, unhooking one of our
prostheses bras first. Its thick straps and vintage-like pattern
were a stark contrast to the black semi-lace bra I threw into
the mix.

"Can I . . . do anything?" I hesitated to ask, feeling as though
my help wasn't needed any longer. Pamela had a process, profoundly different from my own, and I wasn't sure where I
belonged. One of the scars on her chest reminded me of an
expressionless face with a straight mouth. It was clear that her
body had been broken into—deeply and unjustly.

As I stood stationary, watching her place the finely tapered edges of her prostheses into the pouches of a bra, I couldn't help wondering what was going through her mind, especially after our hallway model addressed her man-friend for all to hear.

"My boobs look awful in this!" she yelled. "Ugh, sooo gross!"

With the door handle in my hand, I froze midstance as my stomach plummeted to the floor. *I have a woman who just lost her breasts. Oh my god.*

"You mind helping me with the straps?" Pamela interjected, welcoming me to stay.

"Uh, yeah, sure, absolutely." I turned back around, my heart beating in distress.

Together, we adjusted the placement of her prostheses by moving them up and closer to her sternum. They felt cooler to the touch, having been out in the open and away from her body.

"Wow," she said, brushing the ends of her dark brown hairpiece from off her shoulders so that I could tighten the straps. "These are my boobs."

We both stared into the mirror quietly. I examined the roundness of her silicone as each formation adhered directly to her body, forming a shapely silhouette. I noticed the skin along her collarbone and neck had severe scaling, which made the flesh look tougher and multihued and really uncomfortable as if it had been lit on fire. Perspective poured in as the vulnerability of our exchange intensified. The cellulite on the back of my legs suddenly transposed itself into a worthy asset. The stretch marks on the sides of my titties and ass had never felt so insignificant, like pale strips of minutia atop a well-rounded snowbank.

"Let's get the alteration tickets going," she said, sifting through the row of pocketless bras. "I'll pick out which ones I'd like altered, and then we should be good."

"Do you mind if I bring you one more bra to look at?" I asked, thinking about one of my favorite French bras with just enough cup to successfully add pockets for her prostheses.

"Not at all!" Her face lit up, pushing me to hurry back.

As I moved toward the exit, I walked straight into another fashion show, this time with the opportunity to view a sheer black push-up bra and a G-string adorned with three cover-up-your-mons-pubis rhinestones. Yvonne was near heart attack.

"What do you think?" the woman asked the man, twirling in circles.

"You need to go smaller in the cups," he replied, quickly moving out of the way for a customer to pass by. "Your boobs look weird. They're all uneven."

"What do you mean they look weird? You don't like it? Can we try a smaller size?" She quickly turned toward Yvonne, whose nonverbal expression said it all.

"Put something else on," the man retorted with a demanding undertone. "You look ridiculous."

WTF? Don't get fired. Keep walking. He's gross and wearing dirt for pants. There's a complaint letter with your name on it. It's not your business . . . or is it?

Following Yvonne over to our French collection, I helped pull a few sizes for her, as well as Pamela's black piece.

"Sorry," I said, knowing she was about to explode.

"Almost an hour," she replied flatly while holding up her pointer finger. "One full hour with this couple I'll never get back. That asshole just keeps making her change."

Back inside Pamela's dressing room, I noticed that she had chosen a few bras for me to take down to alterations.

"Here." I held up the French style. "They run small."

"I like it," she replied, examining the thin layer of lace along the top of the cups. The fit was hard to gauge as we worked to fasten the band and place her prostheses into the pocketless cups for an idea of how it would look.

"You've got this down," I said, watching Pamela reposition her breast forms.

"It's taken some time, let me tell you," she replied, shaking her head. "But I'm grateful I'm here."

"Long road?"

"It's crazy how life can change so quickly. One day you're loving life, and then the next day you're wondering if there will be any more of it. I was thirty-eight when I was diagnosed. And then chemo and radiation and a mastectomy followed, not to mention the devastation and depression that came along with it."

I shook my head, imagining her all alone.

"It was really grim for a while," she continued. "I didn't think I was going to make it. And now that I'm here, looking at a body that still works . . . it's pretty great. Life is . . . great."

I remained steady on my feet, completely enamored by Pamela's strength and honesty. "You're a warrior."

She laughed. "I don't know about that! But I know that I've been given a second chance."

Her truth hit hard, as did the depth of her stare.

"I actually finished chemotherapy today," she added with a sense of relief. "Three hours and seventeen minutes ago."

"Congratulations!" I held onto her victory, thinking of my mom's struggles—cavernous mouth sores, tin bowls filled with vomit. "You've got to be exhausted. What on earth made you come get bras?"

Deep in thought, Pamela dressed slowly.

"I've always hated coming in here, like a lot of women do. I haven't been able to look at my scars and breastless chest for a long time, or in a mirror for that matter. But then I heard 'cancer free,' and my whole world changed again. I experienced profound gratitude for the first time in my life. Much greater than any feeling of disgust and self-loathing I fought with for so long. I figured, as I sat crying in my car, that I'd start celebrating by doing something that's made me feel bad about myself. I wanted to celebrate by looking in the mirror."

I swallowed. "Wow."

"And you're having your sale," she joked, gathering her bras and alteration tickets.

We both stood for a minute, taking in the moment. I had no idea how to keep the conversation going, or how to give Pamela a proper goodbye. But I hoped that her brief time in the fitting room made her feel good.

"Don't let that bother you," she said, referring to the couple's not-so-charming banter right outside our door as they left Yvonne high and dry. "I'm not."

I nodded my head quietly, saddened that Pamela acknowledged it, though I knew she felt my own discomfort for her. Balancing the dialogue that transpired along the dressing rooms was challenging and hard to dismiss at times. A lot of us unconsciously—and consciously—fed off one another's cutting regard for a body part, as well as any newfound love, which is why I stood marveling at Pamela. Her courage in the face of adversity was like nothing I'd ever seen inside the dressing room. I was inspired and humbled. And as we hit the sales floor, I noticed her stride, revived and full of purpose. I followed it all the way to the escalator, quietly breathing in life.

BUSTING OUT

With deflated balloons, large gaps in every sale rounder, and Farah in San Francisco, the pace had finally started to slow down as everyone returned to their "normal" selves. The sales floor had also begun its transformation back into non-sale mode with our unrealistic mannequin team dressed in some of fall's new merchandise. Lingerie sets had become darker and richer in hues, setting the tone with velvet burgundies and more classic black. It was a needed change for sure, as was my looming exit. I prayed deep down that my time in the lingerie department had reached its expiration. Summer had spread all its grand splendor. And though the energy felt strange with everything shifting, I was comforted by Diane's trusted mantra on change. It was a constant, an inevitable passage filled with all things scary and all things new. Precisely the problem.

"We have an issue." Yvonne cornered me as I pretended to organize a new slab of Spanx.

"Okay." I stood staring at her. "Harry?"

"No, that couple from the other day is back. They're roaming toward the front. I can't do it. I won't do it."

I took a step behind Yvonne and glared through the legs of a pair of Spanx. The woman had already gathered a fair amount of lingerie to try, including all our smallest pieces. She had strings, pads, garters, and a few sheer negligees. Her male counterpart, wearing the same distinguished boots from before, followed close behind, picking up his own desired pieces.

"Alright," I said, straight-faced. I looked around the floor for Rachel or Michelle but only spotted Tabitha, also hiding in a corner pretending to organize merchandise. "Looks like I'm it."

Treading carefully, I approached the couple from behind.

"How we doing?" I asked, smiling.

"Can we get a room?" the man inquired, trying to take the lead.

"Yeah, no problem, but I'm going to need you to remain outside the dressing rooms."

He nodded in affirmation, passing off his pile of lacy bras and G-string thongs. As soon as we got back to a room, I helped establish a quick try-on method, recommending the bras first.

"Do you need help with a fit?" I asked the woman, moving toward the door as she began to disrobe.

"Umm, I think I'm good."

Trying not to get too invested due to the frustration I felt from them bolting on Yvonne, and maybe their lack of respect for other people's privacy, I resumed my duty and rehung a pair of Spanx. I figured it was easier to just let them be, allotting space and however much time they needed to figure out the lingerie. Of course, right as I sought refuge, the woman emerged onto the floor wearing a sheer black push-up bra and a lacy boyshort. My eyes immediately bolted over to Yvonne and then over to another man waiting for his wife, his stare long and self-conscious.

"I like that," I heard a deep voice say from across the department.

"Are you sure?" the woman asked, almost pleading with his response.

"Where's the red negligee I picked out?" he asked, moving them both closer to my corner of comforts.

Damnit.

"I'll go put it on right now." She disappeared without a second to lose.

I started to feel conflicted about what I was supposed to be doing. It wasn't really fair of me to let Yvonne's experience take away from my own because it could've just been a bad day for the couple. We all had needs. But the pacing and the loud echoes and the sick feeling I'd felt with Pamela present overshadowed most of it. Plus Yvonne still had a bitter taste in her mouth, considering they left the dressing room a mess and then bolted. I was up against a no-win situation, with a job to do, while trying to end my shift. Déjà vu had hit its peak.

"You like?" the woman asked, walking straight out onto the sales floor for a second time, her large breasts propped up against tight-fitting wire and her backside exposed on each side of a thin red string.

"I do," the man replied, looking her up and down. "Go put on the other one."

The thump against my chest began to speed up from the boldness in his pitch. Once again, I had no idea what I was supposed to be doing as their honorable sales associate. Yvonne had already disappeared into the stockroom, which wasn't a surprise, and management was still out of the picture, leaving me with a few other customers and growing demands.

"I don't like it. It makes your boobs look weird again," the man said, leaning against a rounder of pajamas after his companion came back out in another sheer negligee.

"Really?" the woman replied with a distant whine.

"Go." He quickly pointed to the dressing rooms.

What? I watched her back away.

"I think it looks great," I stepped forward holding a pair of Spanx, my opinion far from welcome.

He looked at me and then shrugged his shoulders.

"Hey, I'm paying for it all."

Still questioning my role, I headed straight for the woman's dressing room. I had exactly twenty-two minutes left in my shift, and I was determined to make it out on time. So when I approached the customer's door, analyzing her movements through the cracks, I went all in, with absolutely nothing to lose. "You doing okay in there?"

She quickly repositioned herself.

"Yeah," she replied with zero confidence. "This is always so hard with him. What do you think of—" The door flung open. "This?"

She stood with her arms out, modeling a one-piece teddy pulled well into the folds of her ass.

"I . . . think it looks great." I pondered its implications, wondering if any of my words transferred over. Her need for his approval was hard to watch.

"Is that your husband you're with?" I asked.

"No," she replied quickly, fluffing her long, flowing hair. "He's my boyfriend. Rick."

"Huh." I nodded without speaking, watching her walk back out onto the floor.

Keeping a thoughtful distance, I checked the time on my watch, ticking with twelve minutes left. I began cleaning out the back dressing rooms, all of which hosted stray bras, wadded up panties, and measuring tapes crinkled in corners. As I closed the door to one of the rooms, my customer came back noticeably flustered.

"Is there any way you can grab me a smaller cup size in this?" she asked, holding up a black push up.

"Sure. What size are you looking for?"

"How about a 34 D?" she replied, uncertain of her size.

Looking at her breasts spilling out from every slice of satin, I hesitated to offer something different.

"Are you sure you don't want to be measured?"

"No way!" she snapped abruptly, sounding both playful and defeated.

When I arrived at the entrance to the stockroom, her boyfriend, Rick, managed to find his way into the entrance of the dressing rooms, his presence and oversized leather jacket overwhelming the tiniest of spaces.

"I can't come back?" he asked, trying to feign ignorance with a policy we had already covered. I stood staring at him as his eyes drifted along my collarbone and down around my boobs.

"We established that," I replied, cautiously short.

"I don't see a lot of women back there." He peered his head around the corner.

Temporarily deprived of any speech, I tried my best to find patience and professionalism.

"Well, that's beside the point. We have a policy in place for privacy reasons. You are welcome to stand outside the entrance."

"That's ridiculous," he retorted, shaking his head. "It's nearly empty back there."

"There's a men's department downstairs if you'd prefer to wait there."

His facial expression became hard to look at, as it morphed into a culmination of anger and a strong lack of control. I hurried into the stockroom, grabbing what I presumed to be his desired sizes and headed for my customer, knowing none of them would fit properly.

"I've got a couple 34 Ds, a C, and one of our new satin push ups."

"Wow, thank you," she replied, studying her ass in the mirror. "Is he still trying to come back here?" she asked, slightly perturbed.

"Uh, yes."

She stared at me wistfully, making it hard to turn around and exit as my time ticked to a remaining seven minutes.

"He's relentless sometimes." She stuffed her boobs into one of the bras. "Sorry about that."

Flinching to the sound of the door slamming shut, I waited while she modeled the bra out front, quickly igniting a series of opinions before they exploded into the hallway.

"He's not back here, is he?" A woman threw open her door, sticking only the top portion of her body out.

"No," I responded. "I'll make sure he's—" My customer heatedly turned the corner before I could finish my sentence.

"I guess we'll just take the negligees," she said, unhooking the bra.

I stood in the doorway and analyzed her growing piles of lingerie, from the thin strings to the stiff push ups, wondering what she wanted, if anything. Part of me just wanted her to go, by herself, alone, with nothing. But another part of me wanted her to leave with something she liked. Something she felt good in. Something *she chose*.

"The negligees are beautiful," I said, walking closer into the fitting room.

She stopped and ran her hand through her hair, looking at the floor. "Men can be so complicated sometimes."

I immediately met her gaze, not expecting her to say what she said. "I think we can all be complicated sometimes."

She thought about my statement as I thought about what to say next. I sensed a push into tricky ground, making me hold back on all the questions I so desperately wanted to ask her. It wasn't the first time I felt dumbfounded with partner plays. However, it was the first time I had a man try to dismiss our dressing room policy with such blatant disregard.

"Have you guys been together for a while?" I asked, watching her try on another bra.

"Yeah." She paused before looking up at me. "Maybe too long."

"Things run their course sometimes, I guess."

She quietly hooked the band of the bra around her midsection and pulled on the cups. Though focused on her own reflection in the mirror, she unexpectedly carried on, almost desperate for someone to listen as she vocalized and absorbed her own thinking. "If we could only turn back time," she said, examining her long legs.

I thought about her statement, honest and detached, wondering how long she had felt stuck. And then his voice suddenly hit the hallway, vibrating off walls.

"Let's go, Collette!"

Without a second to spare, she hurried to take off the bra. I stood quiet and consumed, hoping she'd keep talking to me. But she didn't. That was it. Her face was narrow and doleful.

"I, um." Nothing came out right. "I'm going to have Yvonne ring you up for the negligees."

Her pace quickened. "Thank you." She opened the door while pushing for my exit. And within seconds, against the remaining scatterings of his cold demand, I felt like we had exchanged a thousand words. I had come to understand, or at least feel, Collette's fear—and wishes, wanting to choose better and to know better, yet stuck without a compass or the slightest spark of promise.

Signaling for Yvonne to take the sale, I kept a brisk pace straight out of the department and stopped abruptly when I reached the first floor. Customers flocked around the cosmetics counters, as well as the shoe departments, cleaning house on the last day of the sale. I walked over to Chase's department and instantly spotted him working with a customer, meticulously folding the collar of a man's dress shirt. I stared at him for a moment. I pictured his controlled glide passing in front of the lingerie department on his way toward the time clocks, counting how many times I'd waited for it. Everything felt so different and strangely evanescent. Here today, gone tomorrow, disappearing with irreproachable flight.

The store suddenly felt smaller as departments began to spin in my side view. Steven Tyler's "Sweet Emotion" bellowed with wild abandon, during which I stood frozen in the middle of the walkway, forcing customers to walk around me.

Just go. Keep moving. You can't afford Jeffrey Campbell. Chase will always be a favorite hello. He was a summer fling, and you knew it. This is it. No more inflamed joints, Roxanne Michaels, pageant moms, or your name on the schedule. You're free. It's over. Seattle awaits. Your father awaits.

And then before I could blink, an imaginary fork in the road gave heat to my own stride. The glass doors opened, and I slowly began to back away, all the way up to the seventh floor of the parking structure, just in time to witness the dying sun disappear behind the Hollywood sign's big white letters, creating a halo of pure gold.

ROLLING STONE

As Tina Turner blasted from the living room downstairs, casting an astounding realization that I wasn't in LA anymore, I mentally checked the distance between us—all 1,136 miles of it—while I staggered to my feet. Quietly closing the bedroom door, I moved toward my parents' bedroom at the end of the hallway, welcoming the break of day and absolute heartache. Somewhere in my chest sat a feeling of hopelessness and despair, striking with an iron fist as I inspected my surroundings. A floral duvet spread to each corner of my parents' bed without one visible crease, reinforcing Larry's rigid, lonely routine.

After finding my mother's satin brief underwear and thick padded bras folded along the inside of a dresser drawer, I moved to the bathroom. All her belongings remained untouched. Her Sonicare sat in its holder next to the sink. Body lotions and perfumes covered half of the counter. The clothes in her closet, organized by season, hung on hangers directly above her extensive shoe collection. I kept thinking she was going to walk in and ask why I was in her closet, bowled over and stuck in a misery I had yet to fully unload.

"There she is!" Larry smiled with enthusiasm as I entered the kitchen. "Coffee?"

My eyes darted in every direction, moving from the kitchen table over to a freshly painted office.

"Forest green," I remarked, studying his makeover.

"Yeah, you like it?" he asked, guiding me over to a painting of the Old Course in St. Andrews, Scotland.

Nodding gently, I stopped at a handcrafted tic-tac-toe game that still sat on top of the coffee table. Another iron fist came hammering down as I remembered the quiet matches held days before my mom's death. "Sit with me, Nat," she'd say, easing her way down onto the couch. I made sure she won every time. The raid happening inside of her brain as the cancer settled into the back crevices made her question her own sanity, and it was terrifying to watch. I understood it as an ink spill, sullied and reckless, covering every last portion of clarity. It didn't seem fair to have her lose at something so trivial, especially when I saw her at her most vulnerable, deep into the night, desperately trying to piece together a pulverized existence.

I'd lie on the couch next to her while she rocked in agonizing pain. First, she'd take a winter jacket from the hall closet and wrap it around me so that she could have all the blankets, and then the darkness would slowly envelop us. I fought to sniff back tears as the rocking chair clicked with every forward motion. Then I'd wait.

"Natalee," she whispered softly. "You see the fireworks?"

STARING AT THE TANNED CREASES ALONG MY FATHER'S NECK, I sucked down some coffee from his new Keurig coffee machine that he couldn't wait to show off.

"It's genius," he said, pulling out tiny containers of tea and hot chocolate.

"You drank instant coffee for years," I replied, looking around for an old jar of Taster's Choice.

Pulling on his golf shirt's collar, he smiled demurely. "Well, you know, I'm trying new things."

Examining the silver linings along his mustache, I was happy to see that he had created his own private space, though it felt weird and difficult to digest. I had so many questions about how he was feeling emotionally, but I didn't want to make him uncomfortable as he struggled immensely with my mother's absence and internalized every throbbing emotion he ever had. But I always chalked it up to his capacity for reasoning. His aptitude for grasping truths was unparalleled, making him one of the most intelligent and deeply enigmatic people I'd ever known.

Six days, three hours, and seventeen minutes later, I sat drinking more Keurig coffee at the kitchen table, knowing I had reached new levels of desperation. Per the usual, I hadn't thought everything through as far as bringing in money while I lived rent-free for the next six months. I couldn't exactly sign up for a teaching job and expect an employer to understand a sublet in LA. Not to mention I missed all the deadlines while still feeling emotionally inept for the part. I heard "defer student loans" and sprinted toward whomever was going to make it happen—and then the lingerie department, reluctantly.

"You're fit certified!" the lead manager, Kristy, shouted through the holes of the phone, barely controlling her excitement. "Can you come by today to meet?"

My head dropped as my stomach sank. Visions of swaying boobs, lost dollars, and a profusion of shoppers overcrowding every pocket of space bombarded my thoughts.

Damnit.

"Uhhh." I tried delaying the process as I noted the time. Rush hour traffic was soon to be in full swing, and I dreaded the idea of being around large groups of people. But I knew the right answer; it beckoned all along.

"Absolutely," I finally replied, gritting my teeth. "Can't wait."

SCOPING MY NEW DIGS, I BARRELED STRAIGHT INTO FAMILIAR territory and parked my Ford Escort right next to a shiny Benz on the second floor of a parking structure. Well-groomed shoppers emerged from all over, holding multiple retail bags, designer handbags, and fancy cell phones.

Dollar signs came rolling in as I spotted the sign to my department store, a short sky bridge away. I hadn't been in the parking structure for more than five minutes and I could already feel suburbia's chokehold cookie-cutting its way into my soul. And though I purposely chose Seattle's largest suburb, bustling with high-tech employers, affluent residents, and guaranteed foot traffic, it was hard to dismiss how misplaced it made me feel. It didn't have LA's quirky charm and diverse landscapes. Instead, I had Microsoft, Amazon, and American Express in my corner, fueling my drive to get in and get out.

"You can do this," I whispered quietly, thinking about Gladys and her wise words as I leaned into the steering wheel. "You can do this."

When I approached the lingerie department on the third floor, I froze in awe. The department was ginormous, taking up two sections while successfully owning the floor. Sexy, modern, well-placed lingerie reeled everyone in, stopping shoppers on their way to the store's café a mere five feet away. Crystal chandeliers hung brightly overhead, shining just enough light on a mannequin's strategically chiseled bones and well-built cleavage. Bra fitters hustled around the sales floor, plucking items from a wide variety of merchandise. This lingerie department carried everything from an entire Spanx collection to every kind of bra, panty, negligee, and body adhesive possible.

"Oh my god, welcome!" Kristy burst out, gripping my hand at the counter. I smiled as she moved her frenzied gaze along my double-Ds, clearly checking to see if I was wearing the right size bra.

"Thank you." I tried returning a quarter of her enthusiasm. "I'm excited to be here."

My throat nearly closed from lying.

"Come with me," she said, leading me toward her office in the stockroom. "Let's talk!" I quietly took in her energy as I followed her back, realizing nothing much had changed about the trade as far as management went. Our superficial exchange was par for the course. She had a checklist to manage, consisting of two key points: One, will I show up for work? Two, can I make her enough money so she can keep her job?

Amazed by the size of the stockroom, I took a seat next to Kristy and began answering a set of light interview questions, allowing the formalities to pass. Her desk was crammed up against the back wall and covered with business cards from vendors, stray measuring tapes, illegible paperwork, and the proverbial wedding snapshot of her saying "I do" to an exceptionally tall man. Various styles of panties and heavy-duty body slimmers lined rows of bars, forcing fitters to climb ladders in order to retrieve needed items. Size rings were jammed into bundles of bras, separating the 30 A cups all the way down the alphabet to 44 Js. It was packed to the brim, like nothing I had ever seen, including more J cups.

"It's always so nice to get return bra fitters," Kristy said while opening up a screen on her computer. "And you've been with us for a while." I thought about her statement at length, going all the way back to my first day as a nineteen-year-old college student hustling to make a dollar.

"Off and on," I replied, looking over the dark roots and yellow-blonde waves of her hair.

"And now you're a full-timer!" Her lively zest returned. The impact of "full-timer" almost made me choke on my own saliva. *Full-time bra fitter? No. Hell no. I'm going back to LA. I will not get stuck here. I have a plan. Sort of.*

"Alright." She enlarged the schedule, adding my name to the bottom of a nine-woman list, which meant no seniority and a majority of closing shifts. I was peon status, hopelessly treading on vast new shores. "I've got you on as permanent!" She smiled. There was that feeling again. *Permanent?*

"I'm only here for—" I quickly stopped myself. Wait a minute. Why would I disclose my six-month timeline, or sublet, so that I could stay at the bottom of the barrel? I was no stranger to the operation; they wanted lifers, which made sense for business purposes, but I wasn't in the business to stay. Nor was I in the business to lose.

"I'm here!" I recovered, smiling far and wide as she handed me my hours and led me back out to the sales floor.

"Welcome aboard," she replied, picking up a phone call. "See you tomorrow!"

Before heading over to human resources to sign on the dotted line, I decided to spend a few minutes getting acquainted with the merchandise so that I was prepared for the full department tour the following day. While circling a collection of new French bras and matching panties, I noticed a man also moving in circles around a thong tree, his dark hair dripping with grease and his cold stare menacing. I watched as he stuck his head between the small, eye-level gaps in the fixture, carefully observing someone from afar.

"Can I help you?" One of the sales associates approached him from behind, eyeing his scruffy white jawline framed with panties.

I stood glued to the carpet, processing his ET-like hands and black-rimmed glasses.

"Yes," he quickly replied, handing over a pair of black G-string thongs. "I'd like to buy these."

They both walked over to the register. His faded blue jeans barely cupped his flat backside. Something was off. The peculiarity of his movements had me feeling uneasy, as I, too, looked alarmingly creepy with my head lodged between an assortment of thong underwear. But I didn't care. I was convinced I had spotted one of Seattle's top lingerie regulars, whose intentions would soon become clear.

TOTAL BUST

Managing a wad of nerves, I was as ready as I could be for my new lingerie department and new team, leaving me with a series of what-ifs and WTFs. It all happened so fast, so urgently fast, like it always had. I had no idea how to proceed other than to completely throw myself back into the mix. Again. Disoriented and desperately seeking some kind of stability.

"Welcome back." Kristy smiled, rearranging a corner area into a surplus of body shapers. I couldn't believe how many more options existed. Spanx had rapidly taken over the world of retail, offering firm tummy smoothers that hooked to the bra's bands, creating one flesh-sucking bodysuit. The evolution persisted in full force. And as I ran my hand along the shaper's sturdy grip, I noticed an oval-shaped hole in the crotch, allowing for just about anything to peek through or assist with a quick bathroom break. This hot getup was pure genius.

Moving on from the collection of shapewear, Kristy began to lead a tour around the rest of the department until a store page came in, loudly repeating her name overhead. "I'm going to have Caroline finish for me," she said, motioning for help. "Feel free to start taking customers when you're ready." I looked at Caroline and smiled.

She returned the gesture with an awkward hand wave, and then delved straight into the facts. "You gotta be quick around here," she said, taking me back to a second stockroom right next to the dressing rooms. There was a large wooden table that sat in the corner, accruing piles of customer go-backs by the second.

"This is Ruby, Jena, and Susan." She introduced other members of the team as they sat hanging bras and panties on hangers. I nodded with another smile and continued to follow Caroline over to a wall of shelves stacked with plastic containers.

"Your personal box," she said, gesturing to my name printed neatly in black marker. Water bottles, cups of coffee, perfumes, lotions, and piles of receipt paper with obscure markings packed the shelves.

"Thank you," I replied, catching a whiff of Caroline's body odor while she stood fanning herself with a pair of panties. "You okay?"

"Yeah, yeah." She rolled her eyes as small drops of sweat made their way down her forehead. "I'm just losing my hair, and my vagina feels like sandpaper."

Laughter ensued and Caroline joined in. Her contagious giggle and matter-of-fact response made me feel more welcome than ever.

"We love you, Caroline." The girls comforted her from arm's length.

Dabbing her face with a napkin, she erased the subtle remnants of light brown makeup that had spread across her limp cheeks. "You just wait," she added. "Menopause is a real bitch."

Caroline led us back out onto the sales floor as she continued to fan herself with a pair of hardwearing briefs. Her relaxed and easygoing circuit was perfect for my pace. She introduced all the new bras, including new fashion lines, colors, styles, and a surprising availability of sizes. Even some of the "smaller" vendors who historically catered to itty-bitties seemed to have jumped on board, realizing that an abrupt stop toward the beginning of the alphabet wasn't remotely realistic as far as our clientele was concerned.

"There's the sleepwear section, our Hanky Panky thong tables, which is still the number-one seller, high and low rise, though the low gets lower, and the high gets higher, as does the price," Caroline babbled in a subdued manner before exhaling loudly. "What else?"

"Umm." I tried to think of something that I might have missed.

"Oh, yeah!" She perked up. "The Cutlet Collection."

The Cutlet Collection? I followed Caroline to the large stockroom where Kristy's desk sat.

She stopped toward the entrance and said, "Voila," wittily unveiling a bookshelf of stacked breast adhesives cut into floppy pieces of silicone. "You'd be surprised how fast these suckers go," she said, her voice tiring. "Especially the big daddies. Prepare yourself for a lot of back and forth."

Looking around the stockroom, I let it all sink in, mentally placing each item in my head while trying not to feel too overwhelmed. LA's lingerie department was half the size and much easier to manage.

"You'll get the hang of it." Caroline winked, leading me back through the double doors just in time for my first customer.

"We need a fitter," a salesgirl said as she jogged past us.

"She's all yours." Caroline smiled with relief. "I'm off to stick my face in a bowl of ice water."

Cognizant of my newbie status, I didn't waste any time greeting the customer. I needed to get my feet wet so that I could gain momentum and get my name on the payroll. Fortunately Kristy was nowhere to be found, which eased the pressure of having to "perform" in front of our sometimes-needy clientele.

"I think I've got it," I said to the customer before repeating her requests. "A few sexy bras mixed in with a few everyday bras."

"Yep!" She offered a thumbs-up, eager to get started.

Turning the corner, I couldn't believe how long and lit up the hallway was. I'd never seen so many dressing rooms packed in side by side. I opened the first door and immediately noticed the dark floral wallpaper and soft velvet chair planted in the corner.

The room was spotless, providing a contemporary touch with the standard full-length, three-section mirror illuminating every inch of one's body.

"Alright," she said, getting down to business by unbuttoning her top. "I recently underwent breast reduction surgery, and I'm pleased to say that I'm starting all over!" Her bronzed-over face lit up as her own words sunk in. "I'm somewhere around a 36 D, maybe a double-D, but I specifically told the doctor that I wanted to be a D." The first and only word that came to mind was four letters long and passionately unprofessional, so I decided to repeat it ten times in my head before attempting to move forward.

"How about I measure you just to make sure?" I treaded lightly, knowing that the stinging undertone in her voice had potential to boil over at any moment.

She was quiet and extremely focused while she stared in the mirror. I moved in from behind and wrapped the measuring tape around her rib cage, stopping at 37 inches around, and a triple-D—to a possible G—for a cup size. The insides of my hands felt clammy and my chest warm as I contemplated a plan of action. Somewhere along our brief introduction I picked up on her strong need for certainty, which undoubtedly made my role precarious and problematic.

"Okay," I said, considering my revelation. "I'm not sure the 36 D is going to fit you."

"What do you mean?" Her voice cracked.

"Well . . ." I hesitated to form a complete sentence as her eyeballs, bloodshot and topped with winding lines, practically sprung from her head. "I can bring back a few different styles to try, which isn't a bad idea since this is your first time in after surgery."

As soon as I hit the sales floor, I searched the scene for Kristy. And then I walked in circles, desperately trying to find, and gather, a good amount of bras for my customer, including the single-D she thought she paid for. I figured the larger the pile the easier it would be to mask some of the sizes. The process of elimination had to work.

"I've got bras!" I rejoined my customer in the dressing room after a few brisk laps around the department. "And you have options!" Hawk-eyed and unable to control her need to double-check the sizes, she read every tag one by one.

"These aren't all 36 Ds," she said with raised eyebrows.

"They're not," I replied, picking up one of the two 36 Ds to try. "I brought other options just in case."

"In case of what?"

"In case we need to go up a cup size."

The longing that seethed in her veins came rushing forward.

"I told you I'm a 36 D," she countered, her diamond-clad hands moving with every bite.

"Okay." I matched her tone, swiftly unhooking a 36 D T-shirt bra from off a hanger before passing it over. "Would you like me to step out?"

Shaking her head, she eased her arms into the straps. Deep-set scars from the incisions traveled directly down her breasts and around her nipples, adding an array of colors. After she squeezed her way into the bra, she turned her back toward me so that I could fasten the band. Coppery flesh spilled over from every part of the bra's edging, including the sides and tops of the cups. I quickly backed away so she could examine the fit in the mirror without my meaty silhouette crowding her vision.

Silence ruled as our gazes narrowed.

"Do you want to put your shirt on?" I asked, wondering if it would help disguise the large bubble of breast protruding from the cups.

"This is a D!" she exclaimed at full volume, triple-checking the size on the tag. "Oh my god."

She lowered herself into the chair and sat quietly. I delayed every body movement and oral response possible until she was able to speak. The magnitude of her dismay wasn't completely clear. But I didn't know what she needed or wanted to hear. Something was happening inside of her that was beyond my bra-fitting expertise.

"I was told I was a D." She dropped some of her tough disposition.

I looked around the room.

"It's your body; you can wear whatever you want. I just want you to be comfortable. And we have the double-D to try, which could very well offer the little bit of coverage you need." She looked at me as if I was speaking another language. "We can also experiment with the band size." I tried to sound encouraging.

"You can take these," she finally said, handing me all the bras I picked out. "Go ahead and bring back an assortment of 36 and 38 Ds that I can try. There's no way I'm a double-D."

Staring at her boobs pouring out of the cups, I closed the door and set out for another disoriented jaunt around the department. The number of customers seemed to have multiplied during my time in the dressing rooms, making me question whether or not I should pick up another customer. My instincts told me to hold off—it was too early; I would've been shark bait in seconds. So I followed my customer's demanding instructions and gathered a large collection of single Ds. I figured if she was going to buy them and wear them then I had no other option but to sell them to her. What she chose to wear was none of my business; however, my time was.

"Natalee, right?" a fellow bra fitter asked as she moved in from the side. "Are you available to ring up a customer really quickly?"

"Uhhh, sure." I hesitated, stuffing my customer's bras under my armpit.

I signaled for the next customer to step forward.

"Jena was helping you today?" I asked. The woman nodded quietly and placed her credit card on the counter. The screen in front of me was completely unfamiliar and filled with a variety of boxes that read *sale, return, customer info, alterations, time,* and *store numbers.* I had no idea where to start or what to push, given that I hadn't had any formal training with the new high-tech registers, which were already incompatible with Luddites like myself. What the hell happened to keying in the price before hitting the total button? Everything was so complex with too many steps to follow. I was bound to mess something up.

Looking out at the women waiting to be rung up, I tried tapping on a few different options within the "sale" box, but nothing seemed to make sense.

"I don't have all day," the woman snapped, responding to my blank stare as I rushed to understand the order of things.

"This is my first day back after a little break," I replied, still staring at the screen. "I'm learning the new system; bear with me."

Just then, a sales associate finally stepped in and guided me through the process, punching buttons with incredible swiftness as my hands continued to build with sweat.

"Hit this box for credit card." She spoke fast, prompting me to grab the customer's payment sitting on the counter so we could slide it through the computer.

"I have 'see ID' written on the back," she said, pointing to her credit card.

Blood raced down my artery walls. *Yeah, bitch, I see you,* I thought to myself, noting the Roman centurion's headshot against a black backdrop as I placed her plastic alongside her driver's license. I honestly wasn't sure if I was going to make it through my first day back without delivering a left hook straight into a woman's jawbone.

"Thank you, Cheryl." I smiled with my mouth closed while handing over her shopping bag.

And then boorish, crude noises hit the air. "My receipt?"

AFTER GRABBING A COUPLE MORE OPTIONS FOR MY CUSTOMER, I RAN back to her dressing room and quickly hung the bras on the bar, separating sexy from boring.

"All new selections," I said, hoping for some kind of resolution, though that part wasn't my business either.

She hurried to make sure all the bras were Ds, but of course I misread one of the tags and accidentally brought back a double-D.

"I'm not a double-D," she snapped, promptly passing back the bra.

"Sorry about that. I thought I had grabbed a single-D."

"I'll take it from here," she replied, reaching for the doorknob.

I spent the next twenty minutes pacing the department while trying to look busy. I hid behind bathrobes, tidied up a Hanky Panky table, and then wandered across the way to the juniors' fashion section where I attempted to look incognito while trying on a pair of plastic aviators smeared with dirty finger-prints.

Time was a challenging concept for me, ticking slowly at all the wrong moments. And right as I contemplated another visit back to check on my single-D, I spotted her hightailing it out of the department, empty-handed and on a mission. I scrambled to hide behind the small table mirror, clumsily knocking over a display of sunglasses onto the floor while still wearing a pair of teen aviators with the price tag dangling in my periphery.

My heart raced as I watched every one of her long, purposeful steps. I quickly knelt down to the ground, looking out from under the table as customers continued to shop in close prox-imity. I was convinced she was coming straight for me. But then, as the gray clouds parted through the skylight above, she took a sharp turn toward the elevators, leaving me with a short supply of air and questionable security footage.

After picking up my mess, I hurried back to her dressing room only to be greeted with a bigger mess. All but two bras were left on the floor, including scattered price tags and a mea-suring tape. The room was no longer glowing in appearance. My opening record was 0 for 2. And though each scenario was a realistic representation of retail's unfavorable moments, I hoped it wasn't typical for my new store. The thought alone made me recoil. It also drove me to feel anxious and extremely frustrated with myself.

What am I doing? My decision to sublet my kickass apartment in sunny Los Angeles suddenly seemed impetuous and irre-sponsible and so fucking far away. But I had to stick it out. I had to find my groove, sort of similar to my first customer's needs, but with vastly different frameworks. She needed to find what was going to make her new breasts, and body, feel good to her, even if she never surrendered to a size she refused to wear. Though crushingly difficult, she was the only person who could make things better, a reminder that came with another iron fist. Change was hard. So goddamn hard.

Slowly closing the dressing room door, I left the bras on the floor and eased my way into the chair. Every tight punch of panic shot through my body. My vision went fuzzy as my head spun in circles, making all four of my limbs feel overpoweringly loose, as if I was on my way to becoming gutted into an outer shell for someone to find sprawled on the floor. I leaned into the bar and closed my eyes, retracing every one of my steps as sand symbolically trickled down an hourglass amid a shield of darkness. Time had a cruel way of showing itself sometimes.

PIGGY IN
A BLANKET

"Are you ready for your first weekend back?" Larry asked with a sheepish grin. Quietly pondering his question, I went through the sequence of events that transpired during my last honorable moments in the lingerie department and the ten hours of sleep that followed. I had to get some kind of harmony in play or else I wasn't going to make it. A total redo was in order, as was a change in attitude. There was no way I could spend another seventeen minutes hiding in a dressing room when I had money to make, even though the thought of returning made me feel dreadfully anxious. I hated the dizziness and the trapped airway and how it all came on so suddenly. Plus the inner interrogation taking place wasn't helping me feel any less irrational, which was a difficult state to measure. I needed to focus. I needed to put my business panties on and start fresh, knowing a new dawn brought a new day . . . and whatever else.

"How about I meet you for dinner and a movie?" Larry proposed. His offer had a way of resonating woefully, bringing to light the aching that anchored itself in seemingly safe places within him. Having observed the day-to-day, I started to monitor his escape routes: the office, golf courses, Google, and two IPAs every evening. I understood that he needed to keep himself occupied and organized, and I respected his plight.

It was a drastic change from my earlier sentiments as an adolescent, however. Our relationship had many long moments of silence. We didn't fully grasp each other's differences. My rebellious acts had resulted in a lot of wear and tear. But he came around in subtle ways when I least expected it and offered a different assessment on things. He was always so sly about it, too, like the time he caught me sneaking back into the house at four o'clock in the morning when I was fifteen years old. I didn't see that he was in the kitchen right next to the sliding glass door, pouring himself some water. I stood paralyzed, wearing my ripped Levi's, an oversized flannel shirt, and a fresh hickey on my neck that was bound to turn into a full lunar eclipse by daybreak.

"Early morning jog?" he'd asked sarcastically, waiting for the darkness to swallow me up whole. "You know, Natalee," he continued calmly, drinking water from his coffee cup. "We were destined to meet."

"Yeah," I had replied, swaying from the Smirnoff.

"Yep."

Fuck.

"Can I offer you some water?" he asked, moving out from behind the kitchen counter, wearing his one and only bathrobe from the year 1975.

"Um, that's okay." The words came out gradually.

He waited as I fought to shuffle saliva around the inside of my mouth, creating a mix of lumbering noises.

"Since you're such an early bird, I'll be sure to get you up tomorrow at the same time. Maybe even the next few days." My tongue felt like cotton as I tried to speak. "Goodnight, Natalee. Glad to see you're alive."

The weight of his words hit like bricks. He never needed to say much to get his point across, which is why his silence often spoke volumes. It was never empty. He'd seen too much in his lifetime to be even remotely free from mental exhaustion. And it all made sense the second my mom became terminally ill. I watched him, watch her, disappear—and it nearly ate him alive. He feared as quietly as he loved.

Back in lingerie, I embraced the last of my shortened "trial" shifts and jumped right into the mix. Kristy had completed an entire floor remodel, shuffling every piece of merchandise into new corners in an effort to keep customers—as well as employees—on their toes. Just as I conquered the lay of the land, or at least half of it, everything changed in the blink of an eye.

"Sales associate to sleepwear. Sales associate to sleepwear." Kristy's call came in over the microphone. The lack of movement from some of the other fitters led me to believe it was my turn to pony up, so I headed over to the other counter and smiled with every ounce of excitement I could invoke.

"She needs some alterations done." Kristy offered context with her smooth managerial charm.

"Sure." I struggled for a response as I stared at a pile of long cotton briefs pulled from a plastic bag and spread out along the counter. A variety of light and dark hues ran parallel to the seams.

"I'm sorry." I tried gathering more context. "What are you looking to do with the underwear?"

She moved in closer and ran her hand along one of the briefs. None of her fingers straightened out and her knuckles looked like rocks.

"I'd like to resew the top stitching on the panties. Do you see that it's coming undone?" Her voice split as she motioned for me to take a closer look. I quickly eyed the department for Kristy, who had conveniently disappeared, and then looked back down at the woman's worn underwear spread out on the counter in front of me. The only thing coming "undone" was me.

"Don't worry, I washed them!" she added, smiling.

Carefully picking up each pair of underwear with the tips of my fingers, I threw them back into the plastic bag and prepared an alteration ticket, refusing to make eye contact with the inner parts of her "white" briefs. I then scribbled down her information as fast as I could and sent her on her way, hoping the packaged deal I was about to drop off for our alterations team wouldn't blacklist me indefinitely. "I'll call you when they're ready."

Though I was hesitant to hang the underwear on our outgoing alterations bar in the stockroom, I did it anyway. My departing duties included alteration drop-offs, so I figured I'd wait and take everything down at once. It was hard to decide where to place the underwear, however. The bar was filling up fast, mostly with bras that required prostheses pockets, therefore leaving no room for a woman's returned chonies absent of price tags. But they still hung on a hanger at the end of the bar, swinging in full view for everyone to see. My "new girl" rank was off the charts.

"There's a woman waiting in room seven who needs a fit," a sales associate yelled from the front. I took one last glance at the briefs, making sure their placement sufficed, and headed back to the dressing rooms.

"Welcome." A tall, fifty-something woman smiled. I stepped inside and stood in front of the full-length mirror, stunned by the color of her blue eyes. I waited as she readjusted her purse and shopping bags on the hook plastered against the wall. A variety of items were scattered around the dressing room, including lace push-up bras, cotton briefs, thongs, and beautiful silk bathrobes and negligees. Aside from the briefs, her taste was exquisite, reminding me of a controlled kind of sexy that seemed slightly restrained at first sight.

"I really need some help." She sighed, examining her long, slim body in the mirror, her voice deep and composed. I stood behind her as she talked, easing my stare along her pronounced Adam's apple and then up to the fire red lipstick spread into the corners of her mouth.

"I have new breasts," she continued. "And I know how important a proper bra fitting is."

"Most definitely so," I replied, nodding my head in the direction of her new round breasts as she confidently unveiled their command.

"I've been at this for a while now, and nothing seems to fit right," she added, placing her hands above her head as I unwrapped the measuring tape from around my fingers. "I just want a bra to feel good and look good."

"Amen." I rejoiced, moving her arms closer to her sides. She watched as I examined her broad rib cage and defined midsection in the mirror.

"Have you been doing this for a long time?" she asked, trying not to move while I placed the tape.

"Sort of." I leaned in to focus before taking one last look at her body in the mirror. I could tell her new silicone was going to require a round of trial and error, which wasn't out of the ordinary. But first I needed to rid our space of too many guesses.

"Let's start fresh," I proposed, checking some of the size tags. "I love your style, and I should be able to keep everything you've got, but in different sizes. We're going to go down in the band and up in the cup."

She took in a long breath and looked around the room.

"I should've asked for help a long time ago." She shook her head while passing over a stack of bras. "I'm sorry that you have to clean all this up. I'm so overwhelmed right now."

I could tell she was serious and sincere.

"This is not a problem." I smiled, looking over her tight perm. "I've got you covered."

She picked up on my pun with a nod and then moved her body so that her back was turned toward the mirror.

"I'm so . . ." She hesitated before continuing. "I'm transitioning and trying to get my sizing right. It's been daunting and really exhausting, so I grabbed all of these sizes thinking I could do it on my own and . . ."

Everything suddenly made sense. The bearing of the word *transition* resonated without a trace of ambiguity. I'd wondered if she was a transgender woman but knew not to assume. The exhausted tales of "I'm too fat" or "my tits look like sandbags" or "my vag can't breathe because my thighs are suffocating it" fell short by a good distance given the woman's demeanor. And though my intent was never to minimize one's struggles— because I know what it feels like to have sandbags for tits and two very generous thighs—something felt different about our meeting, and I was eager to understand it.

"Claire Whittler." She introduced herself with poise, firmly gripping my hand.

"Nice to meet you, Claire." I moved toward the door. "I'm glad I got you."

It didn't take long to gather a few different bra options for Claire. I wanted to be thorough and mindful of her needs, so I figured the more the better, throwing in a few sexy push ups I loved to look at as I wandered the floor.

"Excuse me?" A fitter I had never seen tapped me on my shoulder. "You have a phone call." I looked at her, confused, thinking that she might've had the wrong associate.

"A phone call," she repeated, staring at my blank face.

"Yeah, sorry." I headed for the counter. "Thank you."

Preparing for the worst, I offered a reserved greeting as I picked up the phone.

"Hello."

"Hi, I was wondering if y'all carry crotchless panties? The V-shaped ones?"

My eyes darted across the floor, hoping Kristy was far from nearby.

"Farah!" I laughed, missing her playfulness.

"Damnit!" she yelled, wrestling with the phone. "I thought I'd get you with my southern charm. How's it going up there?"

Her question made my heart sink a little. "It's okay, I guess. Still acclimating."

"Guess who came in today?" she asked buoyantly.

"J.Lo?"

"Nope."

"Madonna?"

"Uh, no."

"The dude from *Lost*?"

"No, but good one."

"I give up."

"Harry Curly."

"What!" I nearly spit into the phone. "How could he?"

"I think it was the shipment of crotchless panties," Farah said, laughing.

"So he really did want lingerie for himself?" I asked, happy that Harry found the courage to go in and actually shop without making anyone question his intentions. And then I imagined him buying crotchless panties.

"Wait, you guys actually carry them? To sell?"

"Yep," she answered casually. "They're a real sight."

I tried visualizing what a crotchless panty looked like, as well as where everything would go, but I gave up until Farah did the honors.

"There's basically two pieces of fabric that hang in midair." My stomach started to hurt from cackling.

"And they're cut into a V-ish shape so you can slide your bits right in there."

"What?" I fought for air as I leaned into the counter. "And Harry Curly bought—" I stopped abruptly, spotting Claire standing in the doorway of the dressing rooms holding a red silk bathrobe. "Oh, shit, I gotta go."

"Wait!" Farah tried keeping me on the line.

Running over to Claire, I also noticed a light pink negligee hanging from her hand.

"Wow," she said, her face lighting up from the pile of bras I'd grabbed. "Well done! Do you mind getting me a size up in each of these?" She passed over the robe and negligee. I hurried to grab new sizes, still laughing at Farah, and then headed back to meet Claire. Passing the doorway, I noticed that Kristy had recently moved a rounder of new high-end nighties to sit right off the walkway, so I backed up and snagged a couple to throw into the mix, hoping for a victory.

"I think you're going to be pleased, Claire," I said, organizing her options by style, size, color, and, of course, a group of my French favorites.

"This is so awesome!" Her face beamed with gratitude. "Would you mind helping me?"

I paused from the seriousness in her voice. I was certain Claire had wanted to be alone with her thoughts, dispelling old concepts as she maneuvered under the lights in her new lingerie, uninterrupted and at her own fearless pace.

"Absolutely." I unhooked a red lace push-up bra. "Let's start with this."

I could hear Claire's heartbeat as I slid the straps over her shoulders and hooked the band. "I'm just going to move your breast over this way." I positioned her cleavage while walking her through the steps.

"This looks great!" I cheered, admiring the fit and her silicone.

"Wow." She stood speechless, turning her body from side to side. "This is my third time doing this."

"Remember what you said about comfort? If it's too tight, let me know."

I waited as she wiggled her shoulders and moved in circles around the room.

"It's definitely tight." She slowed her shoulder rolls. "Let's try another band size."

I unfastened another bra and let Claire put it on, encouraging her to hook the band in front of her navel and then pull it up and around her torso. It was far easier than trying to hook the bra from behind. I'd always admired women who had enough skill to fasten their slingers with their hands behind their backs.

"What do you think?" she asked, running her eyes along her chest.

I examined the fit, wondering if maybe we should try one more size up. As expected, her silicone was tricky and looked like it had been smashed into the cups, cutting off parts of her skin. I immediately unhooked another red lace bra and handed it to her. Thankfully she was easygoing and tolerant of my changes.

"I think we've got a winner," I said, smiling as I adjusted the straps.

Claire tilted her head to the side. I could tell she was deep in thought, so I backed into the chair and removed the hangers from a few more bras, as well as her pile of negligees.

"This looks good," she said, smiling at me through the mirror as she placed her hands in the back pockets of her jeans. "And it feels good." I continued to stare at her slender physique, grappling with the thought of asking too many questions about her transition and then with the thought of not asking enough. Either way, the sudden bouts of silence started to make me feel like maybe I needed to give Claire her privacy. She had a lot of merchandise to get through and my awkward presence wasn't always soothing or timely, considering the space we shared. So I waited.

"Are you married?" I asked, forgetting everything I had just overanalyzed. She looked down at the ring on her ring finger and stopped.

"This was my mother's ring," she said, moving in closer, extending her long fingers for a better viewing. The vividness of sapphire blue and small-cut diamonds glowed brightly under the lights. "Too bad my father was such a dick. I'd prefer to wear her wedding ring," she added after grabbing a negligee from off my lap.

Trying to keep up with her quickening pace, I unhooked a couple more double-D bras and remained sitting. "Is he still alive?"

Claire thought about my question. "You know, I don't know. My mother died shortly after my father disowned me, and that was it. I was seventeen and an only child, desperately trying to understand what was wrong with me." She threw up air quotes to accompany the term "wrong" and then drew in a deep breath, sucking me in with every word spoken. "Almost thirty years have gone by."

I sat attempting to do the math in my head but failed. I needed my fingers to count and it certainly wasn't the time or place to start adding like a fourth grader.

"He disowned you because you're transgender?" I hesitated to ask, but pushed anyway, hoping Claire picked up on my sincere efforts to understand.

"Transgender, gay, feminist, you name it," she replied, sliding a negligee over her head. "He came home from work early one day and caught me wearing one of my mom's satin nightgowns. I'll never forget it."

My body twitched from the intensity of Claire's delivery. "Called me a faggot, a fraud, a poor excuse for a son and a man."

"Jesus," I whispered.

"And then he told me to get out," she finished, dropping her jeans for a more realistic assessment, first assuring me that her "piggy was in a blanket."

All I could do was sit, stuck in a cobweb of unspoken words suspended in air. The feeling was awful, which couldn't possibly compare to Claire's reality, coupled with the long, insufferable years of losing and hating and questioning and loving without conditions.

"You look great, Claire," I said, staring at her jeans piled around her ankles.

She drew in another long breath and then slowly exhaled. "It's taken a lot of balls." She smiled, turning around to face me.

I exploded with laughter, completely taken aback by her comment. "I bet it has," I replied, shaking my head. "So why now?"

"Time and money." Claire picked up on my vagueness. "I worked high up in business for years and never felt that I could be myself, so I lived a very private life, putting on lots of fake smiles."

"Makes sense," I quipped, referring to the latter part.

"That was just it, actually," she said, removing both the negligee and bra. "I had to make sense of everything all while trying to wipe out the noise. Thoughts of suicide, couch hopping, and lots of alcohol were my only escapes. I spent many nights fearing my life . . . while fearing for my life."

Completely immersed and feeling every draw of despair, I handed Claire another bra to try and continued to listen.

"I could never understand why anyone would ever think that a person would choose a life filled with so much confusion and self-loathing." Claire's quick wit faded. "I had no idea what was happening to my eight-year-old body. I couldn't understand why I hated dragging around a penis so much. But the hate I received? Now that was clear."

I could feel the fullness of her humanity moving in. "I've got nothing but clichéd compliments, Claire," I joked, feeling the ease between us as I reflected on the gravity of one's identity.

"And a great sale." She winked, throwing another bra into the "yes" pile.

I drew in my own deep breath and evaluated our success. "How about I let you have some time alone?" I stood up from the chair. "You've got a lot here, and you might want to try some things on again."

"You're right." Claire nodded, helping me clean up a small pile of items that needed to be rehung and put back in their designated areas.

"Take all the time you need." I bowed, feeling fortunate to have met Claire.

Upon reentering the commotion that spread throughout the sales floor, I was surprised at how much time had passed. There were breaks and alterations to figure out, which immediately led me right back to the stockroom so that I could gather my task and make the delivery once and for all. I noticed that the outgoing alterations bar had filled up significantly with cups needing pockets for prostheses. Some tickets had explicit instructions and others just hung with a ticket that read "Please pocket right side." My handful of worn-and-returned briefs continued to sway in a plastic bag at the end of the bar. It was obvious that fellow sales associates had separated their customers' bras from the underwear, and who could blame them? It was time they came down, so I grabbed a cardboard box from the corner and filled it to the top, including a bathrobe and two pairs of Spanx body shapers.

On the table next to me, I noticed one of our small gift boxes slightly opened with a card on top. I looked closer to find that it was addressed to Ruby, one of my new coworkers, and resembled chicken scratch for penmanship. Checking over my shoulders to see if anyone was nearby, I peeked inside to find one black G-string thong wadded up. I had no idea what it was all about; however, I did recall a conversation some of the girls had about a mysterious panty delivery for Ruby and only Ruby.

"They struck again!" Caroline walked through the door.

"They're not from her significant other?" I asked, shamelessly hooked on the department's compelling, yet disturbing, quandary.

"Ruby doesn't have a boyfriend," Caroline replied, digging for the G-string.

"Ohhh." My response lingered as I stood staring at the panty's scanty string. "This can't be good."

Happy to see Claire, I apologized for the wait and led her toward the registers, lugging the box of alterations.

"How'd we do?" I asked, looking over her stack of purchases that included a large handful of bras, two silk bathrobes, three negligees, and a huge pile of matching panties. I made certain every item was folded and placed nicely inside the tissue, and I also made sure to throw in a few packets of sample lingerie wash that would last her for months. I had a lot of admiration for Claire, who made our trade meaningful while respectfully acknowledging my role as a bra fitter.

"Thank you," she said, staring at me endearingly with her big blue eyes.

"No," I replied, walking around the counter with two full shopping bags. "Thank you, Claire Whittler."

After Claire left, I gathered my box of alterations and signaled to one of the girls that I was stepping off the floor. With a thumbs-up and a loss of dignity, I hoped that I had followed directions correctly, which was never my strong suit. Rumor had it the alterations "cave" was four stories up and buzzing with tickets. Of course, it was no surprise that when I finally found the secret elevator, there was an "under repair" sign on it, kindly asking employees to try again later. I thought about turning around, but decided that it wasn't an option. The stairs would have to do if I ever wanted to leave on time.

When I arrived covered in sweat, a woman shot up from her sewing machine and walked over to me. She was short, round, and commanding, leading me to believe she was the ruler of the alterations department, a fine matriarch who dominated her land with more order and precision than any other seamstress on the planet. Her dyed orange hair and thick penciled-in eyebrows made a statement that was impossible to overlook, as was the department's output happening in systematized rows. Something about the energy reminded me of the scene from *Rudolph the Red-Nosed Reindeer* when Santa's elves worked feverishly to get presents wrapped and ready to go. The place was overflowing with merchandise and time was of the essence, like always.

"You new?" she asked, running her hard gaze along my face.

"I'm new to the store," I replied.

Eyeing my box of goods, she pointed to a long bar with a sign that read "incoming lingerie."

"They go there," she said flatly. I noticed that a couple bras had already been delivered, presumably needing pockets ASAP, so I pushed them toward the front of the bar and started to hang the remainder of lingerie. She watched with eagle eyes as I organized each item and then moved closer once I hung the bag of underwear on the end of the bar. "What is this?" she asked with a heavy accent while carefully examining the bag.

We both stopped to stare at the pile of washed chonies, long and threadbare.

"Um." I hesitated to explain. "A customer would like to have the top stitching resewn."

The clatter of sewing machines came to a halt as members of Team Seam turned to help investigate.

Fucking great.

"The tops?" she confirmed, looking over the ticket with my name inked in bold print.

"Yeah, my manager passed it off, so I have no idea what the conversation was like. They're coming undone." I pointed to the band. It was clear our matriarch was as perplexed as I was and running on the same level of patience when it came to certain human actions.

"Leave 'em." She turned to walk away, muttering something under her breath in a language I couldn't understand. I quickly moved toward the doors and stopped, offering a kind wave goodbye as a room full of seamstresses and tailors stared on, straight-faced and tight-lipped.

RELAXING INTO THE CINEMA'S PLUSH RECLINER NEXT TO LARRY, I reflected on my time with Claire. I couldn't get her, or her disgrace of a father, out of my head. I was so disheartened by her story, which was something I certainly didn't hear on a daily basis. I couldn't comprehend the idea of abandoning someone, let alone your own child, because of their sexual orientation or preferred gender. The ignorance and bigotry enraged me, like nothing I had ever experienced inside of the dressing room before. And though we only shared a couple hours together, Claire taught me about the true meaning of empathy while shining a light on all the things I had directly in front of me, like opportunity, freedom, and a father who allowed me the time to figure out life because he knew that I was lost without my mother. He knew that I needed him. And while he listened intently about my day, digging into a bucket of popcorn as the lights dimmed, I held onto his whisper with a heart full of gratitude.

"Have you ever thought that just maybe things have a way of working out?"

SOMETHING BLUE

S itting alone in a cramped food court, I chewed the last of my greasy pizza to the tiring cadence of Christmas music. The corny and clichéd songs had come early, playing on a slow and burning repeat. Mile-high Christmas trees, gigantic poinsettias, bright lights, and bold, life-sized nutcrackers started to make their entrance, as did an influx of seasonal shoppers. It was a favorite place among many and a retail worker's worst nightmare. Or maybe just mine.

I paced myself back to the lingerie department, having wolfed down three pieces of mall pizza and one of Mrs. Fields' chocolate chip cookies. Due to a late lunch break, I didn't have much longer to go with my shift, which was always the smartest way to play it. However, when I finally returned fifteen minutes past the hour—with an eggnog latte in hand—Kristy didn't hide her disapproval.

"I need you to take the bridal party on the end." She shot me a glare in appreciation of my punctuality, her eyes wide and pleading. I quickly headed for the stockroom so that I could set down my latte, remembering that I forgot to drive the chalk off my tires. A ticket on my windshield was imminent. But all I could do in the moment was pray for a reasonable bride, who undoubtedly led the pack.

Laughter filled the hallway as I made my way back to their room, confirming the fact that I was moments away from multiple requests and a lot of size runs.

"Knock, knock." I cracked the door open to find a room full of loud, dynamic women talking amongst themselves.

"Come in!" one of them shouted, kindly making room for me in the middle of the dressing room. The smell of alcohol, mixed with an infusion of perfumes, instantly hit the air, suffocating our small zone in big waves. At first glance, I noticed that all the women varied in size, starting with their boobs and down to their backsides.

"I heard someone's getting married." I moved my gaze along the circle.

"I am!" The bride stepped forward, throwing her hands in the air. "And these are my lovely bridesmaids."

I took another look around the group, quietly noting sizes, which became a natural part of my role over time.

"Congratulations," I replied, planting my feet on the carpet while I waited for instructions. "Nice meeting you all."

The bride, who was small breasted, extremely tan, and glowing with excitement, quickly revealed her list of wedding essentials, including strapless bras for the bridesmaids, Spanx for under the dresses, a garter for something blue, and a pair of our popular Hanky Panky bridal thongs with the words "I Do" glued in rhinestones along the side. I had a lot to cover, and time was ticking.

"Do you all plan on staying in one room?" I asked, reaching for a measuring tape.

Without hesitation, everyone in the bridal party nodded in agreement, at ease with the idea of stripping down and baring all. I signaled for the bride to disrobe first, pleased that her intoxicated counterparts followed suit.

"Let the good times roll!" one of the bridesmaids yelled.

"Seriously," another one chimed in, grabbing hold of her midsection.

Given the size of the bride's solid B breast tissue and petite frame, she approved of my assessment and quickly added her strong desire for padding. "Lots of padding!" She laughed, grabbing her boobs while the other women giggled.

"Let's get these bitches strapped in," a busty woman said as she moved toward the center of the room. "I'm going to need all hands on deck."

I laughed, swiftly wrapping the measuring tape around her rib cage. "Let's start with a 40 double-G."

"A double what?" the bride asked, surprised.

"Can we just get this one some Band-Aids, and she'll be good?" The woman responded to the bride by playfully flicking her boobs. More laughter ensued as I moved on to the next three bridesmaids.

"I'm a 34 double-D," a tall brunette claimed while cupping the bottoms of her breasts.

"That sounds about right," I replied, assessing the fit of her T-shirt bra. "You understand that the strapless might require a different cup size, right?" She gave me a quick head tilt forward and moved out of the way for the other two bridesmaids. I chuckled as one of them broke out in Madonna's "Vogue" stances, striking one pose after the next. Her boobs shook all over the place, creating another round of howling laughter. I stepped forward to share in the space, preparing to rattle off one backbreaking order. Each one of them stared at me amused. I exhaled slowly.

"I've got one 32 B, a 40 double-G, a 34 double-D, and . . ." I stopped to look at my last two bridesmaids. "Two 36s, one single D, and one triple."

"Wow!" the bride exclaimed, high-fiving my efforts before they all made me take a bow.

"How do you ladies want to tackle the Spanx?" I asked, laughing.

"Laid out on the ground," a woman with long thick braids replied.

"And with a feeding tube," another one added.

"The dresses are knee-length." The bride offered more clarity. "Maybe just grab a variety of styles and sizes and we can go to town." Happy with her insight, I exited the dressing room, promptly inhaling the upsurge of clean air.

As expected, it took me some time to gather the garments, traveling from one stockroom to another. I climbed ladders, busted open boxes, hassled the women's clothing department for the last pair of extra-large Spanx, and dug far and wide for as many strapless bras as I could find. Caroline even pitched in and offered up two of her customer holds, doubting their return. My party needed options—and I was determined to watch every member leave the department with a shopping bag.

Walking straight into the dressing room, I dumped all their garments on the glass table. "Have at it." I grinned, noticing that they had created a small picnic of Chardonnay minis. "I'll be back with some Hanky Panky and bait for your significant other." The bride smiled, raising her wine in the air as her crew peeled away more of their clothing.

Back out on the floor, I studied the display of wedding essentials. Our department stylists created quite the arrangement, introducing a variety of garters stitched with lace, bows, satin, and pastel beading. The warm presentation also included a few styles of breast "cutlets" just in case one of our brides wanted a little help pushing the girls together and up. I vaguely recalled my customer's request for "something blue," so I grabbed a few options for her to look at and then headed over to the other side of the floor for the fun part.

Beautiful white chemises, gowns, and ivory negligees hung in order of size, capturing a range in length while shimmering with pearls and multicolored rhinestones under the fluorescent lights. I sifted through a variation of styles and pulled as many size smalls as I could find, feeling good about my selection.

"Your party sounds fun." Caroline crept up from behind.

"Are they behaving?" I asked jokingly, adding one more chiffon gown to my forearm.

"They've added music," she said, laughing.

"Great."

"Don't forget to bring the bride a pair of those new Hanky Panky open things."

"Open things?" I looked at her, confused.

"The crotchless panties," she replied, smiling. "Kristy set some out on the counters for stocking stuffers." I immediately thought of Farah and laughed to myself, slowly letting it all sink in.

"Stocking stuffers?"

Turning into the dressing rooms, I froze at the sight of one of the bridesmaids dancing in the hallway to Whitney Houston's "I'm Every Woman." The unrivalled tenor blared from the bride's cell phone as the full-busted brunette sashayed in a tan, high-waisted body shaper and a strapless bra that looked like cardboard. Women laughed while peeking their heads out from their dressing rooms, snapping to Whitney's memorable beat and "hear me roar" lyrics.

"Oh my goodness!" the bride squealed, grabbing everyone's attention. "What is this?" She stroked the gown's fabric.

"That's for Ben," I heard one of the women say while I hung the nighttime requisites on a hook and spread the smaller items out on the table.

"Something blue, and I do!" The bride picked up the pair of Hanky Panky thongs.

"They're low-rise," I added, readjusting a bridesmaid's double-Gs as her body sweat moistened the tops of my hands.

"What the hell does all this 'something blue' even mean anyway?" the bride asked, examining the thong.

"You know." The brunette started to chant. "Something old, something new, something borrowed, and something blue!"

I stopped, thrown by the words and suddenly wanting the early holiday music back.

"It's Ben's reality once the honeymoon ends," the woman in long braids teased. Laughter followed as we all caught on to her quip about *something blue*.

"Marissa's been married for twelve years." The bride offered a friendly sneer.

"And I'm happy," Marissa added, taking a seat in one of the chairs.

"Are you?" The brunette lowered her gaze.

"Yeah, I mean, I don't know." Marissa shrugged her shoulders. "Are we ever fully content as human beings? No. Are there greener pastures? Maybe. Do I fantasize about sleeping with other men? Hell yes."

I appreciated her truth, totally absorbing her contribution. "Happiness is really all anyone wants, right?"

I thought about Marissa's statement as I dressed the bride in another strapless bra. Happiness sounded like a good answer, which seemed to encompass so many facets of life.

"Speaking of happiness," the light-haired bridesmaid interjected, irritably pulling on her 36 triple-D strapless. "Why do women get stuck with all this shit?"

We waited while she sipped her mini Chardonnay, and then she stood tall, looking like her circulation was cut off as flesh poured over the top of her Spanx shaper.

"I've got a war zone in my panties, and my tits feel like hanging bricks ten days out of the month. Some of us are also in charge of pushing heads, arms, hands, legs, and feet out of our vajayjays." She waved her hands in the air. "Like real people with heads."

I had no idea how much the alcohol was talking, but I loved her rant.

"And then when they're here, sucking the life out of our nipples until they're cracked open and bleeding, while also robbing us of sleep, depression hits like a semitruck. And everyone has an opinion about it."

"Amen, sister!" a woman remarked from the room next door.

"But it's so worth it." The bride smiled, poking her new breast pads.

"Yeah, yeah." Marissa sighed, facing the mirror. "Men get off so lucky."

"Not that lucky," the brunette muttered under her breath. "Those gross lookin' hairy berries! No, thank you!"

I laughed at their effortless banter, hearing another "amen" from across the way.

The women rested in brief silence, shimmying around each other for a full view in front of the mirror. Boobs moved atop cups, skin rolled out of body shapers, and stretch marks, cellulite, and unshaven body hair were plentiful. I'd never felt more camaraderie in my life, pleased to see we all shared in the same negotiations.

"Look at us!" The brunette cackled alongside another bridesmaid while running her hand along her midsection. "We look like a couple of Mr. Potato Heads!"

"You all look pretty good to me." I stepped back to examine the final fit of everyone's strapless bras.

"What about these?" Marissa picked up the pair of crotchless panties from off the table. Everyone waited while she unfolded the small pieces of fabric and held them high in the air.

"Look at those things!" The bride broke out in hysterics. "And these go where?" she asked, pulling on the side pieces of lace.

"Around the honeypot!" Marissa joked, reading the name on the tag. "After midnight."

All the women stopped to stare at the panties, analyzing their presence with great concern.

"Why the pressure to wear anything?" the bride asked. "It's always the woman that has to serve things up, right? Am I not allowed to change from my wedding dress into a pair of sweatpants?"

"You wear whatever you want," Marissa cut in quickly.

"It's true, though." The brunette spoke in a serious manner. "Ben's not agonizing over what he's going to wear down the aisle or in the bedroom. It's because we're women . . . with tits and ass and all the things that get put up for show. I say you surprise him in a pair of boxers."

Laughter immediately followed, as if the idea was absolute nonsense.

"We'll get you some white ones."

The women continued to analyze the crotchless thong while I cleaned up a few of the leftover bras and body shapers. The room was a mess, and I could only hope the window for more requests had closed, which was why I made myself invisible and quietly slipped out of the room, leaving the women to talk amongst themselves. As I hit the sales floor, I thought about their conversation regarding happiness and contentment, wondering if Marissa was onto something. Are we ever really content? Will searching for something better always be a part of one's life journey? Happiness has to mean contentment. Contentment has to exist alongside happiness. Lots of people are happy. Right?

"Excuse me." A cashier moved in quickly, shaking me from my monotonous cycle as I continued to rehang leftover merchandise. "Your brother called and said to call him back as soon as you can."

Everything became blurry as my heart railed against my chest. Delivered with swift jolts was the intuition Diane always talked about. The kind of gut feeling that sucked the life right out of you and rigged your breathing into bare blues. *Larry*, I thought, looking around to find Caroline for help with my bridal party while coming to terms with the fact that something wasn't quite right. The feeling was too uncomfortable. Too jarring. And as the music became louder from inside the dressing rooms, gifting roars of laughter to the entire department, I continued to make myself invisible, slipping all the way down to the parking structure with faith that my party would find their happily ever after . . . well beyond the midnight hours.

THE STERILE PULSE OF THE HOSPITAL MADE MY INSIDES CHURN. Every measured beep, combined with the strained uprising of machines, shot terror down my body at lightning speed. Doctors and nurses moved in and out, constantly pulling on the cubicle curtain as it screeched along its track.

I sat next to Larry while he quietly laid in agony from the fluid building in his stomach. It filled up like a balloon, causing a restriction of air—and a rapid decline of faith. Images of him sitting in his reading chair on a Thursday morning with his arms and knees covered in Bengay cream just days before suddenly made sense. The only time he had ever missed a day of work was when we buried my mom.

I spent the next four hours and seventeen minutes pacing a windowless room filled with oversized fish tanks and a surplus of magazine subscriptions. The surgeon's path never left my view as I anticipated her arrival through the double doors. It was eerily quiet with the exception of my brothers' sharing a phone conversation.

Absolutely nothing felt right about our situation. The nausea that continued to rise from the pit of my stomach was becoming insufferable. And then the surgeon's black clogs, donned with blue shoe covers, finally moved through the doors. I stared quietly as her eyes brimmed with tears and then everything went dim while I stood blinking to black: *stage four colon cancer . . . metastasis to the peritoneal cavity . . . lymph nodes . . . and bones . . . going to need strength . . . and a whole lot of time.*

Waiting for Larry to wake up from surgery, I sat against the window of his tenth-floor hospital room, quietly piecing together the puzzle—and Gladys's trust in timing. But guilt placed its chokehold. Bengay cream for the bones, extra-strength Tums for what he thought was acid reflux, and unusual fatigue that put him to sleep by eight o'clock in the evening. The all-too-familiar series of what-ifs robbed even the slightest flicker of light. *I should've pushed harder for him to see a doctor. Nobody eats that many Tums, right? They taste like chalk. Why didn't he just get a fucking colonoscopy? Both parents? What are the odds? I lived with him. I saw him every day. How could I let this happen?*

Larry nodded quietly when we told him the news. "How long?" he asked with his hands behind his head, sharp and poker-faced.

"Six months, maybe a year," one of the doctors replied.

"And a colostomy bag?" he confirmed calmly.

"Yes, and you will see normal bowels at first."

Silence followed swiftly. I turned to watch the cars sit idle down below, afraid to look at my father for fear of losing it all.

"Well." Larry deliberated. "Shit."

HOLY NIGHT

Inside Larry's room was the aftermath of captivity. Empty paper cups, newspapers, nail clippers, an Etch-A-Sketch, and various food wrappings were carelessly strewn about, creating a serious lack of order and hospitality. The days were short and the nights long as Larry fought to gain some semblance of normalcy. He was on the mend for the most part, at least enough to get him home; however, his unruly digestive tract, triggered by a gigantic obstruction and leaking green fluids, kept anything—and everyone—from moving. I was moments away from being canned from the lingerie department if Larry didn't produce a proper bowel movement into his new colostomy bag he, of course, graciously deemed the "shit bag."

"Up and at 'em," our nurse Flossie said. I'd taken her measurements for a bra in the wee hours of the morning when I couldn't sleep. We used paper tape from the nurse's station, and she coached me on what to say to Kristy, and the HR department, before I called the store for the fifth time.

Larry peered over in my direction and stared at the accumulation of hair grease that created an uncanny resemblance to Cameron Diaz's character from the memorable scene in *There's*

Something About Mary. Making the title my own, I came in a close second, wearing ketchup stains on my alma mater T-shirt and sizable holes in my sweatpants.

"You're a good sport, Nat," Larry said, smiling at my polished look.

"Thank you, Larry. Let's get your teeth brushed." I rifled through his Dopp kit in an effort to move our daily undertakings along.

"I don't want to brush my teeth right now," he replied, grabbing onto his IV stand.

"Here, take the toothbrush. Let's just get it done."

"I don't want to brush my teeth."

"But you need to brush your teeth."

"I understand that, Natalee."

"Okay, here."

"I'm not brushing my teeth."

"Take the fucking toothbrush."

Larry stood to his feet, quickly straightening out his hospital gown.

"Why don't you go grab a bite down the street," he said, holding onto his IV in preparation for his walk around the unit. "Get some air."

I dismissed the idea immediately, afraid to leave his side in case something happened, and petrified to be in public due to the severe panic I had yet to shake. All of the long hours sitting on my cot watching life unfold from the streets below only reminded me that the world doesn't stop. It just keeps on spinning, wrapping its heavy web around the shattered and numb. But it started to make sense to leave for a little while as Larry continued to push for my exit. I knew somewhere along my escape was a bartender with a heavy hand. I also started to wonder if he wanted to be alone, relieved to welcome a break from a revolving door as my brothers and I moved in and out at all times of the day, adding to the flurry of foot traffic as his vulnerability sat on display.

Four hours later, my long absence proved to be somewhat helpful. One of the girls kindly covered my shift again after I offered to take all her closing duties upon my return. But unlike my dad, I escaped the gastroenterology unit to process a new truth, which recklessly translated into Jameson whiskey coupled with Seattle's best IPA. I squinted to find the number ten on the wall of buttons back inside the elevator, knowing once again that my decision to flee only generated more disorder, and the most paralyzing of fears.

"Four, five, six, seven, eight." I read the white boxes out loud, hoping Larry was asleep by the time I made it to his room.

"She's back!" Flossie grinned.

"How's our patient?" I asked, grateful to find fresh blankets on my cot.

"He's hangin' on, darlin'."

Leaning over Larry's bed, I tripped on one of the cords, loudly knocking his spirometer to the floor.

"Natalee." He opened his eyes. "What the hell are you doing?"

"Are you breathing?" I whispered loudly, inches away from his face.

"No," he replied, not remotely amused with my drunken antics.

"Did you shit?" I asked, still under the impression that I was whispering.

"No, Natalee, I didn't shit."

"That's okay," I said, patting his head. "It'll happen."

"Natalee."

"Yes, Larry?"

"Go to sleep."

The following morning, with a desert growing in my mouth, I awoke to a team of doctors and interns standing over my cot dressed in long white coats. With one eye open and a delayed hand wave, the permeation of booze hit the air. I heard clapping and laughter as more bodies filled the space. Soggy French fries, spilled chocolate milk, and my brothers' juvenile, X-rated creation on Etch-A-Sketch sat atop a rolling table two feet away from a real life McDreamy, making me wonder how long everyone had been in the room before I became conscious. I had no idea what was going on. Everything moved so fast, including the shuffling of papers and the exchange of handshakes. *Did Larry finally have a bowel movement? I wonder if McDreamy is single? When did I buy chocolate milk? Where the hell is Diane and, goddamnit, Raul?* And then someone finally spoke in language I could follow as Flossie joined the party.

"We've got a winner!"

BARRELING INTO THE PARKING STRUCTURE FOR MY CLOSING SHIFT Kristy so desperately needed me to work, I pulled together whatever professional look I could create after days of sinking into a hospital cot and relentless rounds of shock.

"Welcome back!" Caroline came charging with a hug. "We're closing together tonight."

"Thank god," I replied, relieved that Kristy had already gone home for the day and that my responsibility was an easy five-hour closing shift. The weeknight pace was manageable, or at least I hoped. The lingerie department was certainly no exception to surprises, especially during peak season—and record rain, when most Seattleites congregated indoors. But I was back, literally holding on by a thin string.

After looking over new merchandise and Kristy's long list of evening to-dos, I spent the next half hour stocking the counters with all the necessities, trying to look busy without having to help customers. I noticed that Kristy had set up a box in the stockroom for outgoing customer thank-you notes, pushing a very clear agenda with due dates and more one-on-one weekly meetings to go over personal sales and "growth goals."

"She's been all over the place," Caroline said, referring to Kristy while pointing toward a man circling the panty tables in the front of the department. I looked over to evaluate his attention to detail as he picked up a pair of thongs and studied their backside.

"You don't want him?" I asked, willing to beg.

"Nope!" She turned toward the dressing rooms. "He's not my type, anyway . . . Welcome back."

Dragging my feet toward the customer, I noted my irregular heartbeat, unable to overcome the daze that had transformed itself into an unbreakable bubble. Coming from the hospital to the lingerie department with life-altering news and zero hope was surreal. The backdrop felt strangely unsettling and the mood a drifting downcast. Nothing seemed right.

"Good evening." I smiled, looking over his silver highlights and dark brown eyes as I approached the panty table. He was tall and dressed to the nines, wearing a clean striped button-up with his cuffs turned back and a thick flashy watch sharing in the same gold tone as his diamond-cut wedding band.

"Hello," he replied in a deep, croaky voice, still holding onto a pair of thongs. "I'm looking for a couple gifts."

"Okay." I followed him over to a bra-and-panty display and waited while he examined the sheer crotch of another pair of thongs.

"We'll start here," he said, smiling. "And I'd like only black, mostly sheer, and lace is fine." He pointed to a soft charmeuse bra with transparently thin areas for each of the nipples. "I like this. I'll take a size small in the matching thong too."

His quickness was perfect for my comeback.

"What cup size do you need?" I asked, filtering through the row of bras. His eyes darted back and forth from our mannequin's perky, lace-covered breasts to Ruby's boobs packed tightly into one of our T-shirt bras.

"Uhhh." He struggled to respond, and then fixed his eyes directly on my boobs, moving them up and down and up and down. "She's closer to your size in the chest, I think."

"But you don't know the band size?" I replied, trying to follow his lead while realizing that he didn't have a clue what size bra he needed. So I continued to climb the alphabet and grabbed the first double-D I could find and paired it with its matching thong, knowing most of it would be returned.

I then followed him over to our French display and stopped to observe his attentiveness to each item. He picked up all the black lace bras only after examining the cut of their matching panty.

"I like this too," he said, handing over a demi-cut sewn with intricate black lace around the tops of the cups. I quickly grabbed a size from off the fixture and then continued to follow him over to our lace teddies and ultra-sheer bodysuits.

"Wow," he said, picking up a teddy cut into a deep V with two-inch lace for around the honey pot.

"It's a teddy, alright," I replied. "I believe it's called the 'Oh La La.'"

He laughed, steadily nodding his head. "I'll take a small."

Holding onto his merchandise, I waited as he looked around the department, staring down his face, as well as his nose hairs, visible and protruding, like dark uneven paintbrush bristles.

"I think I'm good there." He met my gaze. "Let's add a bathrobe and then if you could gift wrap them that would be great."

Sauntering over to a rounder of bathrobes, he didn't take long to pick out an oversized gathering of blue terry cloth.

"I'd get a small/medium?" I said, happy to move things along. "If she's typically a small, you could still do the small-medium and she'd be fine."

"I'm going to grab a large in this," he replied, looking toward the back of the rack.

It took me a minute to respond as his objectives—and demeanor—changed. I couldn't help thinking about how different his items were. And frankly it was none of my business, but I was far too curious and suddenly confused after he handed me a size large bathrobe my grandmother would've worn had she still been alive. The combo just didn't make sense.

"Are you sure you don't want to consider a small or medium bathrobe since you're buying small panties? They run really big." He struggled to respond to my question, looking at me as if I was the definition of naivety.

"The robe is for my wife and the lingerie is for someone else." He narrowed his gaze while handing me the large bathrobe, struggling to convey what he was really up to while I was still stuck on the idea of helping a partner feel comfortable in his selections for her. "I . . . uh . . . hope that helps." He stuttered slightly.

"I . . . see." My head bobbed back and forth as I searched for a response. "Let's . . . get you rung up."

As I scanned in his merchandise, he watched the price climb on the screen with every bra and panty added. After totaling up his items, I was hit with my first split transaction.

"I'd like the lingerie on this card, please, and the robe on this one." He handed over two credit cards.

"Oh, uh, I'll need to ring them up separately. I can't accept two cards unless you'd like to buy a gift card," I said, taken aback by his candor.

"Whatever's easier," he replied, checking the time on his watch.

I hurried to redo his transactions, balancing two registers at once, and then headed for the stockroom to gift wrap his good intentions.

"Excuse me, ma'am." A woman stopped me right as I turned the corner to hide, holding a huge pile of satin briefs. "May I try these on?"

After unlocking a dressing room, I spent the next ten minutes hovered over our gift-wrapping station in the back. I prepared the bra-and-panty sets first, feeling uneasy as I laid the panties flat against the tissue paper. And not because I couldn't figure out what to do with the thong's cumbersome design while I moved it around the inside of the box five times, but because my customer's straightforwardness was a little out of the ordinary—and hard to swallow. Helping someone gather their desires over cup size guessing games was a weekly task; I was used to men buying lingerie for other women after years in the biz. However, it still felt strange. And I knew nothing about his life or his marriage. He was a stranger, shopping for merchandise, and I had a job to do. But it was awkward. His response, combined with his flagrant gaze, was too honest, disturbing really.

It was hard to imagine that one woman would be tying up her new bathrobe while the other woman slid her bits into a new pair of panties, all for the same man. It really got me thinking. Maybe everyone involved was privy to the infidelity and my internal conflict was provoked by nothing more than my biased assumption. Either way, I made Caroline deliver his boxes while I watched from afar, trying my hardest to drown out the repetition of "ma'am" coming from the inside of a nearby dressing room.

Caroline quickly placed his boxes inside a shopping bag and walked them around the counter. And off his scandalous operation went, causing me to delve into my own morals and how I would feel had that woman been me. My heart hurt just thinking about it, yet I couldn't decide if I'd even the score, or quietly walk away. It seemed so overwhelming and deprived of all the great things true, devoted love had to offer. But things happen, I suppose. Shit can go sideways. We can fall out of love, or find a new one. We stop communicating. We love the wrong people too hard, which can lead to feelings of time wasted and resentment.

There were so many factors that came into play as I stood hiding behind the doorway, reminiscing about the men I'd experienced as well as my shortcomings. Our department Casanova really split open the compartmentalized mess of monogamy that ran hamster wheels in my head. I wondered if Chase had found his Juliet, strumming away his sweet nothings over wine and one of LA's orange sunsets. I wondered if Michael Morrison ever forgave me for choosing to walk away quietly after years of sincere adoration and unforgettable sex in the backseat of my car. I wondered if Marco, my six-month rebound, found his submissive "soul mate," free from opinions.

My wonderment took me on a sequenced rodeo of intimate discoveries, landing me right on top of an offensive lineman from small town Alaska. He kept me curious and irrational all throughout college. And then it ended as quickly as it began, sending me back to Seattle with unsparing nostalgia and straight into the arms of a dying mother. It was never the right time. But maybe that was the draw. Perhaps we get more out of fractured relationships in the long run, well after the shock waves and afterthoughts dressed in terry cloth.

When I finally answered the nagging woman's call, suddenly remembering that I had unlocked a room for her, she asked if I could come in and sit down. I hesitated at first, peering over her shoulder to find the floor covered in long satin briefs.

"Can I answer a question?" I asked, moving only half of my body into the room before noticing that she didn't double up on underwear and keep her own pair on while trying the new.

"Yes, but I'd like to close the door for privacy."

"Of course," I replied, slowly lowering myself into the chair, stunned by the number of panties she had pulled from the floor.

"This is kind of an odd question." She started in, somewhat bashful. "But I'm hoping you can tell me if the back seam is aligned with the middle of my buttocks."

Flashes of me running off the Santa Monica Pier came quickly.

"I'm sorry, I'm not following." My eyes sprung open as she turned around to point to her ass's crack, and then slowly guide her finger down the underwear's thin seam.

"I want to make sure the stitching is perfectly aligned."

My head fell forward as her request became real. The minutia was dumbfounding. I had no idea what to say, or how to appropriately respond to her lingerie needs. I could barely tell her to put on her own underwear first. But that was just it. We all had our own idiosyncratic needs, a personal requirement that sat somewhere between logic and desire. I chose to remain seated in the chair, awkward and tongue-tied, aligning seams against long, aging flesh, and to give purpose in how I tried to understand. "I think it's aligning nicely down your . . ."

She interjected quickly, overjoyed with my observation as she moved her finger along the back seam. "I'll take all you've got."

HEARTS
AND BONES

Running across the sky bridge and up the stairs to the lingerie department, I struggled to arrive on time for a morning "holiday happy hour" followed by a random day shift I picked up in gratitude for those who covered my absences. With coffee and doughnuts (Kristy's idea of a happy hour), management thought it was a good idea to hold a team meeting before the store opened to go over expectations as the holiday shopping gained momentum. We were encouraged, via the "happy holidays" mantra, to keep smiles in the aisles and pep in our steps. I unfortunately lacked in both areas, barely hanging on as I balanced Larry's trial chemotherapy appointments and retail's nagging hours. I was near a full disintegration of morale, silently preparing for Larry's looming exit while scrambling to figure out where I'd end up. The clouded isolation and fecal incontinence I battled after round one with my mom had returned with full force.

"And, ladies." Kristy continued to talk in front of the Spanx collection wearing one of our winter bathrobes we were expected to showcase during bra fittings. "Remember to greet every customer and please keep the go-backs to a minimum! We can't give customers what they want if it's sitting in a pile in the back." My head jerked from nodding off. I shot straight up, quickly looking around the group to see if anyone noticed. I moved my eyeballs in circular motions, hoping to stay awake without looking batshit crazy.

"Last up," Kristy continued, holding up a new full-figure bra in bright magenta with navy blue flowers. "We've got more Js AND new super breathable butt enhancers! Look! The pads are connected to the shapewear!" Everyone watched as Kristy squeezed the round, abundant seat cushions with her hands.

"This place never ceases to amaze me," Caroline mumbled under her breath. "Have we become that desperate?"

"Alright, lingerie team, doors open in ten. Bring on the Spanx!"

It didn't take long for the early morning, down-to-business customers to arrive, keeping me somewhat focused. "Hi, Monica." I read a woman's name tag pinned against her V-neck sweater as she moved with purpose . . . and confusion. I tried gauging her size, no doubt landing on an HH, or a full JJ.

"Hello," she responded in a chipper undertone, jokingly cupping her hands around an airline symbol next to her name. "I know I'm in the wrong size. What is it? 8 out of 10 women?" She kept talking, antsy and closely watching the time. It was hard to hold back from looking at her boobs, nearly busting open the entire row of buttons on her crisp blue uniform.

"You're definitely in the wrong size by a few cups."

She checked the time on her watch again as I continued to stare at her bulging breast tissue coming out from both the sides and the tops of her bra, mimicking the well-known "double bubble."

"Assuming you have a flight to catch, I can get you out of here in twenty," I said, mentally logging our new J cups from the morning meeting.

She laughed, playfully nudging my arm.

"Is it that obvious? I never know how much time I'll need and always end up just snooping around. Or maybe I'm making excuses because I'm scared to do this."

I appreciated her honesty and sensed a down-to-earth, no bullshit kind of woman. Her charm was quick to surface.

"Follow me," I smiled, urging her to get fitted.

Inside the dressing room, Monica was quick to rip off her shirt and stand awkwardly in front of the mirror. It took me a minute to assess her cup size after seeing her breasts in the flesh. "You'd think, with all of my layovers, I would've had this settled a long time ago! And the fact that people stare at my boobs all day long."

"I don't know a whole lot of women who love bra shopping," I replied, lifting the bottoms of her breasts.

"That's the truth!" she concurred, looking in the mirror as her high energy started to fade. "I'm desperate for help. On a flight, it's like I'm invisible sometimes. I mean, I know my boobs are huge, but come on! Have they not seen titties before?"

Monica was visibly agitated—and escalating the more she spoke about her experience, which sent me right back out onto the floor on a serious hunt for bras. I grabbed an H, a few double-Hs, and a couple Js from the stockroom, impressed with our new, colorful shipment. Designers and vendors were finally catching on, slowly but decisively.

Back inside Monica's room, I was happy to see a smile while she held her boobs in her hands.

"I'm in shock," she said, turning toward the mirror as I placed her breast tissue and fastened the band from behind. "An H?" After a firm push and pull, I stepped back to study the placement of her tissue, looking to see how close the underwire was to her body, followed by the "double bubble" that still would've been noticeable under her uniform.

"We need to move cup sizes." I hurried to place her in another bra, keeping in mind that she had a flight to catch. After stuffing her breasts into a double-H, I tightened the straps and ran my fingers along the underwire, making sure that every last bit of tissue was inside the cups and not cut off by the bra's wire, which was sometimes difficult to see with a lot of breast tissue.

"Wow," she whispered, turning to the side. "This is what it feels like to have a bra on that fits?"

"Go ahead and move around like you would on a plane." I prompted Monica to test out her flight attendant moves. "Reach for luggage," I suggested, smiling, watching her arms move high into the air.

"I feel like . . ." She stopped.

"A new woman," I finished for her, handing over her uniform to try on with the bra.

She shook her head while buttoning her shirt, consumed by her own thoughts. "I had this woman on a flight the other day who straight up looked at me and said, 'Your boobs are gigantic, and your bra isn't even close to fitting you.'"

I stepped back to listen as her voice cracked a little.

"She was serious, too. Drunk, but serious. And she said it so loud that everyone turned to look at me. It just happened to be on a day when I woke up feeling horrible about myself, too. Do I cut them off, or not? Do I just embrace what I have at age forty-two, or not? I went home and cried myself to sleep, which is so stupid because they're just boobs. But this woman really got to me."

I pictured Monica walking up and down the aisle of an airplane, already on display given the nature of her job. I had no idea what it felt like to have J breasts, but I certainly understood the anger and sadness that came from being antagonized by another person who had absolutely no right. How awful can you be? Hearing about Monica's experience made my blood boil.

"That's not stupid, Monica," I finally responded. "And they're not *just* boobs."

"I know, but I really wanted to pop that woman!"

"I bet!" I adjusted the collar on her shirt. "People can be so cruel."

"You're tellin' me. But another woman?" Monica's eyes widened. "I've had a lot of men on flights harass me with their eyes or make side comments. But when other women make me feel bad about myself . . ."

I watched as Monica unbuttoned her shirt and gently ripped the tag from off the side of the bra. "I'll take four of these." She looked in the mirror and then down at her watch.

"You got it." I smiled, taking the tag from her hand. But before I could turn around toward the door, Monica grabbed hold of me, forcefully wrapping her arms around me. I could taste the perfume on her hair as we swayed back and forth inside the dressing room. It felt warm and full of sincerity.

"Thank you," she whispered softly. "I'll shake 'em down the aisle in your honor."

A few minutes later, I watched as Monica bolted out of the department for the airport. She left feeling good, which made me feel good. Though thinking about how she'd been treated because of her boobs, *her boobs*, made me angry. Monica could've dressed her titties any way she wanted to dress her titties. It also emphasized, once again, how judgment always seemed to become a significant part of my conversations in the dressing room. It was a starting point for many, coming in subtly or with a lot of force, often to the detriment of women . . . and women's bodies.

Breathing in a small sigh of relief before the anxiety showed itself, I held onto the customer-free moment, quietly noting how the dressing room had a funny way of creating momentary escapes, but only for so long. My days were numbered in the lingerie department. The combination of terminal and "existing" had become terrifyingly unstable, resting on the brink of unhinged. Larry was dying, quickly and inconsolably dying.

Kristy arrived, startling me out of my erratic daze by holding up our ever-changing schedule.

"Sooo." She stretched out the word, "Jena called in sick, and I need someone to close tonight."

"Tonight?" I asked, feeling both surprised and annoyed.

"You'd be working a split." She continued while straightening a couple out-of-place bras I'd managed to overlook as I hid next to the display. Knowing it was my turn to take one for the team, I agreed half-heartedly before negotiating a three-hour break. I needed enough time to check on Larry and then eat my feelings in the food court.

"Appreciate it." Kristy smiled, leaving me in the middle of the department amid a plethora of push ups and the bitter remnants of Monica's passengers.

―⌒

IT WAS AMAZING WHAT A FEW HOURS AWAY FROM THE LINGERIE department could do to the scenery. Last-minute holiday shoppers landed in droves, making it easier for me to stay parked on the second floor without having to monitor the chalk; there were far too many cars to keep track of. Upon entering the stockroom, I noticed a card had been placed on top of my personal box, inked in effortless cursive. I quickly ripped its edges and read on to find a thank-you from Claire Whittler, including a Starbucks gift card and sincere gratitude for her bras she called "perfect." It was a nice way to come back to the department after already working a day shift, on top of a morning meeting. My drive back felt long and heavy. And though I felt some solace knowing Larry was drugged and comfortable, it was difficult to separate.

I wondered what was going on inside Larry's head. Who was he most excited to see upon transitioning to the other side, if that's what happens? There had to be a welcoming committee, especially for a fellow skeptic like Larry who was about as interested as I was in our Sunday morning church excursions growing up. I understood it completely. On days when my mom wanted solitude, Larry would drop the three of us off, along with our one-dollar donations, in front of a gigantic white building that resembled a section of the White House. What congregated inside was another story. But we didn't have a choice per my mother's requests—and her mother's requests, a somewhat dedicated Christian Scientist who could bake her motherfucking ass off. The treats that followed were sometimes worth the screaming discomfort I felt.

"Take the dollar and put it in whatever they pass around," Larry would remind us, feeling beyond ecstatic to have one full hour of silence to drink his coffee and read the newspaper in his car. He couldn't have peeled off faster, leaving my brothers and me to fend for ourselves amid a strange and questionable meeting of the minds. The place was a walking morgue, equipped with a fit-to-drop pianist who part-timed it on the organ, and a small table library stacked with highly regarded narratives like *The Good Samaritan* that often circulated around my classroom with an overarching theme of "don't be an asshole."

Larry knew the dollar donation had become an issue. Frisko Freeze, a classic burger joint that also served dollar ice cream cones, boomed with business nearby. Roughly one blinker and a quick turn into the drive-thru. We'd often plead with Mom to take us through after church, but her own repetitive mantra on work ethic and "earning" money became exhausting. Larry was an easier bet when it came to Frisko Freeze, mostly because he didn't frequent the grounds and he wanted their menu options just as bad as we did. So we'd wait and plot downstairs in Sunday school, wondering if Dad was going to ask us to fork over our own money for a soft serve, also giving a long spiel on working for what you want, or pick us up ready to indulge, having felt renewed.

The donation bowl came quickly. I'd watch it move from row to row while others sang off-key from the leather-bound hymnals about some majestic shepherd showing the way. *The dollar goes in the bowl.* I'd have to prep myself, evaluating all of my goodness as my feet dangled from the chair. Plus our Sunday morning sequence had become predictable and I needed to be prepared to tell my mother what the lesson was about while quoting evidence from the scriptures—and that I'd donated my dollar bill. But I really wanted an ice cream cone 99.9 percent of the time. And as the giving bowl neared, so did the onset of cardiac arrest as my brother Skeet taunted my moves—flashing a mouth full of silver and his pocketed dollar bill. *Don't do it*, I thought, eyeing its steady route right past dying Dolores and dead Donald. *It's almost here. Put the dollar in the bowl. It's the right thing to do. Somewhere, someone needs Oreos and milk and blue fruit Gushers . . . and Easy Cheese with a Tropical Punch Capri Sun. Put the dollar in the damn—*

"Thank you, sweetheart. God bless." Mrs. Wakefield tapped my nose.

Yeah, whatever.

Thankfully when I saw Larry, waving from the car in the parking lot, I'd run right toward him, clicking my patent leather shoes as my ponytail swung freely, knowing he'd come through.

"How about some Frisko Freeze?"

⌒

"DID YOU HAPPEN TO CHECK ON THE CUSTOMER IN ROOM 8?" RUBY asked, passing by with our new butt-enhancing shapewear and a stack of trendy push-up bras.

"Shit." I backstepped quickly after getting caught up in stockroom banter and a game of "Would You Rather." It was Caroline's turn and no surprise that she chose Brad Pitt and Farah's dream-come-true, George Clooney.

When I knocked on the customer's door, she was slow to answer, making me wonder if I should've moved on.

"Sorry," she said, cracking the door. "Come in." Her alarmingly emaciated frame threw me off.

"Sorry about the wait, it's kind of crazy around here."

She stared at me with red, projecting eyes.

"I just need a couple bras." She ran her hand through a thin layer of hair, stopping abruptly at a patch of exposed flesh.

"Sure." I stood close to the door, feeling like she needed distance, as the space felt strained. There was undeniable tension and I wasn't sure how to respond. Something was wrong. And without overtly assuming, I made it a point to let her lead entirely. I was at a loss just looking at her, wizened into bone, and struggling hard to articulate her needs. "Do you know what size and style you'd like?" I asked, noticing a few of our thickest push-up bras laid out on top of the chair.

"Nothing fits," she responded quietly while refusing to look in the mirror, her hands swelling with pale rows of yellowish bone and her arms, long and threadlike, marked with a few discernable scar lines.

"Okay." I tried coming up with a plan. Her young age suddenly hit me and I was concerned about what would happen if she left empty handed.

"You shopping alone?" I asked.

She acknowledged my question with a slow head nod and then self-consciously moved her arms to cover as much of her midsection as possible. Looking over at the chair of bras, I made a mental note of which ones she grabbed, hoping for a smaller replacement. "Let me grab you some different sizes," I said, reaching for the door. "I see you've picked out padding."

Her lack of response led me to quicken my pace. I could sense that she was frustrated and I didn't want her to give up and leave.

When I returned with more merchandise, breathless and determined, she just stared at the bra's padding.

"They're from our petite section." I unhooked the hanger from off the first bra and passed it over.

She waited.

"Oh, sorry." I quickly slid out, resting against the wall outside her room while she put on the bra. After what felt like minutes, I tapped on the door. Without a word, she gestured for me to hurry inside.

"Alright," I said, studying the fit of a push-up bra as it hung off her body. "And this is the 30 AA, right?"

"Yeah," she replied, still refusing to look in the mirror. The band had slid up close to her protruding shoulder blades, making the cups, accompanied with foam padding, sit away from her breasts. I wracked my brain for options while realizing we were out of sizes. I just stood muttering the word "um" as she looked down at the ground.

"Ashley?" I heard a woman call out. "Are you back here?"

"I'm in here, Grandma." She moved to open the door. I quickly stepped to the side to make room before the door slammed shut.

"Oh my god," the woman said, holding a handful of shopping bags. "Look at you."

I swallowed loudly.

Don't say that to her.

"I know, Grandma." Ashley quickly covered her stomach as I stood behind her, desperate to escape the discomfort.

"That doesn't fit you at all," the woman said, setting down her cluster of bags while staring at Ashley's arms and sunken chest.

"I was just thinking I could have our alterations department try to tighten the band and add a couple hooks." I tried jumping in, hoping to break the cold stares.

Ashley continued to look down at the carpet, her skin turning a soft pink. Something led me to believe Ashley's grandmother had pushed her to try on bras.

"People actually do that to their bras?" the woman asked, surprised, looking over Ashley with a side-eye.

"Happens all the time." I stretched the truth, trying to protect Ashley from feeling even more out of place.

"What about a thicker kind of bralette?" I inquired cautiously, still trying to figure out if Ashley wanted a bra at all. She came in wearing a small cotton sports bra from what I could see on the chair, which made the desire for thick padding feel complicated.

"I'll try one, I guess." Ashley shrugged her shoulders before looking up at her grandmother, who couldn't stop staring at her withered, marked-up body.

I stepped out and headed straight for the back room. A long pause was in order as I tried wrapping my head around what was happening with Ashley, and what she needed. I assumed her days were spent reconciling with secrecy and isolation before the enormity of exposure set in, cutting right into her fragile existence. Seeing the traces of her desperation etched into her skin made everything about our encounter difficult to lead, especially while her grandmother continued to stare in disbelief without any semblance of support. Her gaze, stone cold and beseeching, created an uncomfortable pressure I got to escape, a drastically different reality than Ashley's. What must her day-to-day feel like? Self-hatred, carried by fear and loneliness? At least, that's what I presumed to be true after quietly analyzing her weakened body and small wounds rising along her sides. Ashley didn't need bras; she needed love. *Love.* Reassuring love. Comforting love. Love without all the fucking judgment.

When I returned to the room with one more 30 AA I found buried in the stockroom and a semi-flimsy bralette, Ashley's grandma had found a seat in the corner chair. The tension had intensified as Ashley stood against the wall, away from the mirror, still covering her stomach with her arms.

"Let's try another brand before we move over to the bralette." I tried sounding positive.

Ashley watched as I moved the hanger from off the bra and unhooked the band.

"And again, we can add hooks if need be. I'll make it happen."

Handing over the bra, I opened the door for Ashley's grandma. The awkwardness that followed made my face heat up to a deep red.

"Shall we let Ashley undress in private?"

"She's fine . . . right, Ash?" Her grandmother spoke with a firm push.

"Um." Ashley turned to look at me and then over to her grandma. The vacancy in her eyes nearly killed me.

Only love.

"I think she'd like a moment alone," I continued, panicking for a split second that grandma would come undone. She definitely had a time bomb ticking within, narrow and bold. But I pushed anyway, feeding off my own raw emotions and the grimace alongside her nerve.

"Actually." The grandma stood up quickly. "I'd like to ask you something."

Worried about what she was going to ask with Ashley nearby, I led us out to the sales floor.

"I'm really hoping she can leave with at least one bra," her grandmother said, looking me straight in the eyes. "She can't walk around with her nipples hanging out."

"Well." I paused, wondering if Ashley even looked in the mirror at all. "I think a bralette would be great for her."

"Because of her body?" She pushed harder, but then slowed her tone. "I don't know what to do."

I immediately looked down at the ground, feeling her bewilderment—and her sadness. It seemed obvious she was concerned about her granddaughter but had no idea how to proceed or rationalize clearly. I sensed a complicated entanglement between her thoughts, moving in and out from trying to understand to becoming increasingly frustrated. Her quiet need to mend whatever had bulldozed its way into Ashley's world was evident. The need for surrender was clear, as hard and aching as it was.

"Well," I said again. "I think comfort is really important at this point. I also think—" I stopped, choosing my words carefully. "The wire might add discomfort."

"I just—" She stopped, exhaling softly.

"Would you like me to check on her while you wait here?" I asked, trying my best to keep her out of Ashley's room. She looked at me flat faced, but surprised me with her answer after she came across on the more demanding side of things.

"I suppose."

When I returned to Ashley's room, I noticed that she was standing near the door.

"Hey, Ashley. It's me again, Natalee."

"Hey," she replied shyly.

"How'd the bra work out?"

I watched underneath the door as her feet shuffled closer to the chair.

"I don't know. I'm—"

Silence spread quickly.

"You need more time? It's okay if you do."

Her voice lowered into an almost desperate plea.

"Yeah, maybe."

I waited for a few seconds, contemplating her movements. The space surrounding us became strained and hard to read.

"You good?" I asked in a slow, muted pitch, holding onto her stillness.

"Yeah," she responded gently.

My insides sank as I tiptoed away. I wasn't sure what to do next other than hope that something gave way for Ashley, freeing her from the seclusion while breaking every fragment of fear.

"She just needs a few more minutes," I said, rejoining her grandmother as she paced around a display of bathrobes.

"Sure" was all I heard, leading me to separate myself and meander toward the front of the department. I wanted to look busy, but I struggled to figure out how much distance was needed; I didn't want to leave Ashley in case she needed something. I knew she was lonely and lost, spinning in circles inside the dressing room. But her grandmother headed back anyway, discarding all of it. So I hurried to make myself invisible in the stockroom for the time being, hoping to not have to pick up another customer.

"Can you believe it?" Ruby's voice echoed throughout the back. "I mean . . . this takes some serious balls! This man really thinks this is okay, like I want these panties . . . like I invited this . . . like I don't have an opinion on the matter." I stood looking at Ruby's expression as it transformed from sheer shock to anger. The whole operation was intrusive, but still so shamelessly intriguing. I think we all tried our best not to jump to conclusions about Ruby's random panty deliveries, but it had the potential to explode, and rightfully so. It wasn't remotely flattering or comfortable, but presumptuous and really overconfident. I couldn't help wondering what else the night had to offer and why we weren't just getting quick, in-and-out holiday shoppers with good intentions. But I stood by Ruby's every word, feeling every graze of intrusion, inside the dressing room and out.

Joining the group, equally perturbed, was Caroline, holding Ashley's bralette and push-up bras. "Your customers just walked out." She handed over their pile. My stomach sank again. I was really hoping to get at least one bra down to alterations, or a comfortable win for the bralette. I couldn't help wondering if Ashley's grandmother might've said something to halt the process, or make her give up altogether. The grandmother's grand entrance was hard to shake as her words turned into stones.

Look at you.

My mind drifted as the backroom chatter picked up, becoming nothing but separate noise right up until Ruby held the last

pair of our featured stocking stuffers with an invitation to slip
into their lacy shreds. The combination of predicaments was
hard to fathom. I wished I could tell Ashley to wear whatever the
hell she wanted to wear, nipples blazing. To go home and find
the one thing that would spark joy in every fiber of her being.

Finding a bra wasn't important when the mirror alone
became the antagonist. There were bigger things. Bigger battles.
But it was all easier said than done. The aching had intentions.
Ruby's testimony had resistance. People were dying. And in that
moment, among the lost and hurting, a memory of Gladys came
shining in like the big ray of sunshine that she was.

Give 'em hell, honey.

SPACE BETWEEN

Closing down the department again, I moved with little enthusiasm. Customers tore through every piece of lingerie from the minute the doors opened, creating a cluster of stray merchandise and nonstop organizing well into the night. I was beyond ecstatic to bury the holidays and resume some kind of normalcy, at least inside the store, amid temporary measures.

As I marked down a rounder of holiday bras into hot new sale items, a woman approached me holding a well-intentioned stack of boyshorts. Her pile was growing by the second as she added every style from sheer sexy satin to soft cotton.

"Do you know which one of your boyshorts will make my thighs look the smallest?" she asked, adding to her mound. "You know, the ones that won't pinch your skin and create more fat on the sides."

I hesitated, thinking about her question while reflecting on all of the large white flesh I carelessly smashed against string somewhere between retrieving pants from my laundry basket and mismatched socks from a drawer as I rushed to get back to work.

"Well, I know the ones with more spandex in them tend to cut into the skin," I replied, uncertain as to how to respond or, at the very least, appease. "Maybe start with the cotton ones. And some lace?"

"Okay." She perked up fast, leading me straight back into a dressing room. It came as no surprise that leftover merchandise covered the floor. Shit was everywhere, making it extremely difficult to differentiate between utter laziness and flat-out disrespect.

"Take your time and I'll be back to—"

She interjected quickly, her long curly hair bouncing in bundles as she hurried to unzip her jeans. "You mind waiting outside while I put a pair on? I would love your opinion."

I struggled for an escape, knowing I was being involuntarily thrown into the oh-so-conflicting "thigh gap" slash "side bulge." I didn't even bother to utter a response, as I knew my presence was mandatory in her mind. She was down to business. And my role was to watch, nod, listen, and attempt to control my side of the dialogue.

She flung open the door while pulling down the lacy edging of her first pair of boyshorts. I stood staring with my mouth halfway open, still at a loss for what I was supposed to say— while caught off guard, though intrigued, by the explicit sex scene tattooed all the way down the side of her leg. I saw boobs, flowing hair, feet, a man's lower half, and maybe a sunset?

"Awesome! Looks like you found a pair!"

"Nooo, I don't think so," she replied, turning back toward the mirror. "See all this?" She pulled on her thighs' outer flesh. "They're cutting in!"

Mentally winded, I cautiously moved back inside the dressing room and unhooked one of our top-selling boyshorts, hoping their trusted elasticity would suffice.

"Here," I said, handing over a thin nude short with soft lace trim around the waistband and leg holes. "We sell out of these all the time. I hear they're comfortable."

"Oh, great," she replied, once again taking the lead by closing the door. "You can sit in the chair. I don't care."

"Well, I need to—" barely left my mouth before she stripped down to nothing and moved her feet through the trim.

I sat still, continuing to examine the provocative storyline along her strong build. It was obvious she spent a lot of time defining muscle groups, seemingly bonded with her body while knowing exactly what she was looking for. I respected her pace, and I admired her confidence to bare all. Though I couldn't help wondering if the "perfect" boyshort really existed for her, especially as she continued to pull on the thin fabric tightly covering her thighs.

"Damnit," she complained, turning around to examine the back of her legs in the mirror. "These have the same pinch to them." I moved my eyes along the edging of her thighs, trying to follow the "pinch," though it wasn't my place to do so. I thought they fit like boyshort underwear fit. However, I didn't wear them myself, so who was I to know what a good fit felt like? Struggling to respond, I sat forward on the edge of the chair, hoping an assertive approach would land us on a pleasing pile so that she could find comfort in knowing her efforts weren't wasted or overlooked. "What exactly are you looking to see?" I met her stare in the mirror.

She didn't hesitate. "I want very little side squeezing and they need to separate my thighs. I want to see a gap."

"Okay." I nodded slowly, looking over at her pile of underwear. "Let's try on some cotton."

She hurried to remove her current boyshorts to replace them with a light pink pair I'd quickly picked up before she found our room. They were as stretchy as could be and absent of any additional tight stitching or design that might've hindered my customer's desired thigh gap. Simplicity had to be the answer even though I had no clue what it looked like or, more profoundly, what it even meant.

"Those look good," I said, still nodding my head.

She moved her body in slow circles, studying every inch of flesh and fabric.

"More balanced than the other pair?" she asked.

Balanced? I deliberated quietly before moving my gaze from the space between her thighs all the way down to the lack of space between my thighs. The only gap I saw was the air between my fingers.

"I just hate how they cut into you and create a thigh bulge!" She, too, deliberated intensely. "I can't have my thighs rubbing together either!"

Still straddling the edge of the chair, I examined my own thighs one more time, thickset and squeezed into wrinkled dress pants. Everything about their existence started to feel like gelatin as I began to overanalyze their company. It felt impossible to not scrutinize, considering the feel of insistence and demand shown by my customer.

"I just don't know," she moaned, rotating her body in front of the mirror, her lean muscles tight and uncompromising.

"Have you ever thought about just wearing a thong? Or a brief? Or, I don't know . . . nothing?" I asked, cutting through the nuances.

Her facial expression fell flat, leading me to remain silent.

"I just prefer the boyshorts."

"Alright," I replied, handing her another pair to put on. "Let's find you one then."

For the next ten minutes, we swapped out five more styles of boyshorts. I was at a complete loss in terms of what she was determined to see aside from what she'd already shared. There had to have been more. And though I admittedly grew tired and peeved measuring the space between one's thighs, I sort of understood her private need. I suppose we all have body parts we'd love to exchange, or parts that require more attention. I wasn't completely sure. But I continued to sit, talking panty trims and thigh gaps, chalking it up to a nice break from boobs. She was my leader, and I relaxed into whatever direction she wanted me to go, until Caroline came knocking.

"Natalee? You in there?" She stood outside our dressing room. "You have a phone call."

I jumped up to open the door, forgetting that I had a fully undressed customer standing in the middle of the floor, right under the glaring lights. I bolted straight for the counter, knowing nothing good ever came out of my department phone calls.

"Hey, Nat," Larry said, coughing into the phone.

"You alright?" I asked, trying to catch my breath.

"Yeah, I was wondering if you could swing by the pharmacy on your way home from work and grab my nausea meds. They're open late."

I leaned against the counter, still trying to breathe. "You never call me," I said, realizing he needed help.

A soft chuckle came through from the other end.

"That's because you always call me, Natalee."

"I'll talk to the girls and leave a little early." I paused, sinking into his loneliness.

"What are you doing?"

"Preparing for my 10K."

"I'll see you soon, Dad."

A cloud of dizziness came rushing as I looked around the department for one of my closing teammates. I had to get out of there. Though I also wanted to rewind every passing minute and hide back in the room with my customer and her boyshorts—an easier problem.

⁓

WHEN I RETURNED HOME THAT EVENING, I FOUGHT TO REMAIN level in my reactions, hoping to keep the inarticulate sounds and uncontrolled shedding of tears to a quiet minimum. I couldn't let Larry see me go to pieces. He still needed stamina and resilience—and high doses of Oxycodone that I had to cut and manage and not ingest. A blubbering mess would've only made him more uncomfortable and I had never, ever, seen him need someone the way he needed me.

"Sorry I got you out of bed, Nat," he said, expelling questionably colored liquids from his nose as he fought for air. The gurgling rising in his chest, paired with the verdant fluid coming out of the sides of his mouth, had me running back and forth, gathering hand towels and whatever anti-nausea meds I could find among his packed pillbox.

"Do you feel like you need to go to the hospital?" I asked, getting up to flush his innards down the toilet, marking 3:00 AM on the microwave. He thought about it for a second while I cleaned out his bowl.

"Not yet," he whispered softly.

"Are you sure?"

"I'm sure," he wheezed.

I stood in a panic.

"This is it, isn't it?" I said, looking right at him. "You're dying."

"This isn't it, Natalee."

"You're not dying?"

He laughed, shaking his head. "Not at the moment."

Goddamnit, he's dying.

"You want bagpipes, Paul Simon, what?" I asked straight-faced as I began to pace the living room. "I can play *Graceland* . . . or Streisand."

His laugh fell into another labored wheeze.

"ABBA's 'SOS'? Earth, Wind & Fire?"

"Natalee."

I examined his hands covered with residual purple markings from all of the trial drugs that never worked. They only prolonged the inevitable while creating insufferable agony. His last CT scan lit up like a Christmas tree and a menorah combined from his shoulders to his shins, making the likelihood of dissolving even a fraction of his malignancy pretty much impossible. He was dying, quickly and inconsolably dying.

As he rested against the arm of the couch, I noticed his fingers had become more skeletal, causing his wedding band to slide down to his knuckles. I instantly thought about my mom's final days before we green-lighted the morphine. She sat on the same couch, crushed and conquered, assuring me she needed to go to the hospital. I ran around the house quickly packing a bag before calling Larry at work to inform him that we were leaving because she thought her brain was going to explode. A strange silence filtered through the house as I stood waiting for her at the front door, realizing a few seconds later that she was missing in action. I dropped her bag and bolted into the living room and then into the garage, thinking that maybe I had moved the car in and she was already sitting in the passenger seat. Trembling and horrified as to what I thought I was about to walk into, I ran upstairs, yelling her name over and over. And then I found her, sitting in front of her bathroom mirror, putting on lipstick.

"You've got to be kidding me," I said, bent over, holding my knees. She stared at herself for a few moments, quietly connecting all of the dots, and then looked up at me while I continued to pant.

"I ain't dead yet."

Pacing the kitchen, I listened as Larry coughed up more fluid. A slew of scenarios raced through my mind, all of which included the reverberation of a flatline. I could see his arms tightly wrapped around the bowl right before he motioned for me to join him on the couch.

"Would you mind massaging my shoulder, Nat?" he asked. I gulped from the vulnerability in his voice, hearing the faint clinking of tin handles while a forbidding malady chipped away at his bones. The man that I had come to know as an individual, and not just my father, had reached his breaking point. His mustache kisses and wet willies and Donald Duck impersonations suddenly reappeared and crystalized into everything I ever knew about true, devoted love. I longed for our Saturday morning Egg McMuffins. Just him and me sitting in the corner of a McDonalds, squirmy from the hard plastic seats, and giggling uncontrollably after he'd pretend to steal my nose from right off my face and wiggle it between his fingers, assuring me he'd stitch it back on. He gave me everything he had, and goddamn, did I love him for it.

As I lowered myself next to him on the couch, I could still hear a subtle wheeze traveling up his chest. The shine from the back-porch light cast its glare into the living room while we moved inside of the darkness, restless and fearful of the defeat rising within.

"Thank you," he said, holding onto my forearm as I helped guide his body into a pile of pillows. He stared at me lovingly, moving his eyes along my face before he tapped on the top of my hand. "You're going to do great things."

BEAUTIFUL
WRECKAGE

G azing out onto a blanket of leaves, I welcomed fall's arrival while I packed the last of my belongings. There was something about its changeover that felt consoling and serene, allowing me to sit for hours and feel a semblance of life after Larry died. The foliage was all the light I needed as I ate off a TV tray and circled through the same three T-shirts and two pairs of sweats day in and day out. I had become a zombie, living in an empty house and following a well-ordered routine of waking before renting out all of Blockbuster Video. I hadn't worked in months, living off a prayer after walking away from the lingerie department, never to look back.

Sometimes I wondered if my nagging presence and lack of structure concerned the Blockbuster employees. I spent six months with them, ordering obscure foreign titles and buying discounted Milk Duds from their display table. We were on an every-other-day status without fail, and I'm certain their collective curiosity about my daily activities slowly evolved into straight-up feeling sorry for me. Their long, awkward stares hit every aisle as I read handfuls of emerging plots. I wasn't exactly dazzling with a come-hither look either: messy side bun, thick bags under my eyes, oversized sweats I found in an old dresser, and dark sunglasses that blocked out all the glowing rays of sunshine that built rainbows around me. I was bitter—and beautiful.

"What exactly do you do, anyway?" the store manager, Paul, finally asked one day, looking down at my sea-blue sock stitched with turtles, and then over to a red sock sparkling with silver poinsettias.

"I watch movies, Paul," I replied, eyeing their new shipment of buttered popcorn as I held onto a pack of cigarettes and a magnum of wine from the corner mart next door.

"Yes, right." He smiled, allowing me to change the subject to his stamp collection, followed by his girlfriend's pestering need for an engagement ring. I lost my sense of self somewhere between the estate sale and the blinding realization that I no longer had parents. The isolation became irrationally dependable—until I came home to a SOLD sign hanging in red and new renters in my LA apartment. Everything changed, just like Larry said it would.

Crying down Interstate 5, I prayed to the shepherds I knew I'd never comprehend that I wouldn't get pulled over. The bed and inside cabin of Larry's old pickup truck were packed to the brim with everything I owned, including suitcases jammed with clothes, shoes of every kind, silverware, random cooking utensils, Swiffer mops, a portable safe, and a long miniature poodle that sat atop the console. Reality kicked in quickly. But as irony and fate would have it, I didn't have far to go, having been thrown a lifeline and a new set of house keys by dear family friends who spent most of their time out of state. The gratitude that followed will never compare to anything, for as long as I walk this earth. However, my unexpected transition still sent shockwaves. I couldn't believe how quickly and drastically my life had changed, moving from my father's house, back to the neighborhood I grew up in. I wanted none of it. The jolt was astounding. But I was stuck and jobless—again, silently floundering against walls and a crippling sequence of more what-ifs. I had suddenly become a stranger to myself and everyone around me.

When I arrived at the house, I headed straight for the kitchen windows. I could almost see a glowing halo as I stared across the lake at the home I had grown up in. Everything looked the same except for the white and burgundy paint job. Thick green ivy lined the front lawn and the edges of the mailbox post. The driveway that we used to sled down when it snowed every other year still looked scarier than it really was.

Taking a seat at the kitchen table, I stared at my mom's bathroom light flickering against translucent glass. Its muted glare brought me to the endless hours I'd spend sitting on top of the toilet chatting about the intricacies of life while I watched her put on makeup. Larry's corner dwelling was lit up, too, bringing me right back to Seahawks football and a few chosen swear words that would ricochet off walls. I had come full circle in the most unforeseen way, slowly unpacking the remnants of what was into what would painstakingly be.

SHELL-SHOCKED, I SAT HUNCHED OVER IN MY PICKUP TRUCK IN THE parking lot of the first store where I learned how to sling bras. A Swiffer mop remained wedged between the console and the passenger seat, and the floor was still covered with family photo albums, sneakers, a skillet, books, and whatever else had yet to show itself amid the confusion. I was desperate to find some

kind of stability; therefore, returning to the lingerie department felt like the only choice I had. It was available, just like it
had always been. And it came to me, anchored in strange pas-
sages and inexplicable timing.

After completing my rehire paperwork in the HR office for
the tenth time, I sat studying the inside of the office, remembering all the customer service plaques while rewinding back
to my nineteen-year-old self. *There had to be meaning somewhere.
With mystery comes magic. It's only temporary. You'll find your way.*

"Welcome home, Natalee," the HR manager said as she
handed over my old employee number. "We're glad to have you
back." I stared at her thick brown hair and smiled. Something
about the familiarity was oddly comforting. It cut straight
through the purgatory and spread its influence far and wide,
quieting my nerves for a brief moment of time.

As I ventured out onto the third floor, slowing my steps to the
bright lights and moving bodies, I sank into a lingering nostalgia. Everything seemed smaller, including my old lingerie
department, and the pair of thongs hanging from the fingers of
a tall, chiseled mannequin.

"Wow!" Barbara, a veteran bra fitter, grinned from ear to ear,
kindly welcoming me aboard. "After all this time, and now
you're back!"

I thought about my nineteen-year-old self again, timidly
moving through the department.

"Oh, Barbs." I leaned in for a long hug. "Thanks for reaching
out."

She stopped and wrapped her arms around me again. I had
always appreciated Barbara and would call her throughout the
years with random merchandise checks for customers, happy to
keep in touch. I respected her game, too. She was the queen of
bra fitting, hustling day in and day out for more than twenty

years. Women loved her and would come from all over just to see her and purchase lingerie. The receipt rolls during sale time had her employee number printed all over them, all seven digits moving in bold, and it's because she always kept it real. She loved her job; she loved helping women find their power, and it showed.

"Welcome back." Barbs continued to smile, touching my forearm before disappearing into the dressing rooms. "I'd walk the floor for a bit. We've got some good stuff."

Taking her advice, I strolled through the lay of the land, smiling at new teammates as I moved in circles. There was one stockroom, one corner of sleepwear, more modernized shapewear, and every bra imaginable, with a few revolutionized numbers that were bound to turn heads. The department was both small and sufficient, adding just the right touches for a cool and calm ambiance. Its feel was just right, not to mention a drastic change from previous departments, aside from the sink-or-swim mentality, of course. You either moved with purpose or found another dressing room. This I learned would never change. Women had pressing needs—and they mattered. And though my hometown department generated a slow and steadier pace, I could feel the changing rhythms as I absorbed my new surroundings.

"No pressure, but I have a customer if you're ready," Barbs said, returning from the dressing rooms. "My prostheses appointment has arrived, and the woman I started a room for needs some extra care."

"Uh, sure." I struggled to reply, watching the other bra fitters scurry away, leaving me to fend for myself.

"Last room on the right," Barbs said before walking away.

Amazed at how surreal everything felt, I wandered back slowly.

"Hey." A woman stood outside waiting. "Are you Natalee?"

"I am." I reached out to shake her hand, noticing a layer of bandages around her midsection.

"Camille." She smiled, closing the door.

I looked around the dressing room, surprised to see outdated wallpaper and old carpet, though calmed and comforted by the lack of flash. My previous digs sometimes felt overwhelming and ostentatious, a pocket of Seattle I was happy to leave behind.

"Barbara told me I'm in good hands."

I laughed, catching onto her quip.

"Today is my first day back in a while," I said. "Bear with me."

"No problem." She smiled, her teeth a bright white. "You're going to need a little patience, too."

I stood staring at her body, puffy and bruised.

"I've had liposuction, a tummy tuck, and breast augmentation surgery, so as you can see, I'm still healing. The doctor okayed a sports bra, something a little tighter, but no underwire yet."

I nodded, watching as Camille slowly unfastened her cotton surgical bra from the front.

"Wow," I said, staring at her new double-Ds, stuck with square-shaped bandages and deep blue markings. "They look great!"

"And for my tummy and thighs," she continued, guiding me down her body with her hands. "I'm finally allowed to branch out from the compression garments they gave me, but I still need some kind of tight body shaper."

"I think I got it." I nodded, mentally checking each item and then some.

Starting my search for Camille's garments, I located the small corner of shapewear, pulling a variety of styles that covered every inch of flesh from the rib cage down to the thighs.

"The best sports bras for after a boob job are in the stock-room. We don't keep them on the floor," a woman said from behind. Caught off guard, I turned around and stared blankly, her southern drawl still ringing through the department.

"Barbs told me about you. I'm Monique." She stuck out her hand energetically.

"Hi," I said, smiling. "Thanks for the lead."

"Let me know if you need anything," she said, walking away. "We look after each other around here."

Surprised and grateful for the help, I gathered as many wire-less sports bras and sturdy bralettes as I could find and headed back for Camille, thinking it would be a quick "toss over the door" kind of transaction. When I arrived, her door was still open, and she had managed to get herself out of the compression garments, baring a layer of loose stomach flesh and cut-up thighs covered in multihued bruises from dark reds to mustard yellows. Her thinned-out body looked like it had been run over by a bus and left for dead.

"Would you mind helping me get into these things?" she asked. "I need all the help I can get."

Jolting from the door slamming against its hinges, I unhooked one of the sports bras and slowly guided her arms through the straps. I then took a step closer and stood directly in front of her, smelling coffee on her breath as I carefully fastened the bra. She immediately moved her shoulders up and down, feeling out its pressure.

"Look at me!" she said, turning to view the side of her body. "I'm a hot mess!"

I didn't respond to Camille's comment and continued to unhook a pair of Spanx. It was apparent she was figuring something out in her head.

"Higher Power Spanx?" she said, reading the tag before grabbing ahold of both legs.

"And a hole for the bathroom," I added, helping her into the chair.

She paused and took in a deep breath. "Man, the pain is still going strong."

"I bet," I replied, guiding her feet into the holes of the shaper. She held onto my shoulders as she slowly rose to her feet, and then helped pull the Higher Powers up and over her loose cotton briefs.

"It'll be worth it," she said, staring at herself in the mirror. "And I own every slice and dice of it."

"Good for you," I replied, moving out of her way. "Your body, your choice."

"That's right." She looked in my direction.

Treading lightly, I asked what first came to mind, having heard so many different reasons for wanting to go under. "What made you do it, if you don't mind me asking?"

"A lot of things," she said, ripping off the tag from the Spanx before unhooking another bra. "For starters, I was in a horrible marriage for twenty-three years."

I stared, wanting more while quietly acknowledging the ease between us.

"He was a powerful man who couldn't keep his penis in his pants."

"I'm sorry," I replied, carefully helping her into another bra.

"All he did was cut me down," she said, shaking her head. "Made me feel worthless every day. I was fat, lazy, a bitch. He hated everything about me . . . and himself. But I wasn't a saint either. Two wrongs made a right for me, and I ended up cheating, too. It was just—" She paused, sighing. "Really, really toxic."

"You guys have kids?"

"Two," she replied, glaring at her body in the mirror. "And they were the only reason I tried to keep it together for so long."

"And now?" I asked, testing the waters while fastening the last front clasp.

"I'm free." She smiled, waving her hands. "And rich."

I laughed loudly, startled by my own sound.

"So, this is a post-divorce celebration," I said, acknowledging her transformation as I watched her look over the fit.

"You got it."

Camille slowly unhooked the bra and threw it on top of the first one she tried on, happy with the sizing. "One more," she signaled, grabbing a light gray cotton sports bra. I helped move her arms through the straps again, standing inches from her face.

"Whatever you do, live without regrets," she said. "Life is too damn short."

Struggling to connect the clasps on her bra, I fell into her comment. "Life really is too short," I replied, gently pulling on the straps.

Camille stared in the mirror, examining the depth of her nips and tucks, seemingly in awe of her new body under new light.

"So what was your breaking point?"

"You know," she replied, genuinely thankful that I was willing to listen, which kind of broke my heart. I felt like Camille had struggled for so long and just needed to vent. "My fifteen-year-old son came to me one day and asked why his father and I continued to stay together. It killed me. I never wanted my kids to feel or see our destruction as a couple, especially how we talked to each other behind closed doors, which inevitably spread throughout the house. And then the cheating started."

I sensed Camille's rising power as she spoke sincerely. "We both hated ourselves, he and I. He was miserable at his job, and I allowed myself to become some pathetic servant, losing myself in the process while becoming really volatile. And then one day I woke up, right after my son, Carter, found me crying in my car in the garage, drinking vodka at ten o'clock in the morning. I drank in my car a lot. It was awful."

Camille stopped to think about everything she had shared, her voice strong and commanding.

"Carter reminded me that I was failing at my job as a mother, a role model for love. I'm doing me for the first time in my life, forging my own way at forty-five."

A role model for love. Forging your own way. I felt every part of her drive, resurrected and persevering.

"It's scary as hell though, Natalee." she added quickly. "I've never been on my own. Sometimes I wonder if it's too late. I wasted so much time, you know? But then I think, no, I didn't. I'm exactly where I'm supposed to be. So what if I'm in my forties. I'm here, showing up."

Absorbing every word, I continued to stand directly in front of Camille, wondering if I was going to start crying or hug her until our bones broke. Though we had lived completely different experiences, having made totally different life choices, we still felt the same fear. But I was meant to hear her words, I was convinced, just like she was fated to free them. And as I stood staring into Camille's dark brown eyes and bruises, something began to shift. I felt a different kind of understanding that I had yet to experience in the dressing room: a compelling need to understand why I was brought back to the lingerie department and connected with individuals—strangers with wreckage and wonder—who were bound to play roles I never saw coming. "It is scary as hell," I affirmed.

She looked at me before shifting her attention onto her mending body. Together, we stood in front of the mirror, scared and uncertain, quietly assessing her transformation as the banging of dressing room doors filled the hallway. Camille's stare was long and reflective. And then it faded, graciously overruled by a winning grin.

"My tits look fantastic."

FINDING YOU

S till acclimating to my new, old digs, I wandered around the store during my lunch break, naturally stopping in the shoe department before gathering a collection of perfume samples. Camille was still on my mind, as her purpose-driven makeover made me reflect on the certainties of life and the choices we make in order to evolve as people—as women—boldly forging ahead after a devastating defeat. It was no coincidence that I got to experience all of her, every guiding word and silent reflection. Camille's strong and mending presence stuck—and I needed it. So I grabbed hold, quietly acknowledging what I had initially intended to be a "quick sale" so that I could find my way onto payroll. I couldn't have been any hastier as I underestimated our time, realizing, more profoundly than before, what exactly the dressing room had to offer. The intimacy felt different, and the closeness even closer, pushing me to take it all in.

Returning to the floor, my manager, Shay, welcomed my arrival with a kind smile. I liked her for this.

"There's a guy who's been circling sleepwear with a young girl and boy. You mind checking on them before you head back to set down your things? I'm working with a gentleman who's looking to surprise his wife with new lingerie after finishing chemotherapy, and I want to give him as much of my attention as possible."

Eyeing the family of three, I moved over in their direction, sensing some confusion.

"How are you all doing?" I asked, holding onto my coffee.

"We're good, thank you," the man replied, looking down at the girl. I watched as his face turned a soft pink, his hands stuck deep into the front pockets of his blue jeans. "Is there any way my daughter can get measured for a bra?" The girl immediately took a few steps back, trying to separate herself from her dad.

"Of course," I replied, trailing his gaze back over to his daughter. "You ready now?"

"She's embarrassed that I'm here, but she really needs to get some bras," her dad cut in.

"Ah, I see." I peered in the girl's direction again. "Why don't you come back in thirty minutes? You can wander down to our men's department if you'd like, or there's a coffee bar and food court close by."

He looked down at the young boy holding onto the side of his jeans. "What do you think, sport?" he asked, running his hand through his hair. "Shall we find a snack?"

We both smiled at the boy's shy innocence.

"Lily," the man yelled softly, motioning for her to come back over after she had drifted farther away, lost within a display of trendy push ups.

She hesitated to make eye contact as she said hello, gently pushing her long brown hair away from her face. We waited as her father and brother disappeared down the escalator, leaving just the two of us in the middle of the department.

"So . . . you need bras?" I worked at sounding as warm and welcoming as possible, sensing her reserve.

"Yeah, I like the ones over there." She pointed to a rounder of pastel bras.

"Alright." I nodded in agreement, discreetly noting her size. "Are you okay if I measure you really fast? I have a sense of your band size, but not your cup size."

She also nodded in agreement, following me back to a fitting room while scoping out the scene. Upon closing the door, her instincts led her to quickly disrobe, unveiling a larger size than I had thought.

"I'll grab a few C cups just in case the Bs don't cut it."

She became contemplative and focused as she looked in the mirror at her breasts.

"You can put your shirt back on if you'd like. I'm going to be a moment."

She stared at me softly.

"I'm still learning where everything is around here."

"That's okay," she nearly whispered, pulling on the torn straps of an old bralette.

"Let's talk style." I moved closer to the door, sensing her need for my release. "You mentioned pastels."

"Yeah, any of those are fine."

"Are you wanting underwire?" I asked, uncertain as to whether or not I should've been suggesting underwire at all. However, all of our pastel bras that she had been looking at carried underwire.

"I guess I'll try one." She shrugged her shoulders, just as confused as I was.

Lily was far removed from her comfort zone and I wanted to make sure she left feeling secure in whatever she chose to wear, given that her dad approved. Rarely, if ever, had I helped a father-daughter duo. It was difficult to navigate, which was why I tried letting Lily guide me through the process, and also why

I was strategic in my pursuit in finding her the right options. A stronger bralette wasn't off the table, prompting me to grab a couple of our newly padded styles as well as a couple T-shirt bras before rejoining Lily.

"Alright, Lily," I said, hanging a few smooth-cup bras on the bar. I waited as she looked them over and checked the size on the tag. "Let's start with a 32 B and move from there."

Bashfully facing the mirror, Lily stalled while I slid out and rested against the wall. I listened as she wrestled with the hanger and then repositioned her body somewhere in front of the mirror.

"You can come in," she said, reaching for the doorknob. I checked her fit before moving in to tighten the straps. "Let's try a C."

Resting against the wall outside the room again, I tried sparking conversation with the intention of making her bra fitting somewhat less awkward. A silent dressing room had a way of making things feel painfully uncomfortable sometimes. There was so much inner conflict and reflection happening from just being inside a dressing room. Remove a shirt—and a bra—and things immediately changed, bringing a potent mix of emotions.

"So, is that your little brother?" I asked, adjusting her straps again.

"Yeah, he's kind of annoying sometimes."

I laughed, recalling strong sibling rivalries growing up.

Lily turned toward the mirror and analyzed her new bra. "Can I try that black and white polka-dot one?" she asked shyly. "It's toward the front."

"Sure." I hesitated, picking up one of the padded bralettes. "I say throw on one of these and let's see how you feel for comparison."

As soon as I made it back out onto the floor, Lily's dad had returned with her little brother, standing right next to Lily's requested polkadots.

"How's she doing?" he asked, concerned. "We're back a little early."

"She's good!" I amped up the enthusiasm only to have it dissipate moments later.

"That's great," he sounded relieved. "Thank you so much."

The shade of his skin color changed again, making me look over in the young boy's direction as he tore apart a Rubik's Cube. Tenderly placing his hand on the boy's shoulder, the man's words became slow recollections of long and desolate verities. "Their mother recently passed away, and we're out trying to regain some kind of normalcy. Getting bras was always her mom's thing and I just want her to be comfortable in whatever she needs." My heart bounced against my ribs as I looked down at the young boy, who continued to manipulate his cube, and then back up at the father.

"I'm ... so sorry," I responded slowly, trying to hold eye contact while my body turned to Jell-O. "I'll make sure Lily is comfortable in whatever she chooses."

"I really appreciate it," he replied, pulling his son in closer. "She's had a tough go of things lately."

Everything felt different as I dragged my feet back to Lily's room. She was so young, too young, to not have a mother. And here I had her all to myself, shredded into sorrow, while trying to understand her evolving identity as a young, motherless daughter. I fidgeted with her polka dots I'd snagged from the display tree once her father turned around and waited by her door.

"How are you doing, Lily?" I asked, relaxing my approach even more.

She welcomed me in and then stepped back toward the corner, wearing the light-colored T-shirt bra I had started her in.

"You like that one." I smiled, still standing by the door.

"It's okay, I guess." She looked down at her chest.

"Here." I passed over a polka dotted push-up bra. "Let's try this."

Back outside her room, I continued to rest against the wall, listening to her movements as she experimented with another bra. I wondered how her father was doing with everything, having two kids and a completely different lifestyle thrown at him out of nowhere. I also couldn't help wondering what all Lily had been exposed to. It's terrifying to watch what happens to the mind and body when death becomes frighteningly close. *I hope she saw the sky when it parted to make room. I hope that whatever is burned into her memory won't deprive her of living fully. I'm sorry you have to experience this. I'm sorry you were cheated. Losing is the worst.*

With unmeasured mania, I recalled my mother's final hours. Her eyes sunken and her lips splintered. "This is big," she'd whisper, waiting for me to respond as I plummeted into her vacancy, hoping to say something that would put her at ease. But I always failed, encouraging her to let go. Game over. Battle lost. Defeat strong. There has to be something better.

"Yes, Momma, this is big," I'd say to delay my hopeless come-back, slowly gliding a small sponge around the inside of her mouth, releasing just enough coldness to soothe the aching from her ulcers. They were crowded and red around the edges, taking over her once eloquent speech.

"Really big?" she asked, holding onto my finger, her fixed stare moving from the bottom of my chin up to the dark lines stretching along the ravaged bends of my eyes.

My knees buckled as my face landed in her palm.

"Bigger than us."

"Well," she said, running her fingers through my hair. "How do my boobs look in this gown?"

BRINGING ME BACK TO REALITY, LILY OPENED THE DOOR WEARING exactly what she wanted.

"That looks great." I smiled, admiring the black polka dots and soft pink edging. "How do you feel?"

"Good. I really like this one." She nodded, moving in closer to the mirror. The room became quiet, yet peacefully numb. Everything that was going on inside of Lily had showed up in waves of recognizable redolence. I knew better than to strike up a conversation about her mom dying, but something in me wanted Lily to know that I knew all about her loneliness and longing. I understood her need to hide in her bedroom all day, away from people with opinions so that she could dream privately. I knew that the hallways at school appeared smaller and louder, making the long stretches between classes a crowded maze with no way out.

Staring at the bags under her eyes, I reached for the doorknob. "Your dad told me about your mom. I'm really sorry."

Her head shot up as I stood gripping the coldness of the handle.

"She's with you, Lily. I promise you that."

She paused, surprising me with her response and long stare. "Do you really believe that?"

"I've never been more certain about anything in my life."

She looked down at the ground and then back over to me.

"I just wanted to fix her."

Heaviness pulsated all around us, nearly dragging me to the floor.

"I know," I whispered, trying not to cry. "I know."

Giving Lily privacy to try on another bra, I slipped out of the open crack in the door and rested against the wall again. There was a long, forbearing silence as I made the decision to stay, free from interruptions and unimportant demands, happy to tighten strap after strap while Lily quietly determined her needs. She was steadfast in her pursuit and held in a deep dolefulness. It didn't take long for me to internalize a series of apologies. Lily's forthcoming years weren't empty. Not completely. But they were going to be confusing as hell. I quietly acknowledged the significance of my return to the lingerie department again, and how different it felt. Camille was right. I was exactly where I was supposed to be, fumbling toward every guiding measure of Lily's grace. "How are you—"

Lily interjected as I re-entered the room, catching me off guard with how forthright she had become. "So when does it all go away?" she asked, her eyes pleading.

I stared at the small freckles lining her collarbone, quietly connecting their innocence. "Never," I replied, refusing to lie to her. "But you'll learn how to live with it. Right along with all the wisdom that will set you free."

Lily nodded, moving her gaze to the floor.

"Life, huh?"

I waited, trying my hardest not to come undone, feeling every crashing beat. Finally, eyes brimming with tears, I added confidently, "She'll find you."

MOUNTAIN HIGH

oving into day eight of heavy rain, the lingerie department braced for a busy Sunday. Pockets of deep floods spread throughout Seattle, making the roads impossible and the colors dark and dismal. Sundays had become one of my favorite days to work. The store opened late, our shifts were shortened, and people came to spend money, which always seemed to convey an element of irony for me. It was the only day that carried its own energy, separating itself from the slow ticking of the clock.

As I stood in line to check out the moneybags, my manager, Shay, joined me, looking tense. "There's coffee and doughnuts in the back," she said, nudging my arm. "And two of our girls called out sick. Prepare for a storm."

I hurried to sign my name along the dotted lines, then sifted through a stack of cash for the registers, praying my sloppy count was close to accurate. The department was spick and span with absolutely nothing out of place from the night before. Even the front panty tables, as burdensome as they were, held orderly piles of Hanky Panky thongs and other thin pairings. I didn't have a lot of opening duties to check off other than a quick dusting around the mannequins' edges before I double-checked the customer hold bar for any miscellaneous items.

"Opening in five, Seattle." The weekend manager addressed the store over the speakers. "Make it rain, team!"

Laughter filled the floor as everyone picked up on the sarcasm.

Shay and I spent the next few minutes hanging a new shipment of panties on hangers while talking skincare until our first Sunday morning shoppers arrived, one of them rocking a newborn baby as she approached the counter.

"There's two," she whispered, turning around a stroller where another baby slept.

"Nursing bras?" I asked, walking around the counter.

"How'd you guess?" She smiled, following me toward the dressing rooms.

"You'll have plenty of space in here," I said, unlocking our large dressing room.

Staring at her swelling breasts, I reached for the measuring tape as she slowly lowered her baby into the stroller.

"Please give mommy ten minutes," she murmured, blowing a kiss. "I beg you."

I waited while she unbuttoned her shirt, falling into the quietness of the morning.

"Oh no!" She quickly covered her breasts, startling me. "I'm leaking again!"

I looked at her nipple area, soaked with breast milk, and realized we were out of Kleenex, which usually sat atop the table for prostheses appointments, but unfortunately it always went fast.

"I have breast pads somewhere in here." She unzipped her diaper bag, still cupping her boobs.

I looked down at her babies, staring at me side by side. "How about I gather you some Kleenex just to have," I said, watching her press her shirt up against her nipples. "I'll grab a few nursing bras, too. I'm pretty sure you're between a 34–36 double-D, maybe a triple. I'll be quick."

I rushed for the stockroom, grabbing a few styles of nursing bras and a box of Kleenex for the dressing room. On my way back, Shay stopped me, slightly flustered, and working to strike a balance. "My customer from the other day is back to exchange some lingerie. The man who was shopping for his wife after finishing chemo."

"Yes." It all registered, igniting more heart patters.

"If you need me, know that I might be in the back pulling items for him. Monique is on her way."

Moving faster, I opened the door to my nursing mother's room and found her rocking one of the babies again, pacing back and forth as the crying became more strident.

"I'm so sorry," she said, her inflection rundown. "I thought for sure he'd sleep and now he's refusing to feed."

"Take as long as you need," I replied, casually assessing her nipple area that had large outlines of circles from the breast milk that continued to soak through her bra.

"I grabbed a couple different sizes and styles, and then Kleenex if you need it for anything."

"Maybe I will sit in here and see if I can feed him."

"Absolutely. I'll check back." I smiled, closing the door. "And please, take your time."

Back out on the sales floor, I found Shay and her customer organizing a pile of lingerie at the register. They were focused and meaningful in their search. Bright reds, soft pinks, and sexy blacks covered every inch of countertop, from sheer lace bras to silk negligees.

"Beautiful," I said, hovering next to Shay.

"Isn't it?" she replied, picking up one of the sheer cup bras. "What's your opinion on this one? Too itchy?" I moved in closer to examine the bra, and the man, whose indecisions also spread far.

"I don't want to push her to wear anything she's not ready to wear," he said, feeling around the intricate lace. I could tell he was struggling to make everything about his thoughtful idea perfect, which made it easy to remain devoted to whatever he needed. His patience said it all.

"I say go for it." I smiled, moving out quickly from behind the counter as more fierce crying hit the doorway of the dressing rooms.

When I reentered the room, she looked as if something had broken inside of her, clutching every last fragment of hope while she rocked two crying babies against her naked breasts.

"I'm going to leave here with a nursing bra if it kills me." She spoke sternly as her eyes welled up with tears. I stared at the babies' small round heads pressed against her flushed chest, and then along the floor of the dressing room scattered with diapers, burp cloths, and a couple pacifiers. "I haven't even had a chance to try on one of the bras," she added, rocking back and forth.

"Is there anything I can grab for you?" I asked, feeling slightly hopeless.

"Vodka," she replied with a hard-earned grin.

I laughed, watching her move one of the babies closer to her boobs.

"How about I take over the stroller while you try on a bra," I said, unhooking one of the nursing bras. "I can check the fit quickly and switch out from there."

She took me up on my offer and slowly lowered life back into the stroller. I attempted to quiet the crying by pushing and pulling on the handle, but to no avail. Their tiny wails grew louder as my distressed mother grew increasingly tired. She was done, and I knew it.

We hurried to cover her nipples with Kleenex and fasten a bra. "Let's go up a cup size," I said before I even had it hooked. "I know you need to feed, but you still need a little bit more coverage. Next size should do it. Are you good with pink stripes? I just realized I forgot to grab that one."

She paused and took in a deep breath as I resumed pushing and pulling the stroller.

"I'll take anything right now." She fought to respond.

I watched her run her fingers through her disheveled hair as she sat down in the chair.

"My boobs are bleeding, and I haven't slept in two days."

I looked down at the babies, their tiny tongues flapping with every forceful wail.

"You can always take some home and bring back whatever doesn't work." I didn't know what else to say, so I gradually backed up toward the door, reassuring her that I would be back with a top-selling style.

The sales floor began to pick up as I booked it for the stockroom. With two bra fitters out, the day was bound to become a lively maze, leading me into every corner of the department. After I located the pink striped nursing bra, I noticed that the man was still at the counter with Shay, adding bathrobes and silk pajamas to his purchase. I had no idea where anyone was and only heard Monique's voice as it lingered in and out of the fitting rooms. The department was challengingly bare of bra fitters. But then I spotted Monique, desperate, and marching in place.

"I'm going to pee my pants. You mind bringing my customer in room five these bras and panties?" I looked down at a stack of our finest lingerie, coming in everything from a crotchless

black to hot pink lace. "It's for Hazelle. She's a personal customer of mine. Hopefully she'll keep you around and you can
hear about her life as a swinger."

"A what?" I asked, confused, adding Hazelle's bras and panties to my nursing bra.

"A swinger," Monique shouted as she bolted toward the
women's lounge. "You know, marriage with a few perks."

"Jesus," I muttered softly, wondering what I was about to
walk into.

Looking through the cracks of Hazelle's door, I noticed parts
of her still body in front of the mirror. "Hi there," I said, knocking lightly. "Monique asked me to drop off a few items for you
while she ran to the restroom." The door immediately swung
open and out came Hazelle wearing a leopard G-string and
horseshoe nipple rings.

"Wow," she said, excitedly assessing the lingerie. "Monique
is so good to me."

"She is good," I replied, studying her long flowing hair and
heavy diamonds.

"Thanks, baby," she said, smiling wide. "Appreciate it."

Moving on to my tired mother of twins while quietly embracing the eclectic blend of Sunday stories, I unlocked the door and
let myself back in. The helpless crying had waned; however, it
had yet to cease completely.

"An F for fabulous," I said, holding up a pink striped nursing
bra.

"Thank you," she replied, staring at the cups, her eyes nearly
bloodshot from exhaustion. "This is so hard."

I paused to listen, feeling her frustration.

"Really, really hard."

"You're doing better than I ever would," I said, unhooking
the bra.

"I'm really not. I just—" She paused to catch her breath. "I just don't know what I'm doing, or if I'm even doing anything right."

I could feel the concern in her voice, working to understand her role as a mother—daunted, and moments away from breaking wide open. I loved her vulnerability and absolute devotion. She didn't see it that way, of course, which made the humanity of our moment even more real. She bared every loose piece of herself as her fortitude faded, bit by bit. I grabbed hold of her hands and helped her up from the chair before I rushed to wrap her in a bra while she held more Kleenex to her boobs. I hoped, with all my might, that it did everything it was supposed to do, and then some.

"Oh my god." She stood staring at her breasts in the mirror. The look on her face was triumphant, given that the cups fit, yet completely hollow, putting the focus on how drastically different our lives were, shaded with similar undercurrents of total desperation.

"Look at me," she whispered, studying the long, deep stretch marks along her stomach and hips. "I wish I could say I didn't care."

Her comment hit hard as I continued to stare at her in the mirror.

"What a mess." Her voice became muted and her eyes weepy.

"A beautiful mess," I replied, looking around the room at the contents of her diaper bag. "And the bra fits you perfectly."

She nodded, plopping back down in the chair after handing me the bra. The sincerity that followed made the room feel less tense. "Thank you," she said again, looking up at me longingly as she held onto her bare, aching breasts. "Nobody ever said it was easy, right? Loving you. Loving all of you, no matter what."

Deep in thought, I sensed a private reckoning. Its influence made her "mess" even more beautiful as she delivered it with subtle confidence, a knowing that wasn't made for that moment, but would soon come.

Loving you. Loving all of you, no matter what.

Life continued to explode around us as more tiny whimpers gained speed. Per her request, I slid out of the room and rushed for one more nursing bra, pleased she was able to leave with two. The gentleman shopping for his wife had also shared a victory as Shay continued to ring up his pile of surprises. I didn't know his wife, but I presumed, from her husband's commitment to loving, that they had something good. Good enough to land him in the lingerie department for almost two hours, also prompting Shay to need her own box of Kleenex.

When I stepped back into the hallway of the dressing rooms, I immediately noticed Monique's customer, Hazelle, walking back and forth in her leopard G-string thong and matching bra, rocking five-inch heels and a soundless baby in her arms. Her strides were steady and methodical. I was completely caught off guard from the shift in sound and motion, with the exception of a few small, persistent cries.

The feeling was surreal as I stood cemented in the doorway. Watching. I was back in full swing, living and learning from so many unforgettable women, and from all the young, rising girls I had met along the way. The concept of strangers serving as catalysts became stronger, which prompted me to bury all the self-badgering and embrace the messy complexities of life and all of its uncertainties. I was convinced some kind of weird, indefinable destiny was at play as we moved toward one another like magnets, sharing our bodies, and our hearts, within the private enclosures of a dressing room. The solidarity I experienced gave me a true sense of belonging from an unexpected place and, more profoundly, from women who didn't look like me, or talk like me, or come from where I came from—women who had suffered far greater hardships.

It was odd and inspiring how it all suddenly came spilling, loud and honorable. Time had a magical way of showing itself. We don't always get what we want; we get what we need as we work to love ourselves. And if we open our ears and eyes wide enough to understand what's directly in front of us, from the diverse to the divine, extraordinary things happen, humanity happens, one guiding message at a time. The cliché was exhausting, but the enormity of truth was so real. So remarkably real.

I started to walk back into my mother's room, summoned by a few more tireless cries, but a woman stopped me before I could disappear. Strikingly tall, she opened her door and asked if I would come in and check the fit of her bra. She quickly guided me into the chair and assured me it would only take a few seconds.

"I'm a nursing home entertainer, and I just want to make sure my boobs aren't flopping around in this bra," she said, leaning over to stretch her legs before breaking out into full jumping jacks.

"O . . . kay," I replied in absolute bewilderment as her arms—and boobs—swayed in every direction. A lungful of energetic drills hit the dressing room, counting "one, two, three, four." The sudden urge to escape led me straight into a wide-open grin instead, hoping that somewhere, somehow, my sweet Mabel got to see the magnificence of life fearlessly bouncing in front of me. And just when I thought it couldn't possibly get any better, heartfelt dancing supervened as Tina Turner's "River Deep, Mountain High" poured its unmatched glory from the speakers above.

I rested my body against the chair, taking in another moment of timely gifts. Boobs continued to flap, arms flailed effortlessly, and feet tapped to the beat. Roving thoughts shifted into new, lasting perspectives. We were all just trying to make it, deep within the brevity of life, wild against the world. And as the babies' crying finally ceased, spreading a soft stillness, I sat in awe, thinking about all the women who had lifted up so much more than *just* their breasts.

ACKNOWLEDGMENTS

Full Disclosure: I have some people to thank.

Writing a book is hard as hell . . . and more rewarding than I could have ever imagined. Thank you to everyone at Amberjack Publishing for your collective efforts, my ever-so-patient editors, Cassandra Farrin and Cherrita Lee, and my lovely agent, Jill Marr, for the continued support. I've appreciated every bit of guidance. You are one awesome woman.

I'm eternally grateful for my family of women who've supported me through so many dark, daunting days. Moriah Slater, you are what true friendship is all about. Thank you for being my person. Thank you for always showing up and teaching me about love. Devoted, gut-busting, call-your-shit-out kinda love. When you bury me in leather pants and comb my bangs, remember that you are the one person I was damn honored to meet. I love you. I love you. I love you.

Thank you, Kelly Dunning, for your steadfast loyalty. You never stopped asking how the writing was going, and I can't express enough how much it has meant to me over the years. I cherish you, your beautiful family, and all of our profound, soulful talks. Thank you, Paula Olson, for the best air guitar I've ever peed my pants to. We never miss a beat. My glass is always raised in honor of your laughter, the joy you bring to others, a few Tater Tots, Steve, and 4:00 a.m. Cancun.

A big shout-out to Katie Mills for always being my cheerleader and trusted reader. It's meant a lot, and I've appreciated your time. Thank you to Lindsay Bussoli for constantly pushing me to feel and reflect and embrace the scariness of vulnerability. Twenty-something years of love ain't bad. Thank you, Katrina Stroh, for growing with me. How cool has it been to start little, lose some, love a lot, and come back to where it all started. You too, Mollie Murphy. I knew you were something special when I picked your ass up on my Big Wheel. I love your fire, your wit, and our long, loving check-ins. And last, a humongous thank you to Jen Crofton. You amaze me with your brilliance and insight every other day I talk to you. Words cannot express the gratitude I have for your unwavering support, all of your time reading and editing our work, your life advice coupled with your candor, and most of all, the sincere efforts you put forth to lift others.

I want to thank my brother, Spencer, for anchoring our family throughout the toughest of times. You gave us laughter and consistency. I'm forever appreciative of your thoughtfulness and generosity—and I thank you, deeply. You are an incredible father, and I am so proud of you and all that you've accomplished. Thank you to your wife and my friend, Andrea Woods, for being present every step of the way. Your devotion to love big is most admirable. A sincere thank you to you for always supporting my process, asking questions, making me laugh, finding the good, and being one hell of a mother to your brilliant littles, Silas, Lucia, and Nico. To all three of you: Dream, and then dream again. I love you. And to David and your family, I wish you love and happiness.

I'd also like to thank Dan and Sharon Merryfield for keeping the spirit of my parents alive while continuing to nurture and cherish our relationship. I have treasured our time, and I am so grateful to have you in my life. Thank you for the great conversations and thoughtful check-ins. I'm glad Lar and Jan chose you. Another massively large thank you goes out to my DeMatteis clan. Mama Mary and Papa Jack: You picked me up when I needed it most. You welcomed me into your home at my lowest and darkest with a suitcase and a dog in tow. You fed me, loved me, celebrated holidays with me, educated me on Westerns and reality TV, taught me about leadership, and most importantly, you gave me the time I needed to find my footing. You supported me every single day as if I was one of your own while I wandered lost and heartbroken. You embody the very essence of kindness. You changed my life. And I love you.

To Suzanne DeMatteis, thank you for your compassion and commitment to our friendship. All of your encouragement and support through the years has been most valuable. You've opened your home and your beautiful heart. Keep guiding others with your wisdom, and I will continue to follow.

For my fellow educators, partner teachers, and life-long friends, I'll always cover my heart and take a bow in your honor, Colin Slingsby, Erin Belka, and Rachel Evans. The purpose and passion you put into your teaching is extraordinary. I have learned so much from each one of you. Thank you for your brainpower. Thank you for our friendship. And thank you for making me laugh at the most inappropriate times.

Leslie Ostroff: Listen up, Sissy. You are my one-of-a-kind with a fine behind who gets people in line because you are killin' it with every bit of love you give, teaching others how to live, with your charm and your wit, you are lit. Thanks for knowing we're soul mates. Prince would be really proud. Anastasia Tschida, your vision is most profound, and I so appreciate our bond. A big thank you to Emily Kugisaki for being one of my

ARC readers. I admire your brain, and I am extremely thankful for your time and reflection. My very special Petrie 1 and Petrie 2 (order up for negotiation), thank you. Your generosity and ongoing support has meant a lot. Thanks for being so authentic and setting me up to complete this wild dream. You helped shape this journey, and I'm forever grateful. Thanks for making our world a better place too.

Tim and Lilifer Hogg, you two have been a constant, and I'm filled with appreciation. Ruben and Keri Reyes, thank you for sharing all of your love with my family. Kim Leveille, my counsel and confidante, thanks for always pushing me to surrender to the hard stuff. Mike and Diane Loop, I'm most thankful for all the wonderful memories. Thanks for backing me on this long road. Jaydee Lucason, you are a true inspiration, and I thank the stars we crossed paths. Lucretia Tye Jasmine, you too, girlfriend! Thanks for all your brilliance—and beautiful sentiments. I adore you. And to all the incredible women I had the honor of working with in the lingerie department, thank you for the compassion and camaraderie.

Finally, to Mr. Legan, my ninth-grade English teacher . . . you started this mess. You also showed me what can happen when we stop to listen to others, especially our youth. You watched me receive my high school diploma and then, years later, you drove across states to watch me receive my college degree. People don't forget those things. Wherever you are now, thank you. I've carried your words for many years.

And to my mother, Janet, and my father, Larry, I'm sorry we lost. Never do I go a day without feeling your absence. You two knew how to love, quietly and loudly, while allowing me to be me. Thanks for that. I hope you found Bob Marley . . . and the best dance party in town.

Gratitude changes everything.

ABOUT THE AUTHOR

NATALEE WOODS holds a BA in English from Washington State University and an MFA in Writing from the California Institute of the Arts. Her work has been featured in *The Huffington Post, Chatelaine, Reader's Digest*, and *Salon*. Natalee spent over a decade working in multiple lingerie departments, fitting women for bras in both Seattle and Los Angeles. The experiences and lessons she learned along the way ultimately led her to write *Full Support*.

Natalee currently teaches English Literature and Creative Writing within the public school system. Her teaching has magnified her passion around advocating for socially marginalized youth. Criminal justice reform is also a cause very close to her heart. Natalee currently lives in Seattle and has a penchant for leather jackets. She spends her free time enjoying indie films, local music, and planning her next trip. You can find a complete collection of her work at nataleewoods.com.